PRAISE FOR MORE BOOKS BY JENNIFER WRIGHT

Madame Restell

"Painfully timely...Wright observes that Americans don't take well to learning history. When it is delivered with this kind of blunt force, however, perhaps they might. Whatever readers end up thinking of Madame Restell, they surely cannot miss the core lesson: that there has never been a culture in human history without abortion. The only variable has ever been the cost."

—*New York Times Book Review*

"A searing portrait of an indomitable woman...Wright juxtaposes her subject's story with those of Restell's patients and an overview of the broader conversation surrounding abortion in the late nineteenth century."

—*Smithsonian Magazine*

"Wright's book dances off the page." —*Washington Post*

"Restell is central to the story of the dismantling of American women's reproductive freedom during the last half of the nineteenth century, yet she has largely been treated as a curiosity and a footnote.... [This work] fill[s] a grievous void...Wright...has produced an engaging...chronicle, with clear passion..." —*New York Review of Books*

"This brightly written biography of a fierce woman lost to history will appeal strongly to feminists." —*New York Journal of Books*

"A compelling study." —*Los Angeles Review of Books*

"This captivating portrait of the infamous self-taught surgeon and medical celebrity is also a glance at shifting mid-nineteenth century mores, male power players, and their strategic campaign to curtail female independence and criminalize abortion."   —*Globe & Mail*

Get Well Soon

"Jaunty, lively, and filled with references to contemporary cultural history, making this work a well-researched page-turner. Readers will get an intense dose of history, written in a not-hard-to-swallow style."   —*Library Journal*

"Wright brings a reliably sane and bitingly funny voice to a topic we never realized we wanted to know so much about: historically devastating plagues! Read this...so that you can soon amuse your friends with the best dinner party conversation *ever*."

—*NYLON*, "50 Books We Can't Wait to Read in 2017"

"Wright doesn't simply state gross-out facts or hold up solitary individuals as heroes. Instead, she highlights the issues that impacted our understanding of and response to medical nightmares. Leadership, religiosity, power structures, and science collide...Written with Wright's signature humorous tone, this is a grim but engaging look at some of humanity's most feared foes."

—*Bust*

"Jennifer has a rare ability to make history funny, titillating, and relevant in a way I've not come across before. Her passion and enthusiasm jump off the page and make her most recent book, *Get Well Soon: History's Worst Plagues and the Heroes Who Fought Them*, a most compelling and important read."

—Angela Ledgerwood, *Lit Up*

It Ended Badly

"Wright combines a deep knowledge of her subjects with an abiding love for their depravity; she chronicles their breakups with a wit as sharp as a guillotine's blade."   —*People*

"The tone—intimate, whimsical, smart, and silly at once—continues through two millennia of stories of love lost and found...Wright dishes dirt on all of them...with the gleeful irreverence of your wittiest friend recapping a particularly juicy episode of reality television."   —*The Boston Globe*

"Immensely entertaining...If you've gone through a breakup, stock up on Häagen-Dazs, block your ex's number, get drunk with your friends, and buy this book."   —*Bust*

"This is balm for the brokenhearted: we are laughing! We are learning!... Above all, *It Ended Badly* offers hope: for the late-night drunk texters, the doughnut smashers, and everyone else currently exhibiting bad breakup behavior."   —*Kirkus*

"Although the thirteen stories feature heartbreaking and horrific tales, Wright leaves the reader with positive and hopeful thoughts on love...The writing fits right in with the work of comedian authors Tina Fey and Chelsea Handler."   —*Library Journal* (starred review)

"Delightful...funny, irreverent...The book teaches even as it entertains, and applies modern psychology to the behavior of its subjects, providing both amusements and consolation to people likely in need of both."
                                                —*Publishers Weekly* (starred review)

GLITZ, GLAM,
and a
DAMN
GOOD TIME

ALSO BY JENNIFER WRIGHT

*Madame Restell: The Life, Death, and Resurrection of Old
New York's Most Fabulous, Fearless, and Infamous Abortionist*

She Kills Me: The True Stories of History's Deadliest Women

*We Came First: Relationship Advice from
Women Who Have Been There*

*Killer Fashion: Poisonous Petticoats, Strangulating Scarves,
and Other Deadly Garments Throughout History*

*Get Well Soon: History's Worst Plagues
and the Heroes Who Fought Them*

It Ended Badly: Thirteen of the Worst Breakups in History

GLITZ, GLAM,
and a
DAMN
GOOD TIME

HOW MAMIE FISH,
QUEEN *of the* GILDED AGE,
PARTIED HER WAY TO POWER

JENNIFER WRIGHT

GRAND
CENTRAL

New York   Boston

Grand Central Publishing
Hachette Book Group
1290 Avenue of the Americas, New York, NY 10104
grandcentralpublishing.com
@grandcentralpub

First Edition: August 2025

Grand Central Publishing is a division of Hachette Book Group, Inc. The Grand Central
Publishing name and logo is a registered trademark of Hachette Book Group, Inc.

The publisher is not responsible for websites (or their
content) that are not owned by the publisher.

The Hachette Speakers Bureau provides a wide range of authors for speaking events. To
find out more, go to hachettespeakersbureau.com or email HachetteSpeakers@hbgusa.com.

Grand Central Publishing books may be purchased in bulk for business, educational,
or promotional use. For information, please contact your local bookseller or the
Hachette Book Group Special Markets Department at special.markets@hbgusa.com.

Print book interior design by Amy Quinn.

Library of Congress Control Number: 2025937243

ISBNs: 9780306834608 (hardcover); 9780306834622 (ebook)

Printed in Canada

MRQ

1 2025

For my husband, Daniel, who bought a tuxedo the moment we met

CONTENTS

GLITZ, GLAM,
and a
DAMN
GOOD TIME

INTRODUCTION

*I*T WAS OFFICIAL: THE PRINCE DEL DRAGO WAS *COMING TO NEWPORT.*
In the summer of 1902, it seemed like all of Rhode Island was buzzing with anticipation after hearing rumors that an exotic nobleman was headed for their fair city. Could a prince *really* be on his way to visit them? Then again, it *must* be true. After all, Mamie Fish, the supreme arbiter of society, had sent out party invitations to anyone who was *anyone* in Newport, corralling the toniest of the ton, the very highest of high society—together to welcome him.

For the wealthiest families in Newport, the prince's impending arrival signified more than just fun and festivities. It was the dawn of a new century. One hundred and twenty-five years after the country's founding, perhaps Americans were now finally sophisticated enough to be considered equal to Europeans. Princes would mingle with their daughters. Never mind that their American grandfathers had fought against princes and kings—let bygones be bygones. Though some American families had amassed riches beyond riches at this point, there was still one thing money couldn't buy: a title. And for that, these eligible American bachelorettes were paired up with European noblemen, who found that US dollars went a long way in restoring their dilapidated estates. Songs about these "dollar princesses" rang out through music halls declaring,

> *The almighty dollar will buy, you bet,*
> *A superior class of coronet;*
> *That's why I've come from over the way,*
> *From New York City of USA.*[1]

Everything European *had* to be absolutely wonderful. The satirical magazine *Puck* found this kind of striving faintly ridiculous. They featured one cartoon of an absurd, unwieldy carriage justified by a man proudly exclaiming, "It's English, you know!" The highest goal of many wealthy American families was to marry their daughters not merely into nobility but into *royalty*.

And who could possibly be a better matrimonial target than an actual prince, said to be en route to Newport from Corsica? This was no dour English duke. Ladies did not want to end up in a humorless, perpetually damp castle, like Consuelo Vanderbilt, who'd married the Duke of Marlborough and claimed that she spent her days staring longingly at a frigid lake on her estate where a butler had committed suicide. This man might even have a castle in a *sunny* climate, with a *fun, suicide-free* lake. The possibilities!

A word of caution, though. According to Henry "Harry" Lehr, a close friend of the hostess, the prince could be "inclined to be wild."[2] Furthermore, he could not have too much to drink because "anything goes to his head, and then he is apt to behave rather badly." However, amid this corseted, constrained, and utterly prim and polite society, that *too* might have seemed alluring. When Newport inhabitants wondered if it might be one of the Del Dragos they knew from Rome, Harry Lehr informed them, "They all belong to the same family, only the Prince's is a distant branch."[3]

Perhaps an older, *even more distinguished* branch.

And so, the lucky few invited to Mrs. Fish's dinner were positively aflutter. The beautiful women now clustered within the Ocean Drive mansion were understandably concerned whether their own manners would be up to the task of meeting such an established fellow. They discussed their curtsies. Unmarried women primped desperately, patting their faces with powder and pinching their (subtly!) rouged cheeks. They were ready to fall in love with whoever arrived. They only hoped he would love them back. There was a palpable sense of excitement in the air, ladies already bobbing into curtsies, eyelashes fluttering down appealingly as the wealthy Chicagoan Joseph Leiter walked into the room with the prince in hand.

No, literally, *in hand*.

For the illustrious "Prince Del Drago" was actually a monkey...dressed in a tuxedo.

WHEN ATTENDEES RECOVERED ENOUGH FROM THEIR COMPLETE SHOCK TO look over at the hosts, they saw that Mamie Fish and Harry Lehr were doubled over in hysterics.

This joke had been devised beforehand on Fish's yacht, while they were traveling into Newport with the little "prince"—Mamie's newest pet, affectionately named Jocko. No sooner had they docked than Mamie breezed into the finest tailor in Newport, demanding a suit of custom dinner clothes be made for Jocko. Naturally, the establishment refused. Never one to take no for an answer, Mamie promptly fixed the tailor with a frosty glaze and declared, "Name your price, but start sewing—*quickly*."[4] *The New York Times* would later report that the tailor "was given a large sum of money for abandoning all other work in his shop to make and fit a full-dress suit for the monkey guest."[5]

Back at the party, Jocko's presence prompted "a vast assemblage of bejeweled dowagers to gasp and wildly paw the air."[6] Admittedly, this kind of response feels a bit unfair to Jocko, who—it must be said—was behaving *very well* (although he could not have been very comfortable in that restricting suit). Fortunately, things quickly took a turn for the better. Reportedly, "after the first shock, the diners accepted Jocko with good grace, and he, in turn, handled his fork and knife like a gentleman of the old school."[7] As Lehr's wife later noted, "his manners compared favorably with some princes I have met."[8]

Alas, the slightest semblance of decorum only lasted for a while—largely because the many warnings that the prince was not to be given alcohol were mostly ignored. And so, like many party animals who would follow in his tiny footsteps, the increasingly inebriated monkey jumped up on the table and then began swinging from the chandelier, flinging lightbulb after lightbulb at the assembled guests.

Far from running away in fear, the partygoers loved it. After the event, many of the guests professed that it was one of the most entertaining nights of their lives. It did not matter that the joke was on them. They could surely say that *they* only came to the party because they found Mamie so amusing, not because they were really in awe of nobility. *They* wouldn't preen for a monkey if it had a title in front of its name—but they had some neighbors who would.

Few outside the spectacle found it quite as entertaining. Newspaper reports, for example, could see nothing funny at *all* about the evening, and certainly didn't see it as a jab on Mamie's part about Newport society kowtowing to aristocracy. They only saw a woman who let a monkey run amok for reasons they could not begin to fathom. Journalists "grasped their pearls," horrified by the impropriety of it all.

Why, the monkey had probably destroyed an expensive chandelier!

And what would Europeans think?

Americans through this period seemed to regard all Europeans as wealthy and particularly intimidating neighbors whose approval they desperately craved. Reporters cried out that "it is dreadful to think of distinguished foreigners coming over here and judging us by Mrs. Stuyvesant Fish's entertainments," since, after all, "New York Society represents America in the eyes of the foreign world and we should behave with a becoming sense of dignity."[9] Stories of this affair even made their way as far as France, where denizens of Chartres wrongly attributed the prank to a local French church leader named Henry Lehr, who had to issue a statement to the *Los Angeles Evening Post-Record* saying that "he had never dined with a monkey and was not that kind of man."[10]

Those kind of men were, seemingly, some of the richest and most important men in America.

If anything, these reports only added to Mrs. Fish's delight. Ever a proud American, she did not really care what the Europeans thought in the slightest. She was known for endlessly lamenting the fuss made over their arrival and complaining to anyone who would listen that "this country is making itself ridiculous in regard to titles."[11] No, as far as Mrs. Fish was concerned, wealth and status should be earned through hard work and enterprise—or, at least, through wit.

And she didn't curtail or sugarcoat this opinion, no matter who was in her company. When she met a Saxon prince on a trip to Nice, he expressed shock that her husband worked. With dismay, he declared that he'd thought her husband "came from a fine family."

"Oh, yes, he does," she'd replied. "But, you see, in America, it is not a disgrace to work. How much better it would be if those conditions prevailed in Europe! We in America would be spared so many titled nonentities."[12]

Clearly not everyone felt the same, especially in tony Rhode Island, and *that* was much more embarrassing than someone who'd worked for their fortune.

"Newport," she sniffed, "is paying too much attention to foreign lords. By marrying European noblemen, American girls are laying themselves liable to the ridicule of the world."[13]

The whole exchange reeked of desperation and delusion, as far as Mrs. Fish was concerned. Her thoughts on the topic were mirrored by a poem in *Life* magazine, which ran:

> *Such folly is its own rebuke*
> *so let them pay who can.*
> *But if 2 million buys a Duke*
> *How much would buy a man?*[14]

If the guests at the party were being ridiculed, that is what they had come to expect from a woman who often greeted them by saying, "Make yourself at home. No one wishes you were there more than I do."

By the time Jocko arrived in Newport, it was almost a privilege to be heckled by Mamie—or given any flicker of her attention at all. Mamie was a novelty in high society. For generations, famous families like the Astors had kept the rest of the elite in line, prizing respectability, propriety, and dignity above all else. But many had started to tire of this predictable snoozefest—and Mamie instinctively understood that.

"Society wants novel entertainment," Mrs. Stuyvesant Fish explained. "It is like a child...I try to give it fillips."[15] And when it came to the wealthy, that meant that "you have to liven these people up."[16]

Mamie did not want to be a pale, homegrown imitation of a European aristocrat. Before her, American socialites were primarily distinguished by their refinement and ladylike qualities. They could be glamorous, certainly, and positively gasping for breath under the weight of the jewels and finery, but they were not normally funny.

Mamie, on the other hand, was always the first to crack a joke, even when she knew she shouldn't. By her own admission, she could barely read or write. She had none of the musical skills that characterized upper-crust ladies. But she'd jump into a car and try to drive it, even if it meant a spectacular crash. She was never afraid to have a party, and when she partied, she wanted to have a laugh. She was bold, she was brash, she was sometimes thoughtless and overconfident, but she was *fun*. She didn't want to stay cooped up politely in a tower like a princess; she wanted to ride in streetcars, pamper her dogs, and host the best parties ever thrown.

Essentially, every twenty-first-century influencer owes Mamie a debt. Because she taught American women that even in an era when they might never wield the same power as their male counterparts, they could have as much fun as the men in their lives, and it would not be held against them.

And if you did not agree, if you were stodgy, boring, and rooted in the past, well—Mamie would make a monkey out of you.

CHAPTER 1

WHAT MAMIE WAS DOING WAS SO MEMORABLE LARGELY BECAUSE America was never supposed to be a nation that partied too hard. In fact, the Puritans who founded the country intended it to be quite the opposite.

Certainly, they meant for there to be socialization. Humans need to mingle, they're biologically conditioned to do so. Gathering together protects against anxiety, depression, and all manner of mental health issues. But the Puritans wanted a Godly, virtuous, sensible nation, which meant not replicating the parties they'd seen in Europe.

Up to and throughout the seventeenth century, Europe had been awash in fabulous festivities. In France, for example, King Louis XIV had discovered that if he kept the nobles partying, they would be perpetually too delighted—or at least too hungover—to foment a revolution. And this was a serious concern. In the forty years prior to his reign, nobles had incited a whopping total of *eleven* civil uprisings, all in attempt to seize power. Louis XIV understood that if he wanted to maintain some semblance of peace, he had to find a way to keep the upper class in his thrall.

Offering a sumptuous life at court proved itself to be the answer—at least temporarily. There was gambling. There were sumptuous meals, perfectly prepared. There were intellectual salons, scientific demonstrations, and musical performances. Nobles were assigned apartments according to rank. The higher you rose at court, the better your lodgings. It was like college, with none of the things that might have displeased you about college (unless the thing that displeased you was "intense, cliquey social competition," in which case, you would have had a very bad time).

Court was such fun that exile—or, as it was known, disgrace—was a constant terror. When one duke who displeased the king was exiled to his country home, he responded with such grief that, when he went to tell his wife, she initially assumed from his expression that one of their children must have died. "Living at their beautiful houses in the beautiful French countryside...these exiled nobles were considered, and considered themselves, dead."[1]

Never again could they attend the parties that were the cherry atop the sundae of court life.

Meanwhile, by hosting decadent and over-the-top parties like 1664's "Delights of Enchanted Island," the king could provide the nobles with the glitz, glam, and grandiosity they craved. At that particular six-day-long fete, the Palace of Versailles was lit up by thousands of candles, with ballet dancers prancing amidst elephants and masked servants carrying fruits, candied nuts, and pastries around to the guests. There were endless parades, horse races, and lotteries. It was also during this party that the playwright Molière staged *Tartuffe* for the first time at court, after which fireworks exploded overhead, casting an ethereal glow over the drunken spectators.

Four years later, the king was at it again with the "Great Royal Entertainment" of 1668, which began with a lavish garden tea. Afterward, guests were carried in sedan chairs to view a new play by Molière (the farce *George Dandin*), performed in a new outdoor theater that was illuminated by thirty-two crystal lamps. Later that evening, the guests danced at a ball surrounded by walls of flowers erected for the occasion. They could then wander to a secret cave hewn out of marble to carry on secret assignations, canoodling with anyone but their spouses.

This all ended up being an absolutely fabulous time, provided you were invited—which the many, many commoners were not. Eventually, they got understandably upset about money being spent on such celebrations when much of the country was starving. Consequently, as they were not being offered even a slice of this cake to eat, they staged an entirely different and shockingly bloody gathering now referred to as the French Revolution.

France was hardly the only setting for such indulgent celebration. The Italian city of Venice, which came to be known as "the Republic of Masks" by its English visitors, was defined by its festivals. Every year, from December 26 until Lent, Venetians—and plenty of foreigners—let loose and partook in a season full of Carnival festivities, most of which would make a nun blush. Firework shows were abundant, special dances commemorated Venetian power, strongmen formed "Hercules-strength human pyramids,"[2] and tightrope walkers gamboled overhead as people made their way to feasts and balls galore. Revelers cavorted under the cover of beautiful masks, which meant that anyone could be whomever they wished—at least for an evening or two. This disguise inherently afforded the costumed—particularly women—a certain degree of sexual freedom. Lady Mary Wortley Montagu, the eighteenth-century author, recalled these celebrations fondly, saying that "it is so much the established fashion for everybody to live their own way, that nothing is more ridiculous than censuring the actions of another."[3]

However, not everyone heard about parties where people were having unrestrained, anonymous sex and thought, "Delightful!"

Take America, "Land of the Free," where the Puritans went so far as to ban Christmas.

To be fair, England had enacted this decree first. No sooner did the intensely religious, conservative sect come to power in England in 1649 upon the execution of King Charles I than it immediately forbade Christmas celebrations, declaring that December 25 must instead be a day of "fasting and penance."[4] After all, there was no mention of Christmas in the Bible, and certainly nothing about revelry. This was generally unappreciated by the English populace, who had previously spent the twelve days of Christmas feasting, drinking, and caroling in order to demand entry to rich people's homes, who would then ply them with more food and drink. They would get truly, outrageously drunk. For many Englishmen and women, this period was a bright spot within an isolated, wintry season, but in the Puritans' view, the tradition was nothing short of "wanton bacchanalian" behavior.[5] Philip Stubbes, the Puritan writer, wrote in 1583 that surely everyone realized that at Christmas "more mischief is committed than in all the year besides? What masking and mumming? Whereby robberies, whoredom, murder, and whatnot, is committed? What dicing and carding, what banqueting and feasting, is then used more than in all the year besides!"[6] Meanwhile, in 1632, politician William Prynne declared that if anyone were to learn about Christianity from Christmas, would they not think "our Saviour to be a glutton, an epicure, a wine-bibber, a devil, a friend of publicans and sinners?"[7]

Anyone who has trudged through the vomit-coated streets following a rowdy weekend of SantaCon can probably relate, at least a bit, to these Puritan frustrations.

Puritanic rule in England did not last long, ending in 1660. But thirty years prior, Puritans had begun migrating to Massachusetts, where they established the city of Boston and could wage war on Christmas—and all other forms of excessive merriment—to their hearts' content. Christmas was finally banned in Boston in 1659, and it was decreed that "whosoever shall be found observing any such day as Christmas or the like, either by forbearing of labor, feasting, or any other way" would be fined. Christmas would not become a public holiday in Boston until 1856. And, while other early colonies, especially Southern ones, were more apt to celebrate Christmas with caroling and feasting, Christmas wouldn't even be accepted as a national holiday in America until 1870.

There was not much more in the way of merriment for Puritan society throughout the rest of the year. Dancing where men and women might touch was prohibited because, in the words of the clergyman (and subsequent president of Harvard University) Increase Mather, it was a temptation akin to seeing "naked necks and arms, or, which is more abominable, naked breasts."[8] Mather further regarded the fact that dancing was becoming common among Christians as something that "cannot be thought on without horror."[9]

To be fair, he was probably not watching really good dancing going on.

That's not to say the Puritans disavowed *all* festivities. If the Puritans reaped a good fall harvest, they were allowed to celebrate Thanksgiving where, after spending the day in church, the whole community could feast in gratitude. However, these days were greatly outnumbered by days of "solemn humiliation, fasting and prayer," wherein Puritans meditated upon what they might have done to make God punish them with a bad harvest or poor weather.

Some people have noted that the Puritans have been wrongly described as dour because, contrary to popular belief, they actually enjoyed colorful clothing. Good for them. However, it seems like they were more likely considered dour because penance and fasting were a nearly perpetual part of Puritan life. Guilt and hunger are rarely spirits that lend themselves to the desire to party. It's probably because of those habits that, some time later, author H. L. Mencken noted that Puritanism meant "the aesthetic spirit and its concomitant spirit of joy, were squeezed out of the original New Englanders, so that no trace of it showed in their literature or, even in their lives, for a century and a half after the first settlements."[10]

Ultimately, if you wanted to have a good time stateside back then, you needed to look outside New England, where other immigrant groups brought the celebrations of their countrymen with them to the New World. Like the seventeenth-century Dutch settlers in the Hudson Valley who celebrated Pinkster, a spring holiday similar to Easter. Participants attended church services but also dyed eggs, decorated with flower garlands, and ate sweets such as gingerbread. It was especially important to the enslaved populace, as they were allowed a few days off to visit with neighboring family.

By the mid-1700s, partying, complete with dancing and absent of prayer, became more common in the states. Corky Palmer, the eighteenth-century scholar and dance instructor, remarked that "in Virginia, dance, unlike in parts of puritanical New England, was both accepted and encouraged."

Upper-class children would even be trained by professional dancing masters, because knowing how to behave at a ball, especially when they were of marriageable age, was considered an important part of one's civility. Ladies attending galas were instructed to "let the Eyes appear lively and modest, and the Face express neither Mirth nor Gravity but the Medium, which will form an amiable Mein and always be agreeable."[11]

Meanwhile, festivals—such as those held on May Day, wherein the entire town would paint and decorate a maypole to dance around—emerged as an opportunity for lower-class townspeople to join in the fun. In general, the parties partaken in were open if not to all, at least to many. The "rituals of many festivals allowed for the participation of nearly all parts of society... gentile, or plebeian."[12] The diplomat and later President John Adams noted in 1769 that these celebrations were a good idea for uniting a multi-class society into a single community, as "they tinge the Minds of the People, they impregnate them with the sentiments of Liberty. They render the People fond of their Leaders in the Cause, and averse and bitter against all opposers."[13]

There was, however, still a line to be held. If these parties became *too* extravagant, Americans, still imbued with the spirit of their Puritan forebearers, responded quite differently than their European peers. This attitude was made clear in 1778, in occupied Philadelphia, when British officers hosted a *meschianza* (also called a *mischianza*). The meschianza was a large Italianate festival, and this particular one was intended to honor General Sir William Howe and Admiral Richard Howe, who were soon returning to England. The festivities were positively lavish. They were held at the recently abandoned Walnut Grove estate and overseen by Major John André, who would be most famous for later assisting Benedict Arnold. The meschianza commenced with a nautical regatta, which then segued into a medieval-style jousting tournament among British officers who had each been assigned a "lady" from the loyalist families of Philadelphia. The costumes alone for this event cost $12,000, which would be approximately $274,000 today. At the dinner, attendees were served by enslaved men "in oriental dresses, with silver collars and bracelets."[14] The Europeans appeared to enjoy this party a great deal. As William Howe's aide-de-camp Captain Friedrich von Muenchhausen later wrote, "everything was as splendid and magnificent as possible and all, even those who have been in Paris and London, agree that they have never seen such a luxurious fete."[15]

Sure, Louis XIV might have been impressed. But the Americans, who were already staging a revolt against the British, were not.

The colonists were especially furious when they realized that this party "was reported to have cost enough to feed and cloth[e] rebel armies for the rest of the war."[16] If anything, the outrageousness of this soiree drew the patriots closer together and revitalized their hatred for the enemy. After all, they were watching the British feast and fete about while their countrymen fought for their lives.

Elizabeth Drinker, a diarist from this period mused, "how insensible these people appear…while our land is so greatly desolated, and death and sore destruction has overtaken and impends over so many."[17]

At least some of the British officers noted this animosity—and even agreed with their more prudent opponents. Six years later, the British officer Charles Stedman wrote that "this triumphal *Mischianza* will be handed down to posterity, in the annals of Great Britain and America, as one of the most ridiculous, undeserved and unmerited triumphs ever yet performed." And when one governor leaving Gibraltar was asked by his officers if they could stage some entertainment for his departure, he groaned, "Anything, my friend, but a *mischianza*."[18]

George Washington, who was in Valley Forge when the infamous meschianza was underway, might have been more partial to it than many of the residents of Philadelphia. Washington *loved* a good party (he'd learned how to dance in his teens), and he hosted and celebrated many such occasions, though, quite reasonably, on a far smaller scale than British officers. In 1779, for example, Washington decided to celebrate the anniversary of the American alliance with France in Pluckemin, New Jersey (a convenient spot, as it was where the artillery encampment had been established during the war). A military surgeon to the Continental Army, Dr. James Thacher, remarked that "in the evening, a very beautiful set of fire-works was exhibited, and the celebration was concluded by a splendid ball, opened by his Excellency General Washington."[19] Gentleman George would dance for up to three hours at a time until he ensured that he had danced with every woman at a party, paying special attention to the beautiful women who wanted "a touch of him."[20]

He made sure they all got a touch.

One of the distinctive qualities of parties in America during this age is that most of them were still fairly democratic. Not everyone might have been invited to George Washington's parties. But revolutionary American festivals such as New Year's Eve, May Day, and Pope Day were open to *everyone*—with festivities and parades frequently held in the streets. As John Adams had said, these gatherings were intended to bring people together, not create division. This was supposed to be a country where everyone was theoretically equal.

However, as later eighteenth-century American cities like New York and Philadelphia began to flourish, this "come one, come all" mentality began to change. The rise of commerce meant that new, wealthy merchant classes emerged in the social hierarchy, and they were particularly eager to enjoy the fruits of their labor. People with more disposable income started going to assemblies (a.k.a. ticketed parties) and learning the newest dances from Europe, flaunting their access to leisurely activities. Finding a place on a highly coveted guest list at such parties was a status symbol in its own right, and showing off the latest fashions or trendiest dances might even work to secure a wealthier husband for a young debutante—or, in the case of a young gentleman, a more beautiful young bride.

Even so, keep in mind that these lively urban populations in the United States were still relatively small. While it was true that sixty thousand people lived in New York City by 1800, and women there might have been readying themselves for balls impeccably, 94 percent of Americans lived in rural settings at the time.[21] Living on a farm or even a plantation meant that there was often a great distance to travel between one homestead and the next. For those living in even more remote areas, parties couldn't be held regularly simply because you did not see other people routinely enough.

Kristen Richardson, the party historian, recounts one judge visiting wealthy newlyweds who lived in North Carolina. They lived well, but they also lived eighteen miles from the nearest home at a time when a horse-drawn carriage, at a consistent trot, could only go between eight to ten miles an hour, or at a walk, only two to four miles per hour. At that rate, it could sometimes be faster to walk briskly. Such long stretches passed without company that "when a male visitor told the young bride he would bring his own wife to visit her," Richardson writes, "she wept with gratitude."[22]

Consider the factors that made events like Carnival in Venice so popular. First, if you believe filmmaker Stanley Kubrick, there's always that eternal, innate human desire to put on masks and have sex with strangers. But second, and perhaps more logistically critical, everyone you wanted to party with was already within walking distance. Venetians could easily attend even multiple parties a day on foot. Not so for the average farm or plantation owner in America. One London visitor remarked with surprise that when Southern people visited other plantations for balls, they *slept over at the house*—simply because the travel to and from the festivities took so much time and effort. Going to a party was, consequently, an absolutely huge event.

Circumstances changed as the country urbanized. Though 94 percent of Americans lived in the countryside at the start of the nineteenth century, 20 percent of the population had moved to urban areas by 1860. Forty years later, that number had doubled, and 40 percent of Americans now lived in cities. One of the many advantages of that shift was an increased opportunity to socialize, which meant that parties began to be held on a scale that could rival European events.

Much of the time, it went badly. In 1860, Queen Victoria's son Albert, Prince of Wales, came to visit the states. He loved to dance, and parties were held for him on three separate evenings. On Thursday and Friday, the prince arrived punctually, but the parties and dancing did not actually begin with his arrival—as the hosts had underestimated the amount of preparation they needed to do. "Someone blundered," reported *The Baltimore Sun*, "on the reception day of Thursday, and last night." But now it was Saturday, and it was time to show the prince that Americans could put on a party. And at the ball that evening, held at the Academy of Music, everything appeared set to go off without a hitch. "God Save the Queen" played beautifully as the prince entered. The room was full of flowers that were costly and exotic. And it seemed that all wellborn New Yorkers attended, sporting jewels that would "have driven any particular dowager or dame before you quite mad with envy."[23]

Truly, they came in *droves*.

The party was packed. *Too* packed. As *The New York Times* reported:

In the days of our Grandmothers, who used to have their hair dressed two days in advance of one of these festivities…it was regarded as the height of fashion and the supreme of bliss to fill a house so full with embroidered belles and beaux that they stood upon one another's silken toes in the passages and stairways. Of our own days it may hereafter be said that the finest thing which 'four hundred select committee men' of New York could do to entertain the Prince of Wales was to invite to the Academy of Music, 500 people more than the house would hold, [and] amuse them by opening a pitfall in the floor and crush their toilettes into one indistinguishable mass of splendor.[24]

Less poetically, the stage upon which people had just begun dancing to Strauss's quadrille collapsed directly in front of the prince. The dancers righted themselves and began stammering apologies, at which point Hamilton Fish—who would later be Mamie's father-in-law—"rushed forward to reassure the house"[25] that this was only a minor break. Unfortunately, just as people were beginning to recover from their shock, a second portion of the stage collapsed. The attendees, apparently realizing there would not be more dancing, withdrew to supper. Meanwhile, "carpenters came on the scene, and a sort of modified anvil chorus, not in the original opera, was set up in the heart of the ball." Despite the best efforts of the carpenters to repair the stage, the ball itself could not begin until midnight.

And even when they did dance, it was kind of…bad. Mrs. Van Buren, the wife of President Van Buren, claimed she was continually on the verge of laughter watching the "grotesque figures" and wondering, "why, why will not our people learn to dance?"[26] Though the Prince of Wales was seemingly very polite about the chaos, he most likely wouldn't have counted it among the best-organized events he'd ever attended. As for the rest of the crowd, "some went home disgusted, more disappointed, and all mortified."

Other balls—catering to a very different kind of queen—were more successful, they just weren't being held by the white upper classes. Starting in 1867, the Odd Fellows Ball was held at the Hamilton Lodge, No. 710, in Harlem. Hosted by wealthy, free Black Americans, the interracial drag ball was a "grand jamboree of dancing, love making display, rivalry, drinking, and advertisement. The gala affair coming to a climax at the awarding of prizes for the most beautiful gown and the most perfect feminine body displayed by an impersonator."[27] As far as one can tell, their stages never collapsed. These balls attracted hundreds and then thousands of attendees— but they also attracted the police, who raided them and arrested guests. If you were the kind of person who hoped to mingle with the Prince of Wales, this would be a significant deterrent, despite the fact that these balls sound both more fun and better organized.

But then, not everyone was a dowager sporting stunning jewels. There were wealthy, white, heterosexual men who wanted to party too. Yet another culture of festivities, one which catered to "sporting men" who enjoyed gambling, drinking, and women, emerged in lower New York society during the mid-1800s. Concert halls featuring striptease acts or sex shows were abundant, allowing groups of men to convene and carouse. Anthony Comstock, a public moralist who spent an inordinate amount of time observing such erotic acts before actually calling the police, described paying five dollars to witness a "busy flea" dance. The concept behind this performance was that women had discovered a flea on their clothes and had to strip naked to get it off. Historian Timothy Gilfoyle recounts Comstock's experience, writing that, after he paid, "three women thereupon entered the room, dancing to the house's piano music. According to Comstock, he attentively watched the three women slowly disrobe and seductively expose themselves to several patrons. Then, to his amazement, they placed 'their faces and mouths between each others' legs, and lick or pretend to lick or suck on each others' private parts."[28]

Comstock performed a citizen's arrest on the three women and then immediately went to see another performance before the night was out. Because of course he did. It was for *research*. Needless to say, those dancers were not "respectable" women either.

There really wasn't much in the way of entertainment for respectable women. At least, not the kind of fun, flirty events that you might want to attend today. There were plenty of events where you could wait for two hours to dance, but anything beyond that was considered off-limits for refined ladies.

After all, this was not Europe. In 1840, Matilda Barclay, the daughter of the British consul general, attended a masked ball in the New York City home of former Mayor Philip Hone. She wore a $300 costume (which would cost about $10,000 today) that depicted the character Lalla Rookh from Thomas Moore's popular poem of the period. At the ball, she met her beloved T. Pollock Burgwyn, a young man from South Carolina who was dressed up as a character from the same poem. To her family's horror, "at four o'clock, without changing their costumes, they left the ball and were married before breakfast."[29]

The extent to which someone showing up to a masked ball in a costume that matches yours would read as fate, not coincidence, to two horny twenty-year-olds cannot be overstated. However, if you were a highly respectable man planning a financially advantageous marriage for your highly respectable daughter, this was the embodiment of a worst-case scenario. According to *The Evening World* newspaper, "as a result, masked balls were made taboo, and a fine of $1,000 was imposed on anyone who should give one—unless the giver told on himself, in which event the fine was reduced one-half."[30]

And New York City wasn't the only place where masked balls were deemed a little *too* much fun. In 1849, Boston issued a similar law banning masquerades, insisting that "any person who shall get up and set on foot, or cause to be published, or otherwise aid in getting up and promoting any masked ball, or other public assembly, at which the company wears masks…shall be punished by a fine not exceeding five hundred dollars; and for repetition of the offence, by imprisonment in the common jail or house of correction, not exceeding one year."[31]

The following year, masks were forbidden at a ball in Newport because "a number of papas and guardians had positively forbidden young ladies under their charge attending the ball if disguised faces were admitted."[32] This led to, of course, criticism of anti-mask sentiment in the press, which declared that everything was so much more sophisticated in Europe. In 1858, *Harper's Weekly* magazine bemoaned, "Paris, as everybody knows, abounds with masked balls.…It has been calculated that an experienced ball-goer might spend every night of January and February at a masked ball without going twice to the same place."[33]

And it wasn't just masquerades that unsettled the upper classes. Even costume balls in the 1840s, like the one hosted by the extremely respectable Ann Schermerhorn (the mother of Caroline Astor), were regarded with suspicion. At Schermerhorn's ball, attendees were instructed to dress as though they resided in the court of French King Louis XV. However, only 250 of the 600 invitees actually showed up, as "the invitation plainly stated what costume was required." And even those who hadn't dressed up were wary. Chroniclers of the Schermerhorn party—which was in later decades recalled as being rather splendid—"gave only the first and last letter of people's surnames, as Miss J—Y for Miss Jay."[34] This convention was likely intended to allow those attendees some plausible deniability if anyone found out they'd attended and deemed their presence inappropriate.

Upscale people, particularly women, found themselves in a difficult bind. They wanted to host parties in a way that people might, theoretically, consider to be European in style and sophistication; however, they also had to, somehow, do so in a way that would not offend their straitlaced Puritan ancestors. How, in short, could you host parties that were not going to destroy women's reputations but were still fun and exciting? What would such an event even look like?

This was the world that Mamie Fish was born into. And she was destined to show America how it was to be done.

CHAPTER 2

*T*HE *NEW-YORK TRIBUNE* WOULD LATER CLAIM OF MAMIE THAT "coming as she did from a distinguished line and marrying into a historical family of New York, her position in the world of society was assured from the start."[1] In reality, it was much more complicated than that. It is true that Mamie's story was not one of rags to riches. But neither was it a gilded, glossy upward trajectory of riches to more and more riches.

Mamie was born Marion Graves Anthon on June 8, 1853,[2] in Grymes Hill, an upscale area of Staten Island with great views of Brooklyn and, across Lower New York Bay, Manhattan. The family celebrating Mamie's arrival was extremely respectable. Her grandfather, John Anthon, had been the president of the Law Institute. Following John's example, Mamie's father, William, became a lawyer in 1848 at the age of twenty-one. As his obituary later noted, he was considered to be "a leading lawyer of this city"[3] who was wholeheartedly dedicated to his profession.

In 1850, William married Sarah "Sally" Attwood Meert. Sally's aristocratic legacy vastly outshone that of the Anthons. In their home country of

Belgium, the de Meert family had been added to the intimidatingly named Brussels "List of Patricians" all the way back in 1375.[4] Sally's father still held the title of the Count of Donberg, having ensured that the family's claims to nobility were verified by King William I of Holland in 1812.

Sadly, being a noble didn't make you smart about money. Sally's father spent much of his inheritance buying paintings. Though that pastime may sometimes prove itself to be a savvy investment—the world is full of rich people keeping Picassos in tax-free storage—a genealogy later written by Mamie's son, Stuyvesant Fish, notes that Sally's father was "quite an artist, but from the paintings of his collection I've seen, I think that he must have been a poor judge of other people's work or often swindled."[5] Predictably, the paintings he spent his fortune on did *not* appreciate in value—and ran the family coffers quite low indeed.

Sally's family might have fallen into the category of "Counts without accounts" that Mamie would later decry, but after they married, Sally's fortune greatly increased. William's legal business was thriving, and by 1851 he became a member of the Lower House of the state legislature. A year later, the couple's first child, Maria Theresa Anthon, was born, quickly followed by her sister, Mamie, in 1853. William and Sally then had another daughter, Grace, who died in infancy in 1855, before welcoming their youngest son, George, in 1859.

As happy a time as this was for the Anthon family, significant unrest was brewing in Staten Island, where the Anthons resided. Back in 1800, a quarantine hospital known as the New York Marine Hospital had been erected to treat anyone—immigrant or native—suffering from a contagious disease, such as smallpox, tuberculosis, and cholera. By 1850, all passengers on newly arrived ships to the New York harbor—often immigrants—were inspected, and anyone showing the slightest signs of an illness was sent right to the hospital. While this in theory would help prevent new diseases from entering the country, there was still the matter of hospital workers who went back and forth between communities.

In 1858, an outbreak of yellow fever descended upon the town. A Dr. Anderson wrote in August of that year that the outbreak originated with "some of the employees of the Quarantine establishment" and that such out-breaks were inevitable so long as "the Quarantine occupies its present absurd and dangerous position." Everyone was outraged that the hospital employees were basically picking up diseases, going home, and depositing them neatly into the community, thus defeating the point of a quarantine hospital. Not to mention the fact that, according to the *Springfield Daily Republican* news-paper, "the iron scow upon which the infected clothing taken from the dead and dying patients was burned was frequently anchored so near the shore that the smoke and stench entered the house of the islanders."[6]

In a rage, hundreds of citizens formed a mob and burned the hospital to the ground. William Anthon defended the rioters who set fire to the building, successfully arguing in court that the hospital had become such a nuisance that the citizens' arson was really little more than a form of self-defense. Nonetheless, something about the incident—maybe the dis-ease, the stench, the fiery riots—convinced him that *he* did not want to live in Staten Island any longer, and the Anthon family moved northward to the Manhattan neighborhood of Gramercy Park, near Sarah's family.

This wouldn't be what William Anthon was best remembered for, though. Grandson Stuyvesant noted that during his tenure as judge advocate gen-eral in 1863 Manhattan, William was the one who "drew up the Draft Bill which [ultimately] caused the draft riots in New York."[7] While some news-papers attempted to alleviate the blame from him, William *had* been pub-licly commended for carrying out this bill to "completeness"[8] in *The New York Herald* about seven months before the riots began.

Written in response to growing anxieties centering on the country's gruesome civil war, the Draft Bill exempted wealthy men from serving in the Union Army if they could pay $300 for a poorer man to take their place. The bill also dictated that Black people were exempt from the draft entirely—because they were "not citizens." In retrospect, it seems fairly obvious that this would be a recipe for boiling resentment. Many men from lower classes were furious that rich men could buy their way out of the war while they were forced to fight. Rather than taking their anger out on the wealthy, or William himself, they proceeded to massacre the Black citizens of New York—many of them children—over the course of five grisly days. Among the riot's many horrors, the Colored Orphanage Asylum—which was "financially stable and well-stocked with food, clothing, and other provisions" and considered to be "a symbol of black upward mobility"—was attacked by the white mob as "the children, numbering 233, were quietly seated in their school rooms, playing in the nursery, or reclining on a sick bed in the Hospital."[9] It wasn't long before the building was burned to the ground.

If anything could mar one's personal and professional legacy, contributing to an atrocity on this scale *certainly* could. Although William remained a chairman of the Republican Committee of the Sixteenth Assembly District until his death, his private practice suffered, and so did William's general demeanor.[10] In his youth, he'd been known as a formidable and captivating speaker; those who remembered him later on, however, recalled a man obviously beset by anxiety and concern.

Of course, he did have plenty of other things to worry about too. Even though William had an estate worth the modern equivalent of around $900,000 ($25,000 in 1860),[11] he was known to spend money freely and was often short on ready funds. Sadly, that liberal spending did not extend to his daughters' education. By her own account, Mamie could barely write, though this wasn't *exactly* true; there are documented letters written by her to her family members that are perfectly intelligible, though those letters do parenthetically note her difficulty spelling certain words.

Limited educational opportunities were not uncommon for young women back then, even wealthy young women. Though the New York newspapers were filled with advertisements for girls' schools, that education wasn't formalized, even while the instruction at boys' schools during these years was still consistent with what we might expect today. In 1856, *The New York Times* described a boys' school in the Fourth Ward in Manhattan where young men were trained and tested in "reading, grammar, arithmetic and minor studies."[12] However, the same newspaper notes that the girls' school, located only one floor above the boys' school, only offered training in . . . singing. Singing without even the aid of a piano (for what it's worth, they were said to be quite good). Believe it or not, this same "schooling" was actually an improvement over the educational standards a few decades prior, insofar as young women were able to regularly gather together, socialize with their peers, and learn *something*. Up until the 1820s, schooling for girls had largely taken place at home, where women would be taught household skills and basic literacy by their mothers. Even in the event that girls were educated outside the home, that education generally ended around the age of twelve.[13] It was only in the 1830s that women began to receive higher education at institutions like Oberlin, as it became increasingly acceptable for some women to become teachers for younger grades.

Newspapers from the time chronicle the myriad opinions across society regarding how women should be educated. As such, by 1860, "the world is full of schools for girls, but we have never found a dozen men perfectly agreed as to what is best for schoolgirls, or, in fact, what schoolgirls are for. One man...associates them with ideas of music and dancing. Another believes they were born to be cooks...another suggests French...a fourth has no doubt that any mother's daughter of them all will be a clever woman if you only give her a chance, and talks of a vote and oration."[14] The result of this wide spectrum effectively meant that one supposedly educated young woman might be a very competent pianist but barely know how to write, whereas another might speak perfect French but have no mathematical knowledge whatsoever.

That's not to say that skills taught at girls' schools were wholly useless; for instance, a young woman might, indeed, be called on to play the piano at a party more often than asked to do long division (unless the party was full of passionate mathematicians). However, what it really meant was that there was little consensus or coordination on what constituted "education" for young women.

The fact that Mamie's father wasn't focused on giving his daughters an education—however happy he was to spend his money on other diversions—wasn't atypical. Mamie's claim later in life that she could barely read might even have served as a kind of humblebrag, stressing that she came from a traditional family, not a more progressive one that favored female education at newer schools like Vassar, Wellesley, and Smith. She did not need to write, it was implied, because she was not the kind of girl who would *have* to become a teacher when she grew up. Really, she did not need to do anything. In a time when refined women were expected to play the piano or sing, whenever Mamie was asked if she played anything, she briskly replied "a comb" and proceeded to zing on its tongs. She always seemed to stress that her natural wit and aplomb, not any nerdy book learning, was sufficient to carry her through life.

In any event, Mamie's father had spent his money as quickly as he made it, and following his death in 1875, when Mamie was twenty-two, the family found themselves nearly destitute. Mamie's mother was, understandably, terrified. The family "went into a huddle, pooled their resources, and moved to Astoria."[15] This was a significant residential downgrade. At the time, Gramercy Park was seen as one of the toniest portions of the city, boasting stately townhomes and a beautiful private park available only to the residents that the Brooklyn papers derisively termed "the so-called high [born]."[16] That park is still only open to residents today, and Brooklynites regard it with the same derision.

Meanwhile, Astoria in the 1870s primarily consisted of German immigrants. The neighborhood was also known for cabinet and furniture factories, as well as the piano factory of Steinway & Sons, but it was still a far cry from the posh splendor of Gramercy Park. *The Brooklyn Daily Times* newspaper went so far as to report on the sheer unpleasantness of even *getting* to Astoria—since only two horse-drawn trains went out there. Lest you think that it at least was not filled with the stench of burning, infected clothing, well—the *Times also* made note of a profoundly unpleasant smell of grease and smoke that greeted those who made the journey to Astoria. *The Brooklyn Union* seconded this assessment and rather dryly remarked on "the evident prevalence of an unpleasantness between the oil factories of the petroleum capitalists, who don't live there, and the olfactories of people who must live there, resulting in a clamour for a municipal regulation of smells."[17]

Shortly after the move, Mamie's fifteen-year-old younger brother, John, went to work selling dry goods to provide for the family. Now in her early twenties, Mamie was too wellborn to be trained for service, and yet her lack of education also made her a poor choice for a teacher or governess. She could only teach kids how to make jokes, which was not yet a marketable skill. Basically, she had only one option to help her family: She needed to marry *very well*.

Mamie knew it would fall to her to do this, as her older sister Maria Theresa, called Tess by all who knew her, made it clear that she had no interest in settling down and marrying a man. Newspapers at the time did not speculate on her sexuality, but the fact that she didn't seem like the marrying kind of woman comes up a lot. You have to imagine the family was not pinning any hopes on her. She did actually marry in 1896 when she was well into her forties. But even when she did wed, it's worth noting that she married a man who "although he spends much of his time in this city [New York], is a Californian, and lives in San Francisco."[18] Tess, meanwhile, would continue to live in New York.

Ultimately, an unexpected, long-distance marriage, decades into the future, was not going to help the Anthons with their current predicament. If someone was going to rescue this family from the rank smells and scourge of Astoria—and fast—that burden would fall on Mamie's shoulders.

She was not a great beauty. She'd been dismissing every ladylike accomplishment as being for nerds her entire life. She no longer had an admirable Gramercy Park address for suitors to visit. And yet, in a moment that should inspire women everywhere, she had absolutely no problems landing an adoring millionaire.

CHAPTER 3

*E*NTER STUYVESANT FISH, WITH WHOM MAMIE HAD DEVELOPED A friendship during their childhood days in Gramercy Park. Now, *this* was a man who could get Mamie's entire family out of the mediocrity of Astoria. After all, Stuyvesant Fish was born "with a silver spoon in his mouth big enough to be called a soup ladle."[1]

Stuyvesant's family was composed of people somewhat richer and far more serious than Mamie's relations. There would be no frivolous art purchases among the Fish (who, it must be said, were *always* called "the Fish," never "the Fishes"). On his mother's side, Stuyvesant was descended from Peter Stuyvesant, the last governor of New Amsterdam (before it became New York). Meanwhile, Stuyvesant's father, Hamilton Fish, was named after his father's friend, the one and only Alexander Hamilton, a man beloved almost as much by the Fish family as he was by every musical theater student to come. "Absolved from labor by a large inheritance in real estate from his father and his uncle,"[2] Hamilton studied law at Columbia College. He went on to be a New York governor from 1848 to 1850, then a United States senator from 1851 to 1857, and later on, the secretary of state under President Ulysses S. Grant.

That last position was proposed to Hamilton by a man of "African persuasion"[3] named Wormley, who had been enslaved by Cassius M. Clay (a famous abolitionist, but not so devout an abolitionist that he did not own slaves). After Wormley was freed, he opened a hotel, which the Fish family regularly patronized when in Washington. Wormley always "had great admiration"[4] for Hamilton Fish. Most people did. Hamilton was said to be "well bred, well informed, courteous, sound in judgment and thoroughly a man of affairs."[5]

Unlike the attitude that pervaded the Anthon home, a certain degree of care and thought went into the education of Hamilton's children, and Stuyvesant and his siblings spent some time abroad in their youth. In 1857, when Stuyvesant was six years old, the family resided in Paris, and he started studying with a French tutor. Although he was very young, he then begged his parents to attend school in Geneva with his older brothers, Nicholas and Hamilton Jr., and was permitted to do so for several months. In 1859 the family returned to New York, and Stuyvesant attended Charlier's School on East Twenty-Fourth Street. If you thought those girls' schools, which might feature only singing, were weird, just know that at Charlier's, "on Saturday nights certain boys were chosen to fight with each other." In a letter to the politician James W. Wadsworth Jr., Stuyvesant notes that these were referred to as "kid scraps."[6]

This is what happens when all the schools are private and there's no universal curriculum in place: Baby Fight Club.

Nevertheless, Stuyvesant survived these diminutive battles and went on to graduate from Columbia College in 1871. At his commencement, he gave a speech about the study of political economy, noting that "wealth in a nation implies happiness, not the accumulation of wealth, but wealth distributed among the people, as each is best fitted by nature and education to enjoy it... [let us have] a Republic of free enlightened liberty, extending to all citizens the blessings of peace, justice, and liberty."[7]

Needless to say, this was a very idealistic outlook of the world, and one his peers would largely oppose in the coming decades.

Hamilton Fish had initially hoped that Stuyvesant would study law after graduating and was "greatly distressed"[8] when Stuyvesant instead expressed a desire to work as a clerk in the office of the president of the Illinois Central Railroad. To his father, Stuyvesant might have seemed boyishly enthusiastic about the possibilities of railroads, but he was, in retrospect, right to be excited. In 1871, there were forty-five thousand miles of railroad tracks in America. By the end of the century, 170,000 more miles of tracks had been laid down.[9] The first transcontinental railroad, connecting the western and eastern states from Council Bluffs, Iowa, to Oakland, California, had just been completed in 1869. The olden days of covered wagon trails—on which hundreds of thousands of people had traveled west, beginning in 1841—were quickly coming to an end. Suddenly, the average person could travel, with relative ease and safety, from one side of the nation to the other via train.

The entire country was opening up. A generation of young people now realized that they could live *anywhere.* Or else they could pick a city on the map and just visit it, for fun. This would be a feeling akin to technology developing that allowed everyday individuals to travel through space to visit different planets. No wonder Stuyvesant wanted to work in the railroad industry; nothing at the time was more exciting.

His father ultimately conceded and supported his son's decision—provided that Stuyvesant lived entirely off his own earnings, which, at that time, were only about three dollars a week (or around seventy-seven dollars today).[10] Stuyvesant agreed. However, he soon complained to his father that he didn't have enough money to take the streetcar from his boarding house to his office. This was, predictably, especially unpleasant when it was raining or snowing. His *extremely wealthy* father then asked him how much the streetcar cost. When Stuyvesant replied it was six cents (about two dollars today), his father retorted, "Well, I think I would keep right on walking. It's more economical than riding. You'll wear out some shoe leather, but not 6 cents every day."[11]

While Stuyvesant was walking to and from that boarding house, the Fish were masterminding glorious futures for the rest of their progeny. They expected their several daughters to marry wealthy suitors; for instance, it was reported that Edith, Stuyvesant's sister, "should marry a Peer of Great Britain or a German prince."[12] In 1869, older brother Nicholas married Clemence Smith Bryce, the sister of Lloyd Bryce, who would become ambassador to the Netherlands. In terms of their aspirations, these families were well matched. By 1871, Nicholas was the second secretary of legation in Germany, and by 1877, he was the chargé d'affaires to the Swiss Confederation. Both the Bryces and the elder Fish strove for diplomatic appointments abroad and flaunted their foreign connections.

In 1874, even Stuyvesant took a break from his work at the railroad and went abroad. Far from being exciting and taking him to exotic locales, he found that most of the work at the Illinois Railroad simply required him to copy letters long into the evening, after which he presumably had to walk home in the rain. And so, when a position with the bank Morton, Rose & Company came up in London, he readily accepted. There, he was informed, work always ended at 5:00 p.m., precisely when tea was served in the office— truly the nineteenth-century equivalent of luring in promising employees by boasting an office kitchen well stocked with snacks and seltzers. Fortunately, the work/life balance *was* better at Morton, Rose & Company; there was not only tea but numerous holidays and long weekends to be enjoyed with friends in London.

And he did enjoy spending those weekends away from home. Stuyvesant's new accommodations were not quite as pleasant as the office. In his chilly lodgings on Half Moon Street, "the tiny coal fire gave off just enough heat to prevent one's face and hands from chapping and bunions breaking out on one's toes."[13] He roomed with another young man from a similarly distinguished family named George Bliss, though the two had little in common. Simply put, as Stuyvesant explained, they "bored each other."[14] Within a few weeks of living together, they'd run out of stories about their shared experiences and quickly found they had nothing else to talk about. Rather than try to make increasingly awkward small talk with his roommate, Stuyvesant spent as little time in these accommodations as possible and accepted all dinner invitations from anyone who was generous enough to extend them.

When he was not working or attending dinner parties, much of Stuyvesant's time in London was spent in the dogged pursuit of Hugh Leslie Courtenay, a dashing twenty-one-year-old con man who claimed to be related to the Duke of Devon. Early on during Stuyvesant's time in London, Courtenay had met Stuyvesant and persuaded him to loan him five pounds (about $900 today). Unfortunately, Courtenay apparently forgot about the "loan" part of the equation and considered the money a more permanent gift. Stuyvesant—who had, among other indecencies, *walked to work* to save money and was now shivering in a flat alongside an insufferable roommate—was furious. He proceeded to hunt "that man and his alleged relations all over England, interviewed admirals, his supposed uncles, dukes, tailors, etc."[15] Hunting down Courtenay became an all-consuming hobby for Stuyvesant during this period. Courtenay fled to Philadelphia, using the title Lord Beresford, where he was "said to have captured the young bloods who ape the English, and gained admittance to the Union League Club." Even a fictitious title in these times could take you far. Courtenay was eventually brought to justice by a broker he attempted to swindle in 1880, but it seems like he had a lot more fun than Stuyvesant did in London beforehand.

And Courtenay wasn't the only problem on Stuyvesant's mind. Stuyvesant hadn't had particular luck with women, neither abroad nor at home. It wasn't for lack of opportunity; as an eligible bachelor from a good family, he was introduced to many young women, especially as he dined out three or four nights a week to avoid his freezing apartment. However, he found English women "rather plain and excessively poorly dressed." The dinner conversations were also fairly intellectual, and while he found himself trying to keep up by reading Darwin, he admitted in his letters to friends back home that it was very slow going for him. He's not wrong—Darwin is slow going, especially if you're a man whose temperament runs toward "loving fast trains" and "trying to hunt swindlers." As a result, he was quite lonely, and he had no better luck with American women. He assured an associate in a letter, dated March 26 of 1874, that he did not "write to any young lady at home."[16]

That situation changed late in the spring of 1874 when he returned to New York, and presumably a warmer home, to work for Morton & Company. By

May, he was ordering flowers to be sent to Mamie Anthon for her birthday on June 8. Thoughtful as it might be, this wasn't entirely selflessly motivated. She'd previously mentioned in passing that when she'd attended a dance with him in the past, he hadn't sent any flowers, despite their budding friendship. Not to worry, she'd airily assured him, their (extremely wealthy) contemporary, Robert Goelet, had remembered. Perhaps spurred on by a sense of competition, Stuyvesant not only remembered to send birthday flowers but sent a follow-up letter on July 9 to make sure they had arrived.

The fact that Mamie encouraged Stuyvesant's attentions may have been a relief to him. For all his reading of Darwin, women hadn't seemed to enjoy talking to him any more than his roommate had. Though his letters paint a picture of himself as an interesting, hardworking person, he was considered gruff by even his good friends, and somewhat lacking in charm. One woman, Julia Newberry, who had sat with Stuyvesant at a dinner party, noted in her diary, "I went to my first dinner party and never in my life was I so bored. I had the illustrious Stuyvesant Fish [seated next to me] who, in spite of having a grandfather, is less than an idiot."[17]

Brutal.

And also, incorrect! He was simply having a bad time in London, where he found, "time flies, but I wish it went by rail *as being a more rapid conveyance.*"[18] If he'd truly been a fool, it's doubtful that he and Mamie, famous for her wit, could have lived so happily together. Everyone who knew them found them to be wonderfully devoted to each other. It was an "opposites attract" kind of dynamic; whereas he was often seen as being "a big silent man who never wasted words," Mamie was known to "keep up a constant flow of light chatter."[19] He thought she was a hoot, and she loved that he was a constantly amused audience for her jokes and adventures.

By March 2, 1876, less than two years after their reunion, the two of them were engaged to be wed. To her credit, Mamie didn't try to hide her recent circumstances from Stuyvesant. He complained that he spent many days making his way to and from Astoria. Even so, his feelings for Mamie outweighed the fact that, in the eyes of his parents, the Anthons had fallen on hard times, and their daughter was a less-than-ideal marriage prospect.

People would later say of Stuyvesant's regard for Mamie that "whatever she chose to do or say was right. There was something romantic in his devotion to her. Had he lived in the Middle Ages he would have ridden into battle at her lightest word."[20]

The pair married at the Church of the Transfiguration on June 1, 1876. Better known, then and now, as "the Little Church Around the Corner," the name came about when the actor George Holland died. His friends went to see if his funeral could be at a Fifth Avenue church. They were refused once the clergymen were informed it was an *actor* and not a proper, respectable corpse who needed the service. When they asked where they could go, the Little Church Around the Corner on East Twenty-Ninth Street was suggested. A brother-in-law of the Fish, Dr. George Hendric Houghton, had founded the church in 1848, and he swiftly agreed to hold the funeral. By that time, Houghton had been hiding escaped enslaved people at the church for years. During the draft riots, many Black New Yorkers ran to the church for shelter. The police advised Houghton against taking them in, as churches that did so were being burned to the ground. When a mob did arrive at the church, Houghton confronted them, shaking his fist and shouting, "You white devils, you! Do you know nothing of the spirit of Christ?"[21]

The church, and all the souls in it, survived the riots.

This story is worth noting partly because it is lovely to remember that there are people who behave excellently in terrible times. But it also suggests that holding a funeral for an actor seems like one of Dr. Houghton's lower-stress events, and not something he would have thought twice about. Amazingly, that funeral proved to be what he was most remembered for. When news of Holland's plight reached the theater community, actors across the country sent donations to the Little Church Around the Corner. And so, it became known as a church for actors and other creative professionals.

The Fish family held closely with all of Dr. Houghton's views. Nothing made Hamilton's wife, Julia, prouder than that "her grandfather, in 1787, had been on the committee which reported the first ordinance with a clause prohibiting slavery."[22] Considering Mr. Anthon's ignominious involvement in the draft riots, it may have been fortunate that he was dead before the wedding between his daughter and Julia's son.

That June 1, the Little Church celebrated the union of the Fish couple. In addition to the entire Fish clan, attendees included the Pierreponts, known for developing the Brooklyn Heights area, and the Cuttings, who would develop the neighborhood of Red Hook. The service was followed by a reception for the "fashionable assemblage."[23] Mamie had six bridesmaids, including her sister and Edith Fish, soon to be her sister-in-law, who "wore white muslin dresses trimmed with lace, and each carried a bouquet of different colored rosebuds."[24] In a particularly romantic gesture, Stuyvesant, besotted with his new wife, pressed a rose from the wedding and kept it in a book until his death, alongside one of Mamie's love letters to him.

In the newspaper report recounting the wedding, Marion (who was always known as Mamie) had her name spelled Marian. Her wedding might've been the only time in her life that a well-bred woman of this period could expect to have her name in a newspaper, so the misprint seems even more unfortunate. But then again, no one ever expected Marion to be the star of this marriage. That honor would surely fall to Stuyvesant, with his high ideals from Columbia, his business success, and the new house in Gramercy gifted to the couple by his parents.

CHAPTER 4

No SOONER DID THE COUPLE DEPART FOR THEIR HONEYMOON upstate in Garrison than Stuyvesant would be frantically called back to work in the city. Why? Well, because apparently no one else at the Morton office knew how to open the office safe. This was a real "being called back to work because no one else knows how to turn on the computers" situation.

Mamie was—understandably—furious. According to her family, she "never forgave Morton & Company for breaking up her honeymoon."[1] She was fairly certain that Morton & Company was made up of idiots, which does seem hard to argue against considering the safe situation. And boy, was it about to get worse.

The situation at Morton quickly deteriorated. Six months after his marriage, Stuyvesant Fish was welcomed as a broker at the New York Stock Exchange. Upon his initiation, "there was a signal for a general assault, and he was punched from every member of the board from 12:15 until 3 o'clock."[2] It was "kid scraps" all over again. This was just a normal hazing ritual these adult, professional men did.

Less than enthused, and with Mamie's encouragement, Stuyvesant returned to working for the Illinois Central Railroad in 1877. The hours were long, but on the bright side there were no recorded assaults. Mamie was distressed only that sometimes his new job required him to go away on lengthy work trips. During one such trip early in their marriage, she wrote him that "I really don't know what I will do without you all this long time—for it is almost ten days before you will be home again.... I shall not let you go away again without me if I can help it—as I think it's horrid....Do remember what you promised me about not jumping from one car to the other, as you might get hurt."[3] Despite their differing familial circumstances, the young couple were quite happy and very much in love. And while it's true that Mamie had to marry for financial security, it's also true that she adored her husband—and the two remained loyal to each other for the rest of their lives.

Knowing this, it surprised no one that on Tuesday, July 1, 1879, at 10:15 in the evening, Mamie gave birth to the couple's first child, Livingston Fish. His birth was greeted with rapturous delight by his entire family. Instead of employing a wet nurse, she'd even chosen to breastfeed, which had recently become fashionable. Like so many first-time mothers before and after her, Mamie was determined to use the most up-to-date science to do whatever was best for her baby. Also like so many women throughout history beginning their parenting, she wanted to be the perfect mother.

Livingston was christened at the Little Church Around the Corner, where the couple was wed. There, the infant behaved, according to his father, "with great decorum"[4] during the service as "between you and me, he was asleep the whole time."[5] Afterward, his relatives toasted the couple with a bottle of Madeira that had been given to Stuyvesant upon his birth for him to use at a future celebratory occasion. Mamie was there dressed in white muslin and looking wonderful, at least in the estimation of her proud husband, who claimed that she already "looked like her old self."[6] Their new house was similarly excellent, according to Stuyvesant, who wrote to tell his father that "you cannot imagine what a boon our new home has been to her, a flood of light and plenty of air from three sides have, I doubt not, contributed very materially to her and the baby's well being."[7]

Sadly, just six months later, little Livingston died.

In 1880, the mortality rate for children under five was 347 per 1,000 births, which meant that approximately one baby in three would never reach their fifth birthday.[8] These infants were usually felled by diseases like tuberculosis, diphtheria, diarrhea, dysentery, rubella, and typhoid fever. It wasn't until 1880, a year after Livingston's death, that the first organization for pediatricians, the Section of Diseases of Children of the American Medical Association, was established. Doctors working with children implored women to breastfeed or use a wet nurse, as formula did not yet exist, and babies were otherwise fed a deadly diet of "pap" (mashed bread mixed with milk) or "swill milk," which came from cows housed in filthy conditions that had often contracted bovine tuberculosis. Studies found that "more than half of New York's infants who were spoon-fed (not nursed or wet-nursed) in the summer, died before fall."[9] When people on social media talk about how women don't need formula, well, this is what the world looked like prior to the invention of infant formula.

Heartbroken, the young couple went on, enduring the tragedy as so many others during the era did, and continued to have children. A year later, in 1881, a baby girl named Marian was born. She was soon to be followed by Stuyvesant Jr. in 1883, whose birth gave his mother an "awful time." That may have been because he was born weighing a whopping thirteen pounds (notably, the family had to borrow a neighbor's scale as their own only went up to *twelve* pounds). After the birth, Stuyvesant Sr. wrote that "Mamie mends slowly and does not sleep well...[but] the heathen is very hearty and noisy—blissfully unconscious of all the trouble he has caused."[10] Their next son, Sidney, followed two years later in 1885. In a stroke of great luck, the three of them all lived to adulthood.

Later in life, Mamie would wax rhapsodic about the joys of motherhood and lament that "we have too little of the children, and the word 'mother' sounds old fashioned and prosaic to the growing generation." Considering the circumstances of her second-to-last child's birth, that's an impressive attitude. Anyone who gives birth to a thirteen-pound baby without medication deserves accolades—and possibly a medal. However, what "mothering" meant for middle- and upper-class women during this period was very different from what "traditionally minded" people would have you believe today. There is a modern notion that in the past, women—*happily!*—minded their offspring round the clock while also cooking and baking and cleaning their homes, but the reality for middle- and upper-class women was quite different.

Later in his life, Mamie's son Stuyvesant Jr. recalled that on a typical day, he and his siblings would head downstairs around 8:00 a.m. for breakfast with their father before he left for the office. Mamie preferred to sleep in and take her breakfast (prepared by the cook, brought to her by a maid) in bed while reading the letters she had received, which was a common practice for married women at the time. After finishing their own breakfast, the children would come up to their mother's bedroom to chat with her, where she would be "propped up in bed with the breakfast tray in her lap."[11] The children would get morning cuddles and, one assumes, age-appropriate updates on Mamie's correspondence. Afterward, the children would receive "sketchy lessons"[12] in whatever topic seemed to engage them from tutors until about 11:00 a.m.

Then, their governess would take them on a walk to visit with their grandparents if they were in the city. The Fish residence was located at Twenty-Second Street and Second Avenue, and fortunately for Mamie and her little ones, their grandparents and their beloved aunt, Tess, Mamie's sister, lived very close by. Aunt "Tinie," as she was affectionately called, lived just a few streets south on Fifteenth Street (in a house paid for by Stuyvesant) and was known to be "the confidante to whom every member of the family told their griefs and joys."[13] The Fish grandparents resided on Seventeenth Street, and the children loved visiting their grandfather's abundant gardens—comprising an orchard—filled with fruit trees, upon which the siblings loved to play. Stuyvesant Jr. was especially fond of his grandfather and recalled him being surrounded by books and newspapers and sporting "a mop of untidy grey hair, with a beard of the same description." Their grandfather would also entertain them with wild stories; as Stuyvesant Jr. fondly recalled, "Grandpa talked interestingly. I know of few men of 81 or 84 who could hold the attention of a boy of 6 or 9."[14]

Later in the day, the children would be tended to by their governess or visit with Mrs. Fish before she departed for dinner or the opera, all before being put to bed themselves by the governess.

The Fish children's lives did not appear to have been made unpleasant by the fact that their mother did not spend every moment with them. Nor was Mamie considered a neglectful mother in any sense; if anything, she was considered a *good* mother because she shared lunch with her children and made time to see them in the mornings and some evenings. Not all mothers in similar circumstances could say the same; in fact, some found that they really preferred not to see their children on a daily basis.

If this description makes you feel that modern-day motherhood is more difficult by comparison, you are correct. The village of people, paid and unpaid, who surrounded Mamie Fish and helped her raise her brood has largely been replaced by a single coffee machine. Rather than being brought their breakfast in bed, women who stay at home today are often expected to do everything without asking for any help, and they're told that's the way it was in "the good old days." On top of that, they're supposed to be *grateful* to have the privilege of doing everything, given that many women cannot afford to stay home. In the actual past, however, everyone of means understood that it required a great many people taking turns to raise children happily, so that all the adults could have many hours a day to themselves—a concept that seems to have evaded the "traditionalist" social media influencers now longing for the "simpler" days of yore.

In addition to time with her children, Mamie's days involved balancing numerous social engagements, which she thoroughly enjoyed. Certainly, this was expected of many monied women in New York. One of the fascinating shifts during this century was that more women could begin to curate their own social circles. They were not weeping with joy just because they would maybe get to meet another woman on their remote farm. No longer confined to conversing with neighbors or the spouses of their husband's friends and colleagues, these women could actually pick their *own* friends, based on shared interests or personalities.

And personality, in a woman, suddenly mattered more than it used to. Some women were simply more fun to hang out with than others. In the rural past, a good woman was one who worked on or managed the farm and bore and raised her children to be similarly hardworking and Godly. It might have been nice for her immediate family if she was funny, but it wasn't a huge advantage. The farm would not grow better food because you made terrific jokes.

Besides, there often simply wasn't enough social interaction for that to make a difference. One account from George Washington's granddaughter, Nelly, who had grown up in New York City, demonstrates this. Upon visiting her grandfather's home of Mount Vernon in 1796, Nelly Custis noted dolefully that "I stay constantly at home...I have been out twice since I came here (which is three weeks)." Even in very upper-class rural society, long travel distances to other homes for balls or fetes often meant that it was prudent to sleep over at the host's house. This inconvenience for both guests and the hosts meant that opportunities to mingle were relatively scarce (and explains why a ball being thrown is a huge deal in Jane Austen novels). In a city like New York, you could take a carriage to your host's home in no more than half an hour. So while Custis might have only been out twice in three weeks at Mount Vernon, at her home in New York it would not have been uncommon to go out every day.

There was enough of a dense population for women to form their own social circles and exert power in those circles. And the power of being able to do that well, while being popular on top of that, could increase her family's prosperity. A woman who hosted magnificent parties might, for instance, be able to assist her husband with necessary connections in his career. By allowing another man's son or daughter onto a coveted guest list, her husband might be looked on more favorably in his occupation. As an added bonus, she would also have the personal pleasure that came from the power of making that guest list in the first place.

And just as Stuyvesant seemed to sense that railroads were going to be huge, Mamie seemed to understand that extroverted, exciting women who loved the spotlight were the future.

Mamie's in-laws did not expect to see their daughter-in-law spreading her social butterfly wings very widely, particularly because their generation's social vanguard was expected to be led by Nicholas, Stuyvesant's older brother, and his wife, Clemence. At the time, it was thought that "the eldest branch of the house was the head of the line, and to it, deference, dignity and all courtesy are paid."[15] Insofar as there were any rules on socializing, Mamie and Stuyvesant were expected to defer to the older siblings.

But Mamie had very little interest in observing this convention. To be fair, she didn't like obeying *any* convention, but especially not this one. For starters, she did not like Clemence, largely because she felt threatened by her sister-in-law's refinement. Mamie was always quick to point out that Clemence's father had actually been named Joseph Bryce Smith at birth. He'd only changed his surname to Bryce because it was more illustrious— in the same way you might change your name to John Rockefeller if your name was John Rockefeller Smith. It's polite to call people what they want to be called, even if it does seem a bit pretentious. So, everyone basically accepted the name change, calling him by his preferred surname. Mamie, on the other hand, retaliated by constantly calling Clemence "that Smith girl" or saying, "I always knew Nick would come to no good end—marrying that Smith girl."[16]

Luckily for Mamie, the siblings did not spend much time in the same place, as Nicholas and Clemence moved to Europe when he began work as the United States minister to Belgium from 1882 to 1886. While they were in Europe, "Mr. Stuyvesant Fish and his beautiful, vivacious, daring young wife took a prominent place in the New York social set. The younger Mrs. Fish amazed and amused the fashionable folk."[17]

Mamie seemed to bring a breath of fresh air to even the stodgiest events. The thing people liked about her was that she was *funny*. During these years, the crème de la crème of New York high society often congregated at the Academy of Music to listen, fairly reverently, to the opera. Of these outings, Mamie joked, "I'm never sure I've fixed my face right... for sometimes when it is just right for expressing appreciation of a cradle song, I find I'm listening to 'Cry of the Valkyries.'"[18] Despite her misgivings, she attended regularly and found ample opportunity to use the experience as the butt of a joke. In one instance, when a woman asked Mamie for her opinion of her dress, she replied, "It is just like one I saw in the Opera last night." The woman, flattered, asked who wore it. "Old Trudel," replied Mrs. Fish, "who comes out in the middle of the night and caterwauls in the street."[19] In a world where most people were unfailingly polite, where, as author Edith Wharton wrote, "the real thing was never said or done or even thought," this frankness could read as thrilling—and Mamie was nothing if not frank.

Meanwhile, when Nicholas and Clemence Fish returned from Belgium in 1887, they began hosting a series of very proper musicals. They didn't realize that, while they'd been gone, Mamie had made making fun of musical evenings the cool thing to do.

And if she was shaking up New York, she was going to completely overhaul Newport.

CHAPTER 5

I N THE 1890S, THE POPULATION OF MANHATTAN EXPERIENCED A SIG-
nificant boom, jumping from 1,919,000 citizens in 1880 to 2,693,000
in 1890.[1] And of those nearly three million people, *none* of them wanted
to be there during the summer. There are now eight million people in New
York, and this is still true (the ones who say they "love it when the city emp-
ties out" are lying, but you should smile and nod politely when they say it).

While New Yorkers today might bemoan the smell of sweat and trash
in humid subway tunnels, back then the city itself stunk nearly as badly as
the factories of Astoria. As Manhattan's population had grown, so too had
the waste—and residents were now treated to the smell of manure, urine,
and garbage baking outside during the sweaty days of late May to early
September. It got so bad that in 1881, the Department of Street Sweeping
was established to help remove, for instance, animal carcasses from the city
streets. Today, the internet-famed Pizza Rat may be adorable (and an excellent provider), but dead carriage horses in the street were decidedly *not*. Still,
by 1890, there remained a sense that "the streets were not kept within the
meaning of that statute because no proper system had ever been adopted," as

The New York Times remarked.[2] And if you were fortunate enough to have the funds to leave a city where a ninety-degree sun beat down on a horse corpse, its flesh rotting away beneath a hovering cloud of flies—well, it's not exactly a surprise that you'd want to head for greener, more pleasantly fragrant pastures.

While many resort towns existed outside New York precisely for this purpose, one place in particular popped up as the elite's preferred refuge: Newport, Rhode Island. As the Rochester *Democrat and Chronicle* cheekily reported, on the third week in June, just in time for the first polo match of the season, "The Nobles of Damascus will make a pilgrimage to Mecca—in other words, to the Newport House."[3]

As popular as it became, many people were still excluded from this pilgrimage. In 1889, *The Buffalo Sunday Morning News* wrote that "the name Newport is one thoroughly known to every reader...[but] Americans in general have a fear of coming to Newport on account of its exclusiveness."[4] This was not, the paper explained, a town where you would enjoy picnics and make chance acquaintances with people who were staying at the same resort. If you wanted *that* kind of experience, you could go to Saratoga Springs or Long Branch. No, Newport was a verdant land of tennis courts and polo fields, showing off "the magnificent summer houses of the Vanderbilts, the Astors...and others upon whom Jove has rained his golden shower."[5] And while the reporter felt everyone should visit—if only to experience the sheer beauty of the town—he also admitted that you would have very little fun there unless you knew the right people, the kind of people who would invite you to come by their "cottages" and private beaches, or join them for nights out at the casino.

By the summer of 1889, Mamie was ready to take Newport by storm and really make a splash.

Unsurprisingly, Mamie found that she adored the social whirl of Newport from the moment she stepped foot there. She routinely sent the elder Mr. Fish letters detailing the two or three social engagements they had every day. Hamilton Fish seemed to think that was a few too many parties, but he shrugged it off.

"Vive la bagatelle," he reportedly said. "We are young only once in our lives, and Newport is Newport."[6] Mamie was thirty-six at the time, so it's nice to know that thirty-six was still considered young.

With their parents living it up in Rhode Island, the children went to stay with their grandfather upstate at Glenclyffe. Stuyvesant Jr. would later recall that the estate, bought by his grandfather in 1850, was not known for its architecture. "Coming up the drive, which was shady and pretty, the great red pile of bricks slapped you in the face."[7] Nonetheless, everyone in the family loved it despite its ugliness. The estate boasted a moderately decaying old dock, which the kids dove off whenever they went swimming, and it also had a "picnic rock" that was perfect for dining.

As much as their grandfather loved having the children around, he didn't want to babysit 24/7, so he gifted them a pony and a donkey and sent them out unaccompanied to amuse themselves by galloping across the grounds. At this point, the younger Fish were aged nine, six, and four, or, as a responsible person might say, probably too young to be riding animals without an adult present. While the donkey was dismissed as being too slow, the children mounted the pony and raced around for about half a mile, at which point Stuyvesant Jr. fell off, leaving him with a concussion. And yet Hamilton was still considered to have been a good grandfather! His grandkids did not hold the concussion against him. Remember this if you've ever felt guilty about plopping kids in front of the TV to keep them entertained.

In future years, Stuyvesant and Mamie (perhaps wisely) decided to take the children along to Newport with them during the summer. The family rented a small gray house near the public beach, which they found appeased everyone. The children could easily walk to the beach to mingle with other visitors and play in the sand. Despite their name, the Fish children were allowed only twenty minutes of actual swimming in the water due to concerns that they might catch cold. During their swim, their governess, carefully clocking the time, observed them "like a nervous hen watching a brood of ducks."[8] Afterward, they'd return home for lunch with the family. Then they would play outside with a pony—safely harnessed to a cart—before coming back for baths and supper without their parents around 6:00 p.m. As was often the case, "After supper, if we behaved ourselves, we were allowed to watch our mother dress for dinner and leave for the party she was going to that night." If the party was being held at their own home, the children would stay up late to spy on the beautifully dressed guests, creeping out of their rooms as quietly as possible to sneak a peek through the banisters. After those guests withdrew, they would all run downstairs to raid the leftover cakes.

They had excellent priorities.

There were already numerous parties being hosted in Newport by the time Mamie and Stuyvesant arrived on the scene. During their initial visit in 1889, a Mr. and Mrs. Best recruited the orchestra from the local casino to put on a musicale, and a Miss Leary invited Mamie to a ladies' luncheon in a house that was apparently prettily "decorated with potted plants."[9] And that's nothing to speak of the dinners. The elite could dine out every night for an entire month, at stately dinners that comprised up to nineteen courses ("our gay modern belle," quipped the *Boston Evening Transcript*, "stands at the opposite food pole from Dr. Tanner, the celebrated modern faster."[10])

However, most parties—full of food though they might be—were still fairly sedate. By and large, in 1889 the residents of Newport seemed more excited about the impending arrival of an electric streetcar in the town than they were by any fete.

Mamie, who was out nearly every night, saw what people were doing—and she wanted to start hosting parties of her *own*. She began somewhat timidly. For someone who was openly disdainful of tradition, her first party was fairly similar to every other one held in Newport. In 1890, *The Sun* reported upon a breakfast she arranged. Even though the family was still in their rented house, and not a grand mansion of their own, the gathering was described as "a stately and beautiful function."[11] The flowers were nice. The food was plentiful. People enjoyed themselves. Everyone likely went away thinking, "That was pleasant."

Though the event had by all accounts been a success, it was not the kind of party people talk about for years to come. And by many standards of the time, that was a good thing! The stage had not collapsed on a prince. Everything ran on time. But Mamie was a creative and ambitious person, and it left her to wonder—what she might do better in the future? How could she throw parties "different and more original than that of other Newport hostesses"?[12]

If this was an interest of Mamie's, there was one person who would stand in her way. And that person was Ward McAllister.

WARD MCALLISTER HAD ABSOLUTELY *NO* INTEREST IN SHAKING THINGS UP, and yet, McAllister—referred to throughout the 1870s and 1880s as the "autocrat of the drawing rooms"—was the one person who you would *need* to impress.

Ward was, admittedly, an unlikely choice for social arbiter of high society. Born in 1827 to a Georgia attorney, Ward was considered a handsome young man who stood five foot nine and kept his beard neatly trimmed. Still, it was surprising that a Southerner should wield such power in the time following the war. During these years, many Southerners who moved to the North were, understandably, disliked, even ones who affected a British accent as Ward perpetually did.

When Ward moved to New York, he lived with a godmother whom he wrote that he "always felt would endow me with all her worldly goods."[13] His feeling was incorrect. She preferred the Presbyterian Church and the Georgia Historical Society. She gave them a million dollars, and she left Ward $1,000, which he immediately spent on—what else?—formal attire to wear to a ball. He departed, briefly, for California before returning to New York in 1853. There, he would meet Sarah Taintor Gibbons, a wealthy heiress who was apparently charmed by his deportment, at least enough to share her sizable inheritance with him.

Following their marriage in 1853, Ward bought land in Newport and, in his words, "turned farmer in good earnest."[14] He planted ten thousand trees, "and then went to Europe to let them grow expecting a forest on my return, but I only found one of them struggling for existence three years later."[15] He wasn't a great farmer, apparently. By all accounts, his farm served largely as a spot for socializing more than anything else, and he soon began hosting the townspeople of Newport, claiming that "the most charming people of the country had formed a select little community there; the society was small, and all were included in the gaieties and festivities."[16] Though a transplant himself, Ward wished to maintain Newport's quaint appeal, stressing that, in his opinion, "the charm of the place then was the simple way of entertaining; there were no large balls; all the dancing and dining was done by daylight, and in the country. I did not hesitate to ask the very crème de la crème of New York society to lunch and dine at my farm, or to a fishing party on the rocks."[17]

Of course, that's not to say that his lunches or fishing parties or picnics— of which he was particularly proud—were simple affairs. As he recorded in his diary, a typical day of picnic planning might entail:

Monday, 1 P.M., meet at Narragansett Avenue, bring filet de bœuf piqué, and with a bow am off in my little wagon, and dash on, to waylay the next cottager, stop every carriage known to contain friends, and ask them, one and all, to join our country party, and assign to each of them the providing of a certain dish and a bottle of champagne. Meeting young men, I charge them to take a bottle of champagne, and a pound of grapes, or order from the confectioner's a quart of ice cream to be sent to me. My pony is put on its mettle; I keep going the entire day getting recruits; I engage my music and servants, and a carpenter to put down a dancing platform, and the florist to adorn it, and that evening I go over in detail the whole affair, map it out as a general would a battle, omitting nothing, not even a salt spoon; see to it that I have men on the road to direct my party to the farm, and bid the farmer put himself and family, and the whole farm, in holiday attire.[18]

Ward decided at one point that it still didn't look quite right, and he realized that it was because there were no animals on his farm. Afterward, he rented sheep for the event.

If anything says "casual," it's forcing a farmer, who is not invited to the event, to dress up and tend to your loaner sheep.

Ward was essentially turning an accessible and endearingly rustic form of entertainment into the equivalent of an upscale, formally dressed, nineteen-course dinner. But the fact that it was outside, in fresh air, did make it novel.

As much as Ward liked to host picnics, he was not necessarily as popular as you might think. Indeed, the brutality of summers in the city and the fact that McAllister had funds to turn his farm into a festive hot spot may have had more appeal than Ward's personal charms. Many people disliked him, finding him needlessly snobbish. Others felt that they could certainly host picnics too—though Ward insisted it wasn't quite so easy.

Ward felt that buying a farm in Newport early on gave him the distinction of being the first and most prominent citizen of Newport to host such an event. And he took no small pleasure in knowing that he—and he alone—had the power to choose whom he invited to his gatherings. Ward would later write, "Do not for a moment imagine that all were indiscriminately asked to these little fêtes. On the contrary, if you were not of the inner circle, and were a newcomer, it took the combined efforts of all your friends 'backing and pushing' to procure an invitation for you. For years, whole families sat on the stool of probation, awaiting trial and acceptance, and many were then rejected."[19]

Part of Ward's inclination toward being extremely selective stemmed from a desire to start an aristocracy in New York like that which he had seen abroad in Europe. For much of his life, he'd observed, correctly, that "Southern people...worshipped the English nobility."[20] Ward, himself, certainly did. He considered them "the first gentlemen," and in associating himself with this nobility, he hoped to raise his own status.[21] Throughout his memoir, he quotes his supposed friend, the Earl of Rosebery, with truly impressive frequency.

Not everyone felt this much admiration for the English, though. Indeed, this may have been a very early divide between McAllister and the Fish family. Stuyvesant Fish's memories of England were dogged by the facts that he had found it very cold, fell victim to a con man, and, perhaps worst of all, spent months trying to understand Darwin to impress women before ultimately deciding he didn't really have an opinion about evolution. He remembered specifically a time when he had watched the royal family in a rainy parade and thought, "Poor things...I looked at them wet and shivering in the cold and wished less than ever to be 'As happy as a Queen,' the only one I have ever seen looking anything but awfully jolly."[22]

Stuyvesant wasn't the only one who would find Ward McAllister's desire to create an English nobility in America rather silly. Years later, in *The Age of Innocence*, a novel about the Gilded Age in New York, Edith Wharton would create a character who greatly resembled McAllister, and who enthused over people serving their dishes "in the new English fashion." Countess Olenska, the book's savviest character, then muses, "It seems stupid to have discovered America only to make it into a copy of another country."

That seems like the kind of witty line that might have come directly from Mamie Fish.

CHAPTER 6

WARD McAllister may have been pretentious, but he was not without friends—including one incredibly important friend.

Unlike Mamie, Caroline "Lina" Astor was precisely the person you would expect to lead New York society. She was born Caroline Webster Schermerhorn, the daughter of New Yorkers who could trace their ancestry back to the early Dutch settlers who colonized Manhattan. Unlike many families with such a prestigious pedigree, they had retained their wealth as well as their reputation. The family's affluence largely came from their shipping dynasty. That, combined with hundreds of acres in Gowanus, a region in Brooklyn, meant Caroline was born into a family worth about $500,000 ($16.5 million today).

From early childhood, Lina's life was defined and confined by an excess of caution on the part of her parents. She was the youngest of nine children. The eldest of those, Henry, had died at the age of one. Then, in 1839, when Lina was only nine years old, her older sister, Cordelia, died at sixteen. Perhaps because of these tragedies, Lina was treated with a watchfulness that is typically only seen with members of actual royal families. Brought up on Washington Square, Lina was never permitted to go outside alone. According to *The St. Paul Globe* newspaper, she was "a genuine blue blood" and had been raised "with as much formality as a young princess." Instead of mingling with others her own age, "for three hours every day, she played the harp, read French and embroidered."[1] Although she was physically quite plain, it was expected that Lina would marry well—and this strenuous training would thus be worth its weight in gold.

At the age of twenty-three, she found a match, at least financially, in William Backhouse Astor Jr. And, look, it was a financial match. Astor biographer Virginia Cowles notes, "She had married unambitious William Backhouse for his money, not because she loved him."[2]

That's unromantic. Still, if you're going to marry for money, it's wise to marry for a *huge* amount of money. Enough that you can be loveless on a spectacular yacht. And Lina managed that.

John Jacob Astor, William's grandfather, was the wealthiest man in the United States when he died in 1848, leaving his family $20 million ($790 million today). But despite his flush funds, John didn't have the best reputation or long-standing community ties, as he was a German immigrant who had been known to be miserly and difficult to work with. To the Astor name (and its accompanying bank account), Lina brought "beauty, family, and social power"—in other words, valuable social legitimacy.[3] The combination of blue blood and green money meant that "a few years after her wedding she stood at the head of society."[4]

William might have admired Lina's socializing savvy and connections, but he certainly didn't share those attributes. He was a true exemplar of the period's "sporting culture," which meant he was a heavy drinker who loved horse racing and spent much of his time at his stables. The rest he spent on his yacht, which was said to be regularly filled with showgirls (poor Lina did not even get to enjoy the "hanging out on a yacht while drinking champagne and staring sadly at the ocean" part of marrying for money). He had no real interest in joining the family's shipping business and did not even want to reside in the city. Consequently, throughout their marriage, Lina and William spent only a few months together each year, though they both talked admiringly of each other and shared four daughters and a son. For the most part, at least, Lina was "grateful he did not insist on her company."[5] Distance made the heart grow fonder. In their case, a lot of distance...

In the 1870s, when it was time to try to secure similarly suitable marriages for her children, Lina emerged into society, largely because she was "determined to stop them from meeting the wrong people."[6]

Ward McAllister—a snob to his core who believed that "a fortune of only a million is respectable poverty"[7] and that it took four generations to make a true gentleman—was only too happy to help Mrs. Astor with that. Even when he'd been a lawyer entertaining clients, his motto was to "only invite nice people." By which he meant rich people, specifically those with very old money. McAllister would later say that Lina should rule New York City almost "by divine right."[8] But her position did not occur organically. Instead, it was her collaboration with Ward, and their functioning as a refinement-obsessed team, that helped establish her as the social head of the metropolis.

In 1872, Ward began hosting "Patriarch Balls," inspired by those thrown by the Almack's social club in London. The main thing that defined Almack's balls was that they were exclusive—the patronesses had to formally sign off on anyone who wished to attend a ball. In 1866, Grantley Berkeley, the son of the Earl of Berkeley, described these kinds of parties, which were held at fashionable drawing rooms, as such: "They [the 'lady patronesses' who composed the invitation list for these events] issued tickets for a series of balls for the gratification of the creme de la creme of society, with a jealous watchfulness to prevent the intrusion of plebian rich or untitled vulgar; and they drew up a code of laws for the elect who received invitations, which were as unalterable as those of the Medes and Persians."[9]

The balls were held on Wednesdays since Parliament was not in session then, and *obviously* the patronesses wanted members of Parliament to be able to attend. High society women across the city prayed for invitations for their daughters so they could meet someone eligible to marry. On the flip side, men who remained single after two years of attendance were given no further invitations, as they were deemed insufficiently serious about settling down. Almack's was, in short, a place where women of a certain age and status were able to exert considerable social power.

Ward McAllister was one of the people of this age obsessed with all things British. He had gone to Europe desperate to gawk at nobility. He was devastated that he never got to see Queen Victoria in person, but he did convince her chef to let him peek at how her table was set. If this indicates that his nose was pressed rather comically against the glass in England, he could at least try to turn America into a place where he could playact at being English nobility. Aware that these London balls were made possible "by the banding together of powerful women of influence for the purpose of getting up these balls, and in this way making them the greatest social events of London Society,"[10] McAllister planned to do something similar, save for the fact that it would not be "lady patronesses" issuing the invitations.

Instead, the focus for McAllister's party would be on twenty-five of his specially selected "patriarchs," who were each allowed to invite four ladies and five gentlemen. As McAllister explained, "the object we had in view was to make these balls thoroughly representative; to embrace the old Colonial New Yorkers, our adopted citizens, and men whose ability and integrity had won the esteem of the community, and who formed an important element in society. We wanted the money power, but not in any way to be controlled by it."[11] Essentially, these balls would be "capable of giving a passport to society to all worthy of it."[12]

If this sounds like an uncharacteristically egalitarian attempt on McAllister's part, don't worry—it was not! The list of McAllister's invited patriarchs was significantly weighted toward either huge money or blue-blooded legacy—and ideally both. And the "adopted citizens" among the patriarchs that McAllister describes? Well, they included men like William Butler Duncan, who was, indeed, an immigrant born in Scotland but also a man who notably worked for J. P. Morgan before becoming the president of the Mobile and Ohio Railroad and the director of the Atlantic Telegraph Company. Oh, and he also served on the board of nearly every museum in New York City.

It is theoretically possible that these balls could have been used to introduce people of varying social stations to society, but McAllister was very clear that "we knew then, and we know now, that the whole secret of the success of these Patriarch Balls lay in making them select."[13] To put it bluntly: There would be *very few* attendees who actually had to work for their living.

Even if her grandfather-in-law and husband hadn't been among the first names jotted down on McAllister's list of patriarchs (which they were), Lina wholeheartedly agreed with this elitist approach. She later noted that she was disinclined to invite the department store tycoon A. T. Stewart to one of her own parties, claiming, "I buy my carpets from them, but is that any reason why I should invite them to walk on them?"[14]

But despite not having to work, McAllister's patriarch invitees also had to be rich. In fact, McAllister declared it was not sensible to invite people "solely on pedigree" who had "the aspirations of a duke and the fortune of a footman."[15] This is particularly ironic given that, prior to his marriage, McAllister himself would've been very much in that category.

You do begin to understand, reading about Ward, why his aunt left her money to the Presbyterian Church.

Although these balls would seemingly elevate men—the patriarchs—to the forefront of society, it was commonly understood that someone else "figured prominently in the management of the patriarch balls."[16] And that person was Lina Astor.

Lina helped organize these parties, and she certainly induced members of high society, including her own husband, to be involved. Doing so, she imagined, would help her daughters in society. She could ensure the lists contained men she regarded as eligible while keeping out any dashing but lower-class men. In return, Ward McAllister sang her praises, describing Caroline Astor as being his "Mystic Rose." He made it clear at every turn that he could do nothing without her.

In part because of their known affiliation, McAllister's Patriarch Balls were seen as a mere precursor to Mrs. Astor's annual ball, filled with bejeweled ladies, which newspapers as far away as Tennessee declared to be "paradise in New York."[17] However, far from upsetting him, this seemed to *delight* McAllister. When one socialite remarked to him that she actually preferred Mrs. Getty's Ball to Mrs. Astor's, he furiously declared, "Mrs. Astor is the

Queen of American Society and I have placed her on the throne."[18] He continued that she was a natural head of society because "she has good judgment and a great power of analysis of men and women, a thorough knowledge of all their surroundings, a just appreciation of the rights of others...a good appreciation of the value of ancestry....Having a great fortune, she had the ability to conceive and carry out her social projects...above all things she is a true and loyal friend."

All of this sounds commendable, in much the way you'd expect a respected politician to be admirable. However, it does not necessarily describe someone who knows how to have a good time—or throw a killer party.

McAllister was not alone in his high opinion of Mrs. Astor. Many people considered Lina to be steady and stately in manner, having won the position as the de facto leader of high society largely by ensuring that people had to please her if they wanted to attend her coveted events. She was never extravagant, and she did not try to shake things up, unlike her sister-in-law, Charlotte Augusta. Charlotte had tried to start a creative salon where ladies would read poems or stories they wrote. Every week at that salon, fewer people attended, until a day came when no one showed.

Lina Astor would *never* make that kind of mistake. If her parties were perfectly predictable, they demanded little from the attendees other than an appetite. Everyone knew precisely what to expect from her. It was written that "every year of her life for nearly half a century she duplicated almost exactly the details of its predecessor."[19] She didn't gossip. She did nothing that would cause controversy, let alone scandal. She remained reserved herself, always cautious of saying anything that might be misinterpreted. She made no jokes. The author and socialite Elizabeth Drexel recalled that "she gave friendship but never intimacy. She never confided. No one knew what passed behind the calm repose of her face. She had so cultivated the art of never looking at the things she did not want to see, never listening to words she did not wish to hear, that it had become second nature to her."[20]

Despite the popularity of her events, Lina's husband was rarely in attendance at any of them. Many of the partygoers had never even seen him. When people dared to ask whether Lina might want to join him on his (scandalous) yacht, she merely brushed them off, claiming that "it is a great pity I am such a bad sailor, for I should so much enjoy accompanying him. As it is, I have never even set foot on the yacht."[21]

Certainly, the kinds of parties that Lina held were *very different* from those on her husband's boat. For one thing, there would've been no room at them for any showgirls. On one occasion, her sister-in-law, Charlotte, had invited a very famous Italian actress, Adelaide Ristori, best known for acting in tragedies, to a party. That alone was a scandal. Mrs. Astor would never even consider such a thing, and she expressed horror that one of her contemporaries had allowed performers from the opéra bouffe (who had, at least in the past, performed the sordid cancan!) to entertain guests at a party. Mrs. Astor would not even allow the polka at her balls because it might remind people of the cancan.

It must have been very difficult making sure she never stepped a foot out of line. Very difficult, and rather dull.

Only four hundred people were invited to the (very predictable) annual ball, as "the Astor ballroom only held 400."[22] Naturally, this meant a great deal of aspiring people were left out. Rather than admitting they had not been invited, however, the omitted would flee the city, insisting that they had pressing business upstate or even out of the country. Many, many people killed off a fictitious relative. People in the city noted it was stunning how many grandmothers and aunts died the week of the Astor ball.

But merely being *invited* to the ball wasn't enough to feel totally secure in your social standing—it was only the beginning. Once you entered Mrs. Astor's ballroom and battled your way past the yards of flowers that "it took twenty men from six to eight o'clock in the evening to carry [into] the house,"[23] you would undoubtedly see a raised platform away from the rest of the crowd where Mrs. Astor and a few close friends sat on an enormous divan, which was known as "the throne." Author and socialite Elizabeth "Bessie" Wharton Drexel recalled that "no one ever dreamt of calling it anything else. But, alas, capacious as were its depths, it could only accommodate a limited number on those ample red silk cushions and there was acute disappointment every year when the seats were allotted."[24] Women—like

Mrs. John Drexel—literally ran out of the house sobbing because Mrs. Astor informed them that all the seats were taken.

This doesn't sound like a fun party so much as the worst imaginable day of high school.

It is not entirely a surprise that "no one ever remembered Mrs. Astor's ball[s] as being very much fun."[25] If you were not permitted to sit on the divan, you wandered through the large art gallery that Mrs. Astor used as a ballroom. You could look at the paintings, which were expensive, though not considered particularly good by most attendees. An orchestra played outside on the balcony. Certainly, you could dance and converse with other attendees, though you might prefer to just dance. Writing to her friends, one young socialite described dinner at Mrs. Astor's saying, "I was bored to death. I amused myself by grading the people at the table in terms of dullness from one to ten, with one being the absolute peak of deadliness—and hardly a guest fell above three."[26]

Well, of course not. The point of these balls, of Lina Astor's life, was to avoid doing anything crazy or eccentric.

Being invited to one of Mrs. Astor's parties might have been a great goal for anyone who wanted to achieve social prominence, but not for anyone who wanted to have a good time—like Mamie Fish. Mamie could not stomach being bored for even five minutes, let alone an entire dinner that might drag on for hours. But creating an alternative to these staid, predictable parties would not appeal to everyone.

CHAPTER 7

THERE WAS A NOTION AROUND THE 1870S THAT WITH ENOUGH money and a willingness to live in the right neighborhood, you could simply enter high society. *The Ladies' Home Journal* reported that fashionable folk were defined by the fact that they could "keep carriages, live above Bleecker, subscribe to the opera, go to Grace Church, have a town house and a country house, give balls, and parties."[1]

According to these narrow parameters, Mamie Fish certainly did not qualify...and on several counts, at that: She attended the Little Church Around the Corner, rented rather than owned a house in Newport, and famously hated the opera for being so stuffy. While her soon-to-be-rival Lina was busy heading up the extremely reputable and stodgy Academy of Music, Mamie was described as talking through the entire show and having "not a mouth one would fancy in an adjoining box at the opera, and it is not a mouth that would brook opposition in operatic conversation."[2]

While Lina was so reserved that she never said anything inappropriate, Mamie pretty much *only* said inappropriate things. When one hostess, with great solemnity, showed Mrs. Fish an iron fountain made by Rodin that she'd had shipped from France, Mrs. Fish immediately replied, "I have a trough exactly like it for my farm horses."[3]

Even if Mamie Fish had met the qualifiers as dictated by *The Ladies' Home Journal*, Ward McAllister and Caroline Astor would've *never* found that sufficient enough to deem someone worthy of entering the echelons of their inner circle. There's particular, there's picky, and then there are people like Ward and Lina, the latter of whom once cut a person out for choosing a sorbet she did not think complemented the fruit.

Moreover, no one from a working background—like Mrs. Fish's brother, who had sold dry goods—would ever pass muster with the two because "in England," Lina and Ward agreed, "people look down on tradesmen."[4] When the thought of widening their circle was brought up, Mrs. Astor shuddered that "people seem to have gone quite wild and are inviting all sorts of people to their receptions. I don't know what has happened to our tastes."[5]

Christ, Lina—people met *one* actress, who pretty much only performed in solemn tragedies like *Medea*.

Ward McAllister was similarly selective (about practically *everything*), and rather than bringing them together, the two occasionally came to blows because of their rigidness and perfectionism. And their arguments weren't limited to the guest list either. In one such case, papers reported that "Mrs. Astor found grievous fault with Mr. McAllister's way of serving entrees and now Mr. McAllister is discoursing volubly to [the elite] as to how they must adorn and fill their tables during the coming reception season."[6] Ward, seemingly deciding to heed Lina Astor's criticism, decreed a host could not serve soups *and* escargot (only one or the other) at an event, and that a host could not serve fish, frog legs, Roman pudding (cheesecake), or French pastries *at all*.

If these rulings sound a bit arbitrary, it's because they absolutely were. These may well have come about just because one or the other of the two didn't like frog legs. And yet, McAllister expected people to take these dictates as seriously as if he had carved them in stone.

These were the people whose approval Mamie had to win over if she were to ascend to the summit of New York society. Clearly, she was not going to woo them with cheesecake.

In other words, any potential the trio had to build any sort of friendship was doomed from the start.

Prior to Mamie's developing social ambitions, the Fish had very little to do with Lina or her cohort, Ward McAllister. For one thing, they were understandably proud of their antislavery views and legacy, as well as their support of the Little Church Around the Corner. Meanwhile, as many Southerners did, Ward McAllister romanticized slavery. In his memoirs, he mused fondly about how he'd return home to Savannah and "the colored people would give you in song all the annoyances they were subjected to, and the current events of plantation life, bringing in much of and about their 'Massa' and his family, as follows: 'Massa Ward marry our little Miss Sara, bring big buckra to Savannah, gwine to be good times, my boys, pull boys, pull, over Jordan!'" He delighted in "the old Southern butler, quite an institution; devoted to his master, and taking as much pride in the family as the family took in itself."[7] Many former slaves, who had recently been freed and were sharing truly horrifying stories about the abuses they'd experienced in the South, probably would not agree that they had been part of a big happy family. Most family members do not hunt down other family members who try to move away from home with ferocious dogs.

It seemed very likely that Ward McAllister would've happily left the Fish on the sidelines of New York society forever, even as Mamie was gaining a reputation for being fresh and funny, as she was "very unconventional despite her social aspirations."[8] Alas, it was those very social ambitions that brought Mamie into his orbit, along with that unconventionality that infuriated him, as Mamie "set out to be a reformer rather than a conformer."[9]

Mamie experienced the full weight of McAllister's horror when she at last invited him to dinner. This was to be her first true "society" dinner, one designed to dazzle and delight. She knew that her chef could not outdo the dishes provided by McAllister or Mrs. Astor. The Fish had far less money than most of Mrs. Astor's inner circle. At their peak, they possessed only "a few million," which Ward saw as just scraping by. If she truly wanted to stand out, she knew she had to be inventive.

And so, she transformed her dining room table to represent a pond. She filled the room with flowers, selected green place settings, and completed the look with a glass tub featuring baby ducks paddling about as the center-piece. There was no need, it seemed, to venture outside for a picnic—Mamie had whimsically brought the outdoors right under her roof.

As you might imagine, this whimsy was not exactly in keeping with Ward's dictates. The most inventive he'd ever been entailed hosting a patri-arch's ball where all the flowers were pink. In fact, he believed having too many flowers on a dinner table was vulgar and that "at the best dinners, you see perhaps in the centre of the table one handsome basket of flowers; no bouquets de corsage or boutonnières; the table set with austere simplicity; a few silver dishes with bonbons and compotiers of fruit, that is all."

And that's not even including the ducks. No, there would be no place for ducks at *his* dinners, none at all.

This was the absolute opposite of all of that. Sure, it might be acceptable to rent some cows to line your farm for parties, but that was outside! He might have wanted events to be lavish, but he also wanted them to operate on pre-dictable lines. At dinner inside, a duck belonged on the plate, not frolicking about on the table. According to *The Muscatine Times*, that quirky little detail might've been the one that really set him over the edge, as Ward McAllister "was horrified by the duck pond dinner and read Mrs. Fish out of society."[10]

However, unlike his previous cast-outs and condemnations, this dictate was not effective. People might have truly disliked McAllister, but they also knew he held the keys to many social events. So when he said no Roman puddings, they stopped serving them. Mamie, though, didn't really care about whether she was welcome at Mrs. Astor's ball or the Patriarch Ball (at least, not enough to obey McAllister's dictates). She was perfectly capable of making her own fun. And she was beginning to prove she could make things fun for others. People were charmed by Mamie, admiring that "the lady had spirit." As a result, "she defied McAllister, and plunged right into the middle of society."[11]

It was said that, in this regard, she had a "certain French daring that conservative New Yorkers of her set did not know."[12]

By 1891, the times were changing. It was clear that Mamie did not consider dining to be an event that required terrible solemnity. Instead, she wanted people to have *fun* at her dinners—and she wasn't the only one. Papers at the time bemoaned the solemnity of Astor and McAllister's preparations, claiming "it is simply ridiculous how much time Ward McAllister [and] Mrs. Astor...spend talking and arguing about their menus."[13] The same paper suggested that "the main point of a good dinner is hospitality, a spirit of geniality which is universal with all your guests and well-cooked foods."[14] If people are fleeing your events in tears, like at Astor's ball, because they feel left out, the spirit of geniality is officially lacking.

Mamie was but one among many people who were beginning to chafe at the confines of society as run by McAllister and Astor. It's unlikely, at this time, that they would even have seen Mamie Fish as being their chief opponent. That honor would go to Alva Vanderbilt.

And Alva Vanderbilt would walk, or rather dance, so that Mamie could run.

CHAPTER 8

As much as Ward McAllister and, by extension, Mrs. Astor may have dismissed Mamie Fish as, well, a rude eccentric, they positively recoiled from Alva Vanderbilt. Mamie was at least from a good New York family. Alva came from the South, which is also a reasonable place to be from. But from the way Lina treated Alva Vanderbilt, you would've thought that Alva had grown up in a sewer, Teenage Mutant Ninja Turtles style.

She did not.

Alva came from a very respectable—read: *wealthy*—background. She was born Alva Erskine Smith in 1853 to affluent cotton merchant parents in Mobile, Alabama, and was one of six children (though only three of her siblings would follow her into adulthood). In an era obsessed with railroads, Alva was, basically from toddlerhood, an unstoppable freight train of a person. She preferred playing with boys over girls, and she was confident she could climb higher in any tree than all of them and run faster in any footrace. Boys frequently informed her she couldn't play with them because she was a girl. She promptly beat up the boys who told her this. They soon learned that it was better to just let her play alongside them. First because they didn't want to be pummeled, and second because she was more daring than most boys her age.

In spite of being absolutely steadfast in her desires, Alva said her teachers were kind to her. "Perhaps they realized that I was impossible," she later recounted, "and thought the best thing to do was ignore an impossible condition."[1] This wasn't always an asset. Though she grew up and into her place in the circles of high society, throughout her life she would retain, according to her daughter, "a violent temper that, like a tempest, at times would engulf us all."[2]

In 1860, prior to the start of the Civil War, the Smith family moved to France. Alva's father, a cotton merchant, felt certain that the war would come. He was right. And he did manage to ensure that his family avoided the bloodshed that would engulf the country in the coming years. But following the war, upon their return to America, the Smith family found themselves nearly bankrupt, like many other Southerners. In an attempt to provide for the family, her mother opened a boarding house in New York, and her father began attempting to trade cotton.

In this regard, Alva's circumstances were not so different from Mamie Fish's. The solution for both women, if they wanted to help not only themselves but their families, was to marry a wealthy man. Alva didn't have a childhood sweetheart, but she did have a best friend who was hell-bent on helping Alva find a good match.

Consuelo Yznaga had grown up alongside Alva in the South, but unlike Alva's family, Consuelo's family had maintained their wealth during the Civil War (they had sugar mills in Cuba, untouched by the war). Fiercely loyal and devoted to her friend, Consuelo made it her mission to introduce Alva to every eligible bachelor in New York City—including a man named William K. Vanderbilt.

William was a total catch: handsome, charming, *very* rich, and the vice president of the New York Central Railroad, to boot. Initially, people did not think that Alva—who was never considered to be a great beauty—could ever attract his attention. Even the couple's oldest daughter, Consuelo (named after Alva's dear friend, of course), mused in her memoir, "Why my parents ever married remains a mystery to me. They were both delightful, charming, intelligent people, but wholly unsuited to each other." William, in Consuelo's account, was someone who "found life a happy adventure." Meanwhile, Alva's "combative nature rejoiced in conquests. She loved a fight."[3]

And yet, opposites attract, and perhaps it was this forceful trait that gave Alva the fortitude to pursue someone as seemingly out of her league as William Vanderbilt. People who told Alva what she could do—or could not do—never fared well, anyway. She may not have been a great beauty, and she was certainly lacking in money, but Alva was smart. She was funny. Men considered her to have a magnetic, sexy allure. And, most importantly, she really had no other option. If Alva wanted to succeed socially or financially, she *had* to use all the winning traits she possessed to land herself a successful husband, just as Mamie had. If not, she would merely be considered the daughter of formerly wealthy people who now ran a boarding house. Ever ambitious in her own right, this was simply unacceptable.

Lucky for her, Alva succeeded and married William Vanderbilt in 1875. In a surprising twist, Alva's family was horrified. They simply could not abide their refined Southern belle of a daughter marrying the grandson of a lower-class man. Alva noted that her relatives "cut me dead for marrying W.K. Vanderbilt because his grandfather peddled vegetables."[4]

It was true that his grandfather, Cornelius, did indeed grow up "peddling vegetables"—if that is what you call "being a farmer." But what Cornelius Vanderbilt really represented was the potential for anyone to climb the societal hierarchy and amass wealth in America. He was born in Staten Island in 1794 to a farming family and never even attended school, starting full-time work on the farm by age eleven. America urbanized in part because working on farms is not as idyllic as Instagram might make it seem. Farmwork was backbreaking. Like many people, Cornelius sought other employment. When Cornelius was sixteen, his mother lent him one hundred dollars (about $2,500 today) to buy a boat so that he could work as a ferryman in New York Harbor. He worked relentlessly. Within a year, he made $1,000, which he sent to his mother as a return on her investment. Cornelius was a *very good son.* The other ferrymen grew so used to the sight of the young man hauling passengers (and oysters) to Manhattan that they affectionately nicknamed him "Commodore."

Before long, Cornelius was able to use his profits to buy additional boats. When it became clear that modern steamboats could travel significantly faster than traditional sailboats, he bought one of those, offering passenger and freight runs from New York City to surrounding areas, like Albany, that were far cheaper than any of the more established lines. Yes, the service was terrible—the meals he boasted about often consisted of spoiled meat—but the ride was cheap. At one point, he even offered "The People's Line," a route that ferried people for free—with meals included—to drive competitors out of business. His competitors ultimately paid him $100,000 to stop running this service.

By his forties, the Commodore had made millions of dollars and owned over a hundred ships. He built a $27,000 ($916,000 today) mansion on the farmland where he'd grown up. Despite his newfound wealth, he remained much the same man he'd always been: cheap, coarse, and, according to many, uncouth. He refused to carry a cigar case because it meant that people might ask him to share his cigars, which would cost him money. He took an astonishing *twelve lumps of sugar* in his tea, turning any offered into a tea-flavored sugar mush, much to the surprise of virtually everyone having tea with him. He retained the same filthy mouth he'd had in his youth and often referred to women in his household as "sluts."[5] Though married with thirteen children, he had a near-constant stream of affairs, including one with his children's governess (which was problematic to the upper classes likely only because a more tasteful man would have dallied with actresses and courtesans, rather than someone he encountered domestically). Lest you think he was trying to maintain his humble roots, he also refused to spend money on civic causes, reasoning that there would be no profit in that, and, in his own words, "I have been insane on the subject of moneymaking all my life."[6] If you gave money to a museum or opera or even other people, you see, then you have *less money.* All of society agreed that he was truly brilliant with money, but didn't want much else to do with him.

Following the Civil War, the Commodore took a break from boats to invest in newly developing train lines, the same industry that so fascinated Stuyvesant Fish. He bought up the Harlem Line—the only line that ran directly into New York City—and built the illustrious Grand Central Station in Midtown Manhattan, reasoning, "If I don't get the benefit from this, my children will."[7] Increasingly convinced that "the future in this country is railroading,"[8] he continued to buy up other lines, just as he bought up other boats, and consolidated them. No longer would people have to switch trains dozens of times to get from New York to the Midwest; they could simply ride one line all the way to their destination. Of course, the conditions were, again, terrible. In rain, the train roofs were so leaky that the floors were known to flood. But because the trains Vanderbilt ran were cheaper than the competitors', Vanderbilt was confident that there would always be people willing to endure less-than-optimal conditions to save money.

After all, for a long time he had been one of those people.

When Cornelius Vanderbilt died in 1877, he was worth $105 million, or about $3 billion today—making him the richest man in the United States. Still, he remained needlessly frugal to the end. On his deathbed— and he died from more or less everything; his autopsy found "there was not a sound organ in his body"[9]—his doctor suggested he drink champagne. At the time, it was thought to both mitigate pain and have curative properties. Vanderbilt replied, "Champagne? Champagne! I can't afford champagne. A bottle every morning! Oh, I guess soda water will do." He died shortly after.

In retrospect, he really should have enjoyed the champagne.

Though the Commodore and Alva got along famously (he loved that she didn't seem to be in the least bit afraid of him, and she thought he was simply extraordinary), William did not share much in common with his grandfather, other than his money and his work ethic. Ironically, much of that was *because* of Cornelius's success. William had been brought up in wealth and comfort, the kind of luxury that the Commodore feared would "spoil those youngsters…through petting and indolence."[10] Fortunately, William was still prepared to work to establish his own career, and he started out as a low-ranking clerk, understanding that he would "be promoted only on his merits, and [so] he applied himself with sufficient diligence to win promotion."[11] William was also a great deal more pleasant than the Commodore. Far from his grandfather's ornery demeanor, William was known for having a "generous and unselfish nature; his pleasure was to see people happy and he rejoiced in the company of his children and friends."[12]

Alas, no matter how much money they had and how many industries they dominated, in the eyes of people like the Astors, the newlywed Vanderbilts could not shake their vegetable-peddling legacy. The Astors held the same position toward the young couple as they did for his father, which was that they "did not know him, and they did not want to know him."[13]

The Astors' harsh opinion could not be dissuaded by anyone, even Ward McAllister, whom, to everyone's surprise, the Commodore actually liked. His affection didn't stem from Ward's much-vaunted taste. Rather, it was because Ward once revealed to the Commodore that he had snuck in through the service entrance at Buckingham Palace in the hopes of seeing royalty. To the Commodore, this indicated an impressive desire "to go places and do things." He saw Ward as an upstart, like him. Eager to support Ward's ambitions, the Commodore once advised him, "Mac, sell everything you have and put the proceeds in Harlem Railroad stock."[14] Ward, who believed "society is my business," declined to do so. If only McAllister had taken Commodore Vanderbilt's suggestion, he would have been a millionaire many times over.

But then again, no one took the Commodore or his children seriously, at least at first. The jokes about their family were numerous. People claimed they would rather associate with a cohort who "knows that it isn't a proper thing to drink wine out of a finger bowl," complaining that the Vanderbilt set "blow the tops off of Charlotte Russe [a dessert with a creamy top] the same as if they were glasses of lager beer."[15] And it wasn't just their table manners either. A fellow socialite who had seen the Vanderbilts' art collection scoffed that "the frames are the most expensive part of them."[16]

They might have been rich, but in the eyes of the public, they were still trash.

Other women in her position might have been satisfied simply building a magnificent mansion on Fifth Avenue and living the rest of their lives out there in luxury. But this was not enough for Alva. What was a mansion really worth if it was not filled with the most prominent people in Manhattan? If you were an ambitious woman, you could not go about making millions like Commodore Vanderbilt. You could not enter politics. You could not do much, really, with your ambition, other than climb to the top of the social pile.

Like Mamie, Alva long dreamed of ruling the elite; as her daughter Consuelo recalled, "One of her [Alva's] earliest ambitions had been to become a leader of New York Society."[17] Even though she now had millions of dollars to spend in pursuit of this goal, she couldn't quite buy the approval of her elite peers, and she received a lukewarm response from most of the society doyennes.

Determined to win them over, Alva prepared to give a costume ball in her own home. The fete would celebrate both the completion of the house at 660 Fifth Avenue and her friendship with Consuelo Yznaga, who had since married into British aristocracy and become the Viscountess Mandeville. The lead-up to the ball, which was to be held on March 26, 1883, was extraordinary. *Never* had people been so excited about any party—and the opportunity to showcase both their creativity and refinement. In the weeks leading up to it, "amid the rush and excitement of business, men have found their minds haunted by uncontrollable thoughts as to whether they should appear as Robert Le Diable, Cardinal Richelieu, Otho the Barbarian, or the Count of Monte Cristo, while the ladies have been driven to the verge of distraction in the effort to settle the comparative advantages of ancient, medieval, and modern costumes."[18]

They may have been "haunted" by their own competitive edge, but the whole thing still seems a good deal less stressful than competing to sit on Mrs. Astor's divan.

Soon, word of this excitement made its way to Carrie Astor, Lina's twenty-two-year-old daughter. She, like so many young people in the city, was "intent on seeing the ball."[19] According to the *St. Louis Post-Dispatch* newspaper, so many of her friends had recounted what wonderful costumes they would be wearing that "a great longing arose in her heart to go and participate in the gaieties in the 'plebian' railroad prince's gorgeous mansion."[20]

But, as Alva slyly pointed out, she could not possibly invite Carrie Astor. Why, she couldn't even invite all her own friends, and she didn't even *know* the Astors, as she informed nearly everyone. Such a shame!

Carrie was devastated. She implored her mother to befriend Alva Vanderbilt, saying, "What if Old Commodore Vanderbilt did work on a horrid old ferryboat?...I want to go and have a good time."[21] Devoted to her daughter's happiness, Mrs. Astor dutifully swallowed her pride and, much to the surprise of her household, took her carriage straight to 660 Fifth Avenue, where she informed Mrs. Vanderbilt, "We have been strangers long enough."[22]

And so, Carrie Astor ended up scoring an invite to the party and had a very good time. Everyone at Mrs. Vanderbilt's ball reportedly had a very good time. The rumor that the frames on the Vanderbilts' paintings were worth more than the art they contained was set immediately to rest as guests entered the impeccable mansion. Indeed, the walls were adorned with Renaissance treasures; everywhere guests looked, they might've seen Flemish tapestries or works by Rembrandt—though they would have to spot them through the masses of flowers. According to *The New York Times*, the house had been completely turned into "a fairyland...the walls were nowhere to be seen, but in their place an impenetrable thicket of fern above fern and palm above palm, while from the branches of the palms hung a profusion of lovely orchids, displaying a rich variety of color and almost endless variation of fantastic forms."[23]

Jokes aside, those flowers (the Vanderbilts apparently spent $11,000, or $343,000 in today's currency, on them) were an essential component of the scene, not merely decorative trinkets. Deodorant wouldn't be invented for another five years, in 1888. Until then, balls where people would be dancing energetically for hours on end—and *especially* at balls where many would be wearing heavy costumes—could start to smell really funky very quickly. So the hosts tried to preemptively fill the space with very sweetly scented flowers.

In Mrs. Vanderbilt's case, in addition to the orchids and ferns, there were also "gilded baskets filled with natural roses of extraordinary size, such as the dark crimson Jacqueminot, the deep pink Glorie de Paris, the pale pink Baroness de Rothschild and Adolphide Rothschild, the King of Morocco, the Duchess of Kent, and the new and beautiful Marie Louise Vassey."[24] If the Astors and the Ward McAllisters of the world needed aristocratic names to feel comfortable, you could find them clipped and bundled in the Vanderbilts' rose baskets. You could also look out on the ballroom floor, since the ball's guest of honor, Consuelo, would become the Duchess of Manchester by the end of the decade.

Mr. and Mrs. Vanderbilt presided over the ball in the garb of medieval royalty—the kind that Mrs. Astor so dearly wished was in the Vanderbilt familial line. In dreaming up her costume, Mrs. Vanderbilt had been "inspired by Alexandre Cabanel's painting of a Venetian princess. Her dress was embellished with a light blue satin train, magnificently embroiled in gold and lined with Roman red. It likewise had an underskirt of white-and-yellow brocade, shading from the deepest orange to the lightest canary. On her head, she wore a Venetian cap from which there shone, among other jeweled miscellanea, a miniature peacock of many-colored gems. A covey of lifelike doves served her also as minor accessories."[25] According to *The New York Times*, it was an outlandish outfit that displayed her "irreproachable taste... to perfection."[26]

The ball had cost the Vanderbilts a fortune, and they spared no expense. The champagne alone cost $2,000 ($60,000 today). The total bill for the ball was $50,000 (around $1.5 million), which was akin to the salary of the US president. Still, the expense was worth it to Alva and her husband. Everyone was now in awe of the couple who had managed to bring Mrs. Astor to her knees. And if Mrs. Astor was willing to beg for an invite to the Vanderbilts' parties, they must be magnificent. No one wanted to be left off their guest list in the future.

The Fish family attended the ball. Sadly, Mamie and Stuyvesant's costumes are lost to history; the young couple was not yet well enough established in society for their every move and outfit to merit note in the newspapers. But *The New York Times* reported that Mamie's brother-in-law Hamilton Fish was there, dressed as "a Spanish muleteer, in a brown velvet jacket and breeches, with a blue satin vest covered with buttons."[27] Despite this grandeur, it was actually Edith, Stuyvesant's sister, whose outfit inspired gasps of admiration. She dressed up as the Duchess of Burgundy, the front of her costume copiously embroidered with genuine rubies, sapphires, and emeralds.

But the costumes that emerged as the most memorable of the evening weren't necessarily the most expensive. Instead, they were the ones that were the most creative, and even a bit humorous. For instance, one man who attended the ball with his three daughters went as King Lear, though he stressed that he was still in his right mind. Miss Bessie Webb "appeared as Mme. Le Diable in a red satin dress with a black velvet demon embroidered on it and the entire dress trimmed with demon fringe—that is to say, with a fringe ornamented with the heads and horns of little demons."[28] Miss Kate Strong, who was known more familiarly as "Puss," famously arrived with a cat on her head. Not a fanciful hat crafted to make her look like Catwoman; her headdress consisted of a *real dead cat*. It shouldn't be weirder than wearing a bird on your head or a fur coat, but somehow it is. As for her dress, "the bodice is formed of rows of white cats' heads and the head-dress was a stiffened white cat's skin, the head over the forehead of the wearer and the tail pendant behind. A blue ribbon with 'Puss' inscribed upon it, which hung a bell, worn around the neck completed the dress." Meanwhile, the overskirt "was made entirely of white cats' tails sewed on to a dark background."[29] As startling as this might sound to us today, no one at the party was horrified by this cat massacre. In fact, *The New York Times* declared it was "one of the most striking costumes"[30] of the glamorous evening. It gives you the impression that had *101 Dalmatians* been set in the Gilded Age, Cruella de Vil would have been received quite differently.

Ultimately, the true belle of the ball was Alva Vanderbilt's sister-in-law, Alice, who arrived in costume as "The Spirit of Electricity." Her gown of gold satin was designed by the famed couturier Charles Worth. It was beautifully trimmed with silver metallic tinsel, and across the fabric were motifs of lightning and starbursts. The dress itself might have faded into the background if not for the fact that it contained hidden batteries, allowing Alice to illuminate a torch as she walked. In what was perhaps the most notable picture of the evening, she was photographed holding this light above her head like the Statue of Liberty.

By 11:00 p.m. (parties began late so people could enjoy dinner or the opera before them—think of them as the nineteenth-century equivalent of going to a club), there were so many spectators outside the mansion trying to catch a glimpse of the glamorous invitees that the police were called in to try to help the attendees navigate their carriages through the street. Dinner was served at 2:00 a.m. and was prepared by the chefs at Delmonico's, a favorite restaurant among the New York gilded set. By this point in the evening, the men's appetites were said to be astounding. The plates were laden with the choicest delicacies. Men in evening clothes polished off plate after plate of chicken, pork, and foie gras, as well as ice creams and fruits, with the enthusiasm you might typically see at a barbecue joint. Meanwhile, a "miss in pink satin picked daintily at a salad which she barely touched."[31]

The more things change.

Guests partied until the sun rose the next morning, their extravagant costumes only slightly worse for the wear. And when they rose from their post-party naps, they were greeted by articles announcing that they had enjoyed the best party ever given. *The Courier-Journal* went so far as to declare that "such magnificence was never seen before in Republican America, and those guests who were familiar with the courts of monarchs had to admit that indeed it 'laid over' the levee of modern or ancient kings.... The Czar of all the Russias [would] turn green with envy had he been invited."[32]

Those who were not invited to the grand fete—the Czar of Russia included—were, predictably, furious. Mr. Jay Gould, a Wall Street titan of the time, was enraged to find that he was not included on the guest list and began furiously informing the people around him that "I am going to give a ball, and if William Henry Vanderbilt gets in, I will eat your hat."[33] The fact that it was William K., not William H., Vanderbilt who hosted the ball did not seem to bother Mr. Gould.

The rich—at least in New York—may have been deep in slumber the morning after the Vanderbilt ball. But it was clear to all that a new era was on the horizon. When the haut monde awoke, they couldn't stop fantasizing about the possibilities, the wild parties that could be hosted and who might host them. The Astor balls might remind people of their daily social status, but the Vanderbilt ball was a "scene of magic. Not a man or woman brought to mind the commonplace reality of today."[34]

Parties needed not merely reinforce the elegance and formality of the world you lived in. They could transport you somewhere else. Someplace novel, and exciting, where the rules—like what sauces could be served for dinner—might be forgotten.

Indeed, the ball represented a real turning point. Afterward, the door that had been shut to so many was nudged just the teensiest bit open. As much as people wanted to go to Mrs. Astor's parties for the chance to elevate their status, what they *really* wanted was to have fun—and it was more likely they'd have a blast at parties where people dressed up as counts and cats than ones where people sat around, bored stiff.

From her regal divan, even Mrs. Astor sensed the change. She, too, had been at the party. She had seen what it looked like when people had a really good time.

And so, even the regal Lina Astor admitted, "The time has come for the Vanderbilts."[35] And this new era of elite society would belong not to the most polite or wellborn, but to the most inventive.

CHAPTER 9

FOR WARD MCALLISTER, THE SHIFT IN PUBLIC PREFERENCE WAS positively hellish. He might have accepted the Vanderbilts—he was charmed by the Commodore's affection for him—but he had no interest in opening his world to other members of the nouveau rich. His vision for New York society was that of a tightly contained social universe built on birth, a world where all the money was agreeably aged, a place where tradition and continuity reigned supreme.

Just like in England.

To put it plainly: If Americans could not quite be English—or even European—then they could at least *try*.

But Americans did not have hundreds of years of tradition and royal protocol to guide their gatherings. The country was barely a hundred years old. It had no set formula for parties. They could make up their own rules. And they were going to. In 1884, it was declared that "people who go to parties must give parties."[1] As dancing was all the rage, smaller festivities were suggested for many people who did not have a ballroom. According to the *Buffalo Courier* in 1888, "nothing is more apparent to the thinker and observer of fashion than the dying away of prejudice against the healthy and natural amusement of dancing."[2] The paper went on to offer young people tips on how to behave at parties, like how to politely decline an invitation to dance, for instance, or how to introduce yourself to the hostess. Now that the tides were shifting in favor of inclusivity, the same article noted it was a shame that "in our republican country, perpetual 'Almack's' [the hosts of the London ball that inspired Ward McAllister's highly exclusive Patriarch Balls] arise, offensive and defensive, who give balls to keep people out, apparently a circle who live by snubbing."[3]

They might as well have called McAllister out by name.

Indeed, as early as 1885, people were beginning to complain that the Patriarch Balls Ward McAllister and Mrs. Astor threw were becoming old-fashioned affairs where "the young people are expected to watch [the elder Patriarchs] dance with all the interest and respect due their grey locks."[4] It's a sad fact of life that nothing geared to elderly people is considered cool. A *New York Times* reporter attending a Patriarch Ball found himself hoping that the musician "will put a little more vim into the dancing music than is customary for him, and that he will play some music which has not been played for the past ten years."[5]

Slowly but surely, change was coming.

By 1886, the unthinkable happened: A Patriarch Ball was given with "the Patriarchs issuing their own invitations without Mr. McAllister's personal supervision of the cards." The result was that "the younger society element was much more largely represented than is usual at the Patriarch's."[6] They might even have played hot and sexy modern music, like a polka.

Meanwhile, the Fish had never forgotten Ward's open disgust for Mamie's duck pond dinner, and by 1887, they saw chinks in the social dictator's armor. As long as Ward McAllister existed to sneer at her, she could never really climb to the heights of society.

It was time to rush in for the kill.

That same year, a committee of thirteen formed to plan an official Centennial Ball, a celebration on the one-hundredth anniversary of George Washington taking the Oath of Office on the steps of the Sub-Treasury building on Wall Street in 1789. Stuyvesant Fish was one member of this committee. Ward McAllister was another.

If Stuyvesant was defined by anything, it was loving trains and loving his wife. As with all good husbands, all her enemies were his enemies. From day one of this committee, he was resolved to tear McAllister apart.

From the outset, there was a shared sentiment among the rest of the committee that "Mr. McAllister was doing too much lofty boasting."[7] His ideas and pressure on formality seemed a bit outdated too. As the planning for this party was underway, *The Brooklyn Daily Eagle* exclaimed that young people were indulging in "a new pastime" known as the cakewalk, where a cake was awarded to dancers who stood on a particular number when the music ended. Stuyvesant—with Mamie's blessing—rallied the rest of the members, and they kicked Ward off the committee. Ostensibly, this was because Stuyvesant disagreed with Ward about the sixteen ladies McAllister had selected to lead an opening dance. There was discord over whether all the ladies had to be direct descendants of the ladies who had danced with Washington (though it seems uncertain who fell on which side of this debate). That was a disagreement that, newspapers noted, would have typically been resolved by talking to the other committee members and coming to some sort of consensus. However, in this case, as *The Brooklyn Daily Eagle* reported, "They fired him in their own tender and diplomatic way by making him resign."[8]

Ward declared, "Sometimes it happens...that you have men on a committee with you who are woefully ignorant of the work they have undertaken to superintend, who in one breath tell you 'I know nothing about this business' and in the next criticize, discuss and deluge you with useless and worthless suggestions."[9]

In response to Ward's objections and claims that he had been mistreated, by which he seems to have meant that he was not continually praised, Stuyvesant quipped, "The committee is not one that can be bossed by any demagogue, big or little, young or old."[10] McAllister, horrified, replied that he thought he knew quite a bit more about the planning of balls than the Fish! To this, Mr. Fish merely mused, in what feels like one of history's most devastating insults, "Who is Ward McAllister anyway? McAllister was our major domo, our master of ceremonies, our caterer. As such he was not acceptable to us, and we told him his services were no longer required. McAllister is a discharged servant. That is all."[11]

Undeterred, Ward McAllister attempted to claw his way back into society's good graces. In 1889, he hosted a New Year's Eve ball that was clearly designed to be "revenge upon Mr. Fish for ousting him from the management of the centennial ball."[12] He intended it to combine all the glamour he had seen at balls abroad—especially those he'd seen on his youthful trip to England—and chose the Metropolitan Opera as its location.

Ward invited 1,200 people, claiming that the object was "to enlarge society."[13] This was a huge concession for a man who always wanted to keep society very small. He may have been worried that people would not show up as they had in the past. Or he might have, somewhat clumsily, been trying to embrace a "more is more" approach. This, he promised, "would be no fish ball."[14] (Fish balls were a kind of lower-class snack, and the term was used to describe something tacky, but he did absolutely mean this as a dig at Stuyvesant and Mamie Fish.) Amazingly, Ward invited the Fish to attend, perhaps because he wanted to show off how well he could organize a gala. Or was it because he was officially acknowledging that they were progressing through the ranks of New York society's power players? Whatever the motive, Stuyvesant did not attend, but Mamie showed up out of curiosity.

For all his pomp and circumstance, things did not go exactly as he'd planned. The ball was hindered somewhat by the fact that, after 1:00 a.m., it had to operate without a liquor license. The Police Commissioners had decreed that, as McAllister's ball was being held at the Metropolitan Opera House and not a private venue, "the party may dance until dawn, but after 1 o'clock AM thirsty dancers may rinse their dusty throats with nothing stronger than Croton sec [a reference to the Croton aqueduct which carried New York's water supply]."[15] For a society that was accustomed to swilling champagne until the sun came up, this was a significant drawback.

It was crowded, and it was dry. There was nothing especially entertaining, like a chance to win a cake. People left the ball in search of more exciting venues, or their own beds.

Confronted with a society that had begun to think his outlook was stodgy at best, McAllister began to reminisce about better times. And so, he penned his memoir, *Society as I Have Found It* (1890), and chronicled his adventures among New York's elite, or, as he thought of them, the four hundred most important people in the city. Friends reported that "he had a supreme belief that the American people were simply waiting for his book and that they would buy it by the thousands immediately upon publication."[16] Apparently, he "believed it would net him $50,000."[17]

Alas, he made less than $2,000.

As it turned out, most people did not want to read a book that, when not glorifying Ward McAllister himself, rhapsodized about all the wonderful millionaires he knew. Not even the English he so worshipped were willing to give it a chance. In a manner that must have devastated an anglophile like McAllister, British newspapers sneered that the book was "a guide to authorized vulgarity" filled with "chapters on stationery, mourning, dressing, jewelry, and many other details, which in England—indeed, in all of Europe—we generally regulate by cultivated taste."[18] Americans, the papers concluded, must simply be a less evolved species if they all required *this* much help picking out their jewelry and stationery.

The book fared no better stateside. When he was giving a speech about "Americanism" in 1890, Theodore Roosevelt began "by paying his respects to Ward McAllister's 400 in a few stinging sentences that were received with laughter and applause" as he noted that "socialists were circulating [the book] as evidence of the uselessness of the rich and luxurious classes in this country."[19]

They agreed, given Ward's pronouncements that "up to this time, for one to be worth a million dollars was to be rated a man of fortune, but now, bygones must be bygones."[20] This would be an insane thing to say now, in 2025. In 1890, the average working man's salary was $584 (about $19,000 today). Boy, working men were *really* not charmed by Ward's glib proclamations.

Today, McAllister's book actually does serve as an interesting treatise for anyone who wants to know how flowers would have been fashionably arranged during the period (at least, according to McAllister). It has some very useful accounts of parties. Its greatest literary sin might be that the book is profoundly humorless (except when he recounts catty remarks from his wealthy friends, which, again, did not endear them to the average person). He treats the flower arrangements as a matter of life or death. His positions—for instance, that "madeira [wine] of any age, once moved, cannot be tasted until it has at least a month's repose"[21]—can't help but seem a little grandiose and ridiculous to anyone who was not Ward McAllister.

The members of the upper classes dutifully bought their friend's book, but they weren't thrilled by his insistence on digging his heels in on how, actually, he was right about everything he wrote, and common people just didn't *get* it.

"I do wish Uncle Ward would stop talking," lamented McAllister's niece. "He is making such fools of us all."[22]

To society's general displeasure, he did not.

In fact, Ward became even more driven to show people that *he* was the one who set the standards for society. He was not someone to be laughed at! He was no mere servant to these wealthy people! In Europe, where social position was determined by birth, he reasoned that no one would've laughed at him. He had, by this point, entirely forgotten that he was not to the manner born. He recalled giving friends "the benefit of my European education in the way of dinner giving." However, he also noted that at least some people responded to this kind of education by saying, "Heydey! Here is a young fellow coming out here to show us how to live... let us leave him severely alone."[23] He really was the equivalent of a college student who does one semester abroad and comes back determined to show everyone how breakfast is different in France, and will shove a croissant (pronounced "cwah-sahnt") down your throat whether you want one or not.

Ward was outraged that no one was taking him seriously. Maybe people did not realize he was a person of importance.

How could they? In Europe, everyone at least acknowledged that if you had a title, you were important. It irked Ward that there was no such clearly defined list in America. So Ward McAllister decided to write one. In 1892, Ward McAllister had been boasting to his friends about edits he'd made to a lengthy list Mrs. Astor had previously compiled of possible attendees for one of her balls. He explained that he'd reviewed the lineup and crossed off names until only four hundred, the number her ballroom could accommodate, remained.

Given the forcefulness with which he had boasted, a reporter from *The World* newspaper was surprised to find that in the end, only 150 people were actually invited to Mrs. Astor's ball. The fact that her ballroom could fit four hundred didn't necessarily mean she always wanted to cram it as full as possible. The reporter then cheekily declared that there must not be four hundred members of the elite, but only 150. Ward informed him that "this [number] is incomplete and does injustice, you understand, to many eligible millionaires."[24] He informed the journalist that he would give *The New York Times* a list of the four hundred people who were truly in society in New York City. He then proceeded to make up a list that did not, in fact, contain four hundred names; it contained 269 names.[25] Nevertheless, it ran in *The New York Times*, which claimed it was a definitive list of "The 400." The list included not only the Astors but also the Vanderbilts and even Mamie and Stuyvesant Fish. Ward may have hated them with his whole being, but by 1892 he couldn't deny they were showing up on nearly every guest list. Ward concluded by declaring, "Now, that is all, don't you know."[26]

If you think this response sounds profoundly ridiculous, you're not alone—so did everyone in New York.

This reaction was disastrous for Ward McAllister's hopes of a comeback. For all of upper-class America's obsession with Europe and its many princes and royals, they didn't want their *own* status codified in *The New York Times*. For a country that was ostensibly democratic, it seemed absolutely ridiculous to make a list of who was "in" and who was not. Ward's in/out list read as if someone had composed a list of the most popular kids in high school and then proudly printed it in the school newspaper for everyone to gawk at. Even if most of the people on the list were commonly accepted to be popular (though, of course, there were still plenty who disagreed with names on Ward's list), you were supposed to pretend not to pay attention. And besides, who did Ward McAllister think he was to be so entitled as to make up such a list in the first place?

The New York Times quickly dubbed him "Mr. Make-A-Lister," and Ward became the laughingstock of the town. Journalists made fun of his tendency to pepper the phrase "don't you know" into his speech, with an *Onion*-esque article that bore the title "The Only Four Hundred: Ward McAllister Gives Out The Official List. Here Are The Names, Don't You Know, On The Authority of Their Great Leader, You Understand, And Therefore Genuine, You See."[27] Another paper even quipped that "his 'don't you knows' come as natural to him as does 'I guess' to a Yankee or profanity to a parrot."[28]

Before long, any and all association with Ward McAllister was ill-advised—and being on the list implied you were so associated. As a piece in the *Pittsburgh Post-Gazette* scoffed regarding a diplomatic trip undertaken by the Duke of Veragua, "the only thing derogatory to the Duke of Veragua is that he comes to us highly endorsed by Ward McAllister."[29]

Things went crushingly downhill from there. As Chicago prepared to host the Columbian Exposition—a showcase for people to view new technology, like the Ferris wheel and electricity—in 1893, McAllister popped up once more and tried to teach the city how to put on a "stylish" party, lest the Midwestern town embarrass itself in front of sophisticated visitors from abroad. *The Buffalo Enquirer* reported that Ward McAllister advised the Chicagoans that the champagne should be "served frappe [frozen], and intimates that anyone who would drink it otherwise must be lacking in breeding."[30]

Obviously, journalists immediately seized on this frivolous advice as yet another reason to mock him.

In England, papers pointed out that this advice was simply *wrong*. *The Inter Ocean* wrote that "in the opinion of a properly constructed Londoner a man who would freeze champagne would not hesitate to freeze his grandmother."[31] The *Chicago Journal* took a different approach, assuring Ward that "the mayor will not frappe his wine too much. He will frappe it just enough so the guests can blow the foam off the tops of the glasses without a vulgar exhibition of lung and lip power. His ham sandwiches, sinkers [potato dumplings], and Irish quail, better known in the Bridgeport vernacular as pig's feet, will be triumphs of the gastronomic art."[32] Meanwhile, the *Chicago Tribune* proceeded to run a list of potential names for Ward McAllister, including "alleged leader of society," "damn fool," "chief flunky," and "head butler."[33]

But the humiliation didn't stop there. "Poor Ward McAllister," cooed *The Daily Democrat*. "Chicago is handling him without gloves. It was bad enough to be written down as a mouse-colored ass, but it remained for a still more scathing writer to name him an 'antique male dude.'"[34] *The Minneapolis Daily Times* claimed this description of him as a "mouse-colored ass" was unfair, and that he was really nothing more than "a bulb, a sort of boiled onion with the smell removed...kangarooing down fifth avenue at noontime with dust on his shoulders and the expression of a fainting halibut in his eyes."[35] This feels like way too many animals for a single metaphor, but I'm sure it was withering. *The Chicago Mail* agreed that "the funniest thing about a donkey is the perfect unconsciousness that rules him...the fact that he doesn't know he is funny is what multiplies the humor. It is the same with that two-legged donkey, Ward McAllister."[36]

Poor Ward indeed. He attempted to walk back his advice, claiming that he thought the response was "amusing" but that he "never intended to convey the impression that any New Yorker as a man is necessarily superior to a native of Chicago. There are many wealthy and charming people in Chicago."[37] He was off to a great start on that apology, although it fell apart considerably when he proceeded to add that "the leaders of society in the Windy City, I am told, are the successful pork packers, stock-yards magnates, cottolene manufacturers [a brand of shortening made from beef suet and cottonseed oil], soap makers, Chicago gas trust manipulators and dry good princes."[38]

You know, tasteless garbage humans that Mrs. Astor would've loved to spit on, were she not so elegant and refined.

In response, the *Chicago Tribune* pointed out that, when it came to the wealthy people in Chicago, "they are with few exceptions descended from the best stock on this continent, old puritan families. Most of them are college graduates, and the lavish manner with which these men have poured out money not only for higher learning but for the primary education of the young people of the city, betokens no passive interest in refinement and culture."[39] Still, Ward suggested, these gentlemen, though "nice in their way," were "perhaps in some cases, unfamiliar with the niceties of life and difficult points of etiquette."[40] He then went on to list stupid things he had heard of wealthy Chicagoans doing, like putting ballrooms in their attics.

Maybe someone in Chicago did do this. Maybe they did not. Either way, it was not exactly the best way to win over a city.

As a native of Chicago myself, I am offended by Ward's snobbery over a hundred years later—and so was just about everyone in Chicago back then. *The Chicago World* threw Ward's elitist mentality and hypocrisy back on him, asking, "Can you trace your lineage back to the Chicago fire? If not, how do you propose to square yourself?" and "What valid excuse have you for being on Earth?"[41] Like many a man who just doesn't know when to quit, Ward attempted to explain himself *again* in the *Chicago Tribune*, but to no avail. Finally, he retreated back into New York society rather miserably, sniffing that Chicagoans merely "want to knock me down for telling the truth about them."[42]

Okay, say you're willing to entertain the notion that every rich person in Chicago at that time was a rube listlessly gnawing on a hot dog while slurping warm champagne straight from the bottle. Why not. However, Ward's assumed persona as the master of etiquette was severely undercut by his insulting *an entire city*. People who passed through Chicago for the World Expo were asked by the newspapers whether they agreed that Ward was an idiot. Most happily agreed.

In the span of five years, Ward had fallen from being feared and respected as a King of Society to being mocked as an elitist ass.

Not long after, in 1895, Ward passed away from the grippe (a.k.a. influenza), surrounded by his wife, brother, son, and daughter. He collapsed at his club, where he was dining alone. He was often dining alone, now. Once Ward's closest ally, Mrs. Astor didn't even bother to cancel one of her society dinners when she heard that her old friend and compatriot was on his deathbed. But then, as Elizabeth Wharton Drexel noted, Lina *had* "cultivated the art of never looking at the things she did not want to see."

McAllister's funeral was crammed, although not by the so-called important members of society he had spent his life trying to lead. It was estimated that only about twenty of the people on his list of "The 400" showed up. His obituary noted that a friend of his, who wished to remain anonymous, claimed, "Ward McAllister was a leader in society more than 30 years ago, before the war."[43]

Instead, it was the regular New Yorkers who showed up to see the spectacle. Hundreds stood outside in the snow for what was supposed to be "the society event of the season." The police lined the streets to keep out the common people, who wanted to see how a man who at least believed he had impeccable taste would be laid to rest. Inside, Grace Church was filled with flowers as Ward's casket was buried under a mass of "floral tributes."[44] "The service was scarcely over before the crowd made for the chancel. A woman in sealskin seized a big violet wreath near the altar and hid it under her cloak." Even in death, the *Delphos Daily Herald* couldn't resist a jab at McAllister, noting that stealing flowers at his funeral was "terribly bad form, don't you know?"[45]

It was perhaps a sign that in coming years, the common people would not be content to leave finer things to the wealthy. Indeed, they might begin taking them by force.

One person who did not forget about Ward McAllister, even after all his embarrassments, was Cornelius Vanderbilt, who served as one of McAllister's pallbearers. That family, admirably, never forgot social favors done for them and resolved to treat those who'd treated them kindly with dignity until the end. In that regard, if not many others, they showed far more class than the families that considered themselves the Vanderbilts' betters.

CHAPTER 10

*T*HE VACANCY IN SOCIETY LEFT BY WARD WOULD NOT STAY EMPTY for long. By 1887, a young man named Harry Lehr was already in New York City, trying to establish himself among "The 400." He was absolutely unambiguous about his intent, claiming, "I begin where Ward McAllister left off. He was the voice crying in the wilderness who prepared the way for me."[1]

At first glance, the two would not appear to have anything in common, apart from their mission of becoming social arbiters. Still, Lehr's wife, Elizabeth "Bessie" Drexel, later noted that she didn't think Ward would've appreciated any comparison. Ward's approach to society was so intensely serious that Drexel remarked, "His cult of snobbishness was so ardent, so sincere, that it acquired dignity."[2] By contrast, she found Harry to be "the most amusing man in New York."[3] Unlike his predecessor, he refused to take anything too seriously. Instead, Harry Lehr wanted to make fun of society—or at least make it *fun*—almost as much as he wanted to be a part of it.

Like McAllister, Henry Symes Lehr (known to everyone as "Harry") didn't come from money. His father had been the German consul, and he was the third of six children in a conservative family. Harry grew up in Baltimore, a city where people were "inclined to despise New Yorkers as vulgar and affect disdain of the new aristocracy of wealth."[4] Unfortunately, his family lost their money in the depression of 1886 (truly, everyone except Mrs. Astor seemed to have suffered from a reversal of fortune). When his father died that same year, he found himself penniless at the young age of seventeen.

Harry noted that afterward, the family was not only without funds but without friends. "In our days of success there had been so many invitations," he later recalled, "now we got more snubs than anything else. We could not afford to entertain, so people did not want to bother with us."[5] He remembered those days as being "like Hell. The wretched poverty, the grayness, and the squalor of it all."[6] He just could not abide it, and so he decided to leave Baltimore for New York, where he found work as a wine merchant, specializing in the sale of champagne, which he hoped would attract a bubbly upper-class clientele. His lack of funds didn't deter him from trying to enter New York society, but it did force him to become more creative than the average New York society man. He was determined never to be shut off from society again. He realized that "if I wanted to get back into the social set I had been in in my father's lifetime, I should have to offer something in place of the money and position we had before."[7] So, as his future wife would muse, "he offered them laughter."[8]

Lehr wasted no time making moves. Upon his arrival in New York in 1887, Lehr convinced his tailor, shoemaker, and watchmaker that it would be advantageous to give him wares for free, since he was so fashionable (think of him as a proto-influencer). The clothes did not remain in good condition for long. Shortly afterward, he began encouraging others, like Miss "Freddie" Morris, who was said to be one of the great society beauties, to leave her carriage after a ball and leap into a fountain with him.[9] When word of this got out, other society women—who may also have wanted to be encouraged to do daring things—began asking to meet him. They did, and they loved him.

You may be thinking: Was Harry Lehr really, really good-looking? No! He was not. He was said to be "stout, blonde, with a high-pitched voice and an amazing assurance of manner."[10] *The St. Paul Globe* noted in 1900 that "to succeed in New York society, a young man must usually be either rich, handsome, or clever. Now, Mr. Harry Lehr's best friends do not claim any of these distinctions for him."[11]

Instead, it was his confidence—that assurance of manner—that bolstered him. Where Ward McAllister had been obsequious, Harry Lehr was insouciant. When he met the illustrious Mrs. Astor—Ward's longtime friend and collaborator—he informed her that when wearing her diamonds, she was so overdressed that she looked "like a walking chandelier."[12] He suggested that she wear, instead, a single red rose.

Perhaps because of that mystic rose, on some level he reminded her of her old, cast-off friend, Ward McAllister. Or perhaps she was just delighted by his fresh, new manner. After a lifetime of people pandering to her, she found Harry Lehr's refusal to be deferential positively irresistible. She even allowed him to take her out to lunch at the Waldorf Astoria Hotel. Keep in mind: This was a time when the very wealthy were expected to dine exclusively at their homes, and not alongside the rest of the public (even if they were upper-class). Indeed, "Harry Lehr, and his legs, and his piano playing, and his singing, and his witticisms, and all the rest of it have completely fascinated Mrs. Astor," the newspapers reported.[13] She adored him so much that she hired him as her personal secretary, proving Harry's point that the New York elite "will overlook most anything so long as you entertain them."[14]

And Harry *did* entertain them. He not only encouraged people to jump into fountains, he also posed funny (and subtly provocative) questions at salons, such as "How did Sherlock Holmes pick out Adam and Eve in heaven?"[15] (The answer is that the two had no belly buttons.) It was a question just spicy enough that it held the attention of an audience *and* could still be told in the company of debutantes.

Though Mrs. Astor was fond of Harry, she was by no means his true partner. That designation was reserved for Mamie Fish.

Harry Lehr and Mamie Fish were sympatico from the moment they met. No sooner had she heard of Mrs. Astor dining in public than Mamie Fish and her friend Frances Burke-Roche decided they'd break the taboo against women dining out with their necks exposed rather than wearing high collars in public restaurants. It was, they decided, "absurd that the public should be deprived of the sight of a pretty neck just because an obsolete convention decreed that nice women could appear in evening dress only in the shelter of their own and their friends' houses."[16] Knowing they'd get a rouse out of nearby onlookers, the duo enlisted two seemingly reluctant men to dine with them at the high-class Sherry's restaurant, where their lovely necks were met with abject horror. Throughout the restaurant, "incredulity, horrified condemnation, outraged virtue registered themselves in varying degrees on every face. There were audible comments of 'bold,' 'shameless,' 'disgusting.'"[17] The proprietor was aghast but found he could not turn away "two such celebrated leaders of society."

Mamie Fish and her friends could not have been more pleased. They had, after all, "demonstrated that it was possible to dine in New York as one dined in London without loss of caste."[18] And in doing so, they started a trend. By the next Sunday, women started exposing their necks *and* their décolletage when they were out to dinner.

Provoking outrage was one of Mamie's favorite pastimes. She loved to shake things up. She and Harry were wholly united in their distaste for boredom and their desire for excitement. For instance, they both found the opera "surpassed everything I ever knew in the line of boredom."[19] Instead, the two preferred to go to Barnum's circus, where they could see elephants, contortionists, and a marching band. They could also see what ordinary people seemed *delighted* by. It's little wonder Lehr was later dubbed "the P.T. Barnum of the 400,"[20] and there were descriptions of "Mrs. Stuyvesant Fish's circus set."[21]

For years, Mamie had waited for someone as interested in society who would not only tolerate her duck pond dinners but *love* them. Edith Wharton, perhaps the most flawless chronicler of this period and its inhabitants, once wrote that "the real marriage of true minds is for any two people to possess a sense of humor or irony pitched in exactly the same key."[22] The fact that they were of opposite sexes probably only added to their friendship.

Mamie could bring Harry gossip from women, and he could share with her information he gleaned from their husbands. They both relished in gossip and refused to take anything too seriously. Together, Lehr's wife recalled, "their practical jokes were endless, they were like two children."

Memorably, one day, while walking with Tessie Oelrichs, they saw a finely dressed rag doll in the window of a Newport store. They bought it and then proceeded to walk through Newport with a rag doll baby slung between them. They cooed over it, cuddling it and whispering to it in baby talk as one might a newborn. When other people invariably tried to approach to see the darling thing and then drew back in shock, they laughed hysterically. One paper, outraged, remarked that, in this incident, "the only respectable character is the rag doll."[23]

Another time, Mamie and Harry caught a society lady's dachshund, covered it in flour, and let it loose in a casino. Then they watched in hysterics as well-dressed women ran away from the dog, horrified of the prospect that it might mess up their chic lace dresses. On another occasion, they paid a streetcar driver one hundred dollars to ring the bell for an hour, driving at breakneck speed while they shouted, "All aboard for the cemetery!"[24]

Perhaps one of their most outlandish pranks took place at an auction. After each item was displayed, they groaned or made horrified gasps while covering their eyes, one-upping each other with every turn. At one point, Mrs. Fish appeared on the verge of fainting in visceral disgust. When the auctioneer, fed up, announced that "the sale has been suspended until the lady and gentleman at the back leave the hall,"[25] Mrs. Fish and Mr. Lehr smiled, wondering aloud to whom the auctioneer could possibly be referring. Only when they were told directly that they would be forcibly ejected did they retreat into the street, whereupon Mamie yelled, "Oh, look, look… he can't get the horse to stop. He will be killed; there's going to be a frightful accident!" Thereupon "the audience [from the auction] rushed in a body from the hall to behold the scene of horror, only to be greeted by peals of laughter as Harry and Mrs. Fish drove off."[26]

Other members of society often wondered what point they were trying to make, and the simplest answer is that there often *wasn't* any greater sentiment underlying Harry and Mamie's pranks. The two just loved mayhem for mayhem's sake.

But they could not play like two children forever. Married though their minds might have been, to cement his place in society—and to obtain the money he required to live in it—Harry would *also* have to marry, and marry well.

CHAPTER 11

*I*N 1900, HARRY LEHR BEGAN COURTING THE BEAUTIFUL YOUNG WIDOW Elizabeth Wharton Drexel Dahlgren, often called "Bessie." Since her husband's death the prior year, she had, by her own account, become very lonely. Eager to win her over, Harry swept into her life providing an endless stream of entertainment and engaging parties. In her biography, she recalled that he "informed her that, 'at 32, you are far too young and pretty to remain a disconsolate widow…I am going to wake you up and teach you how to enjoy life again.'"[1] Before long, Elizabeth wrote, "He filled my somber house in West Fifty-Sixth Street with gaiety and laughter…bringing people to see me, arranging parties on the spur of the moment, inviting me out to dine at the house of one or other of his friends."

After some time, he introduced her to Mamie Fish and other society ladies—including Mrs. Astor, Mrs. Stuyvesant Fish Jr., Mrs. Hermann Oelrichs, and Mrs. Oliver Belmont—at a luncheon. All the other women found Elizabeth charming and offered to introduce her to more people. This approval mattered far more to Harry than to Elizabeth. As he later admitted to her, "Much as I wanted to marry you, nothing would induce me to forfeit my position in society to do so."[2] The approval of the society doyennes now secured, he proposed, informing Elizabeth, "I have been in love with you ever since that first evening. I know you don't love me, but you are lonely, you need someone to take care of you. I believe I can make you very happy."[3]

Elizabeth wasn't sure she loved Harry. But she prayed on the matter—considering how much Harry added to her life, and how lonely she had been—and she accepted his proposal. She also arranged to give him an allowance, so he would no longer need to worry about money. On the night of her wedding, however, she was shocked when the servants told her that she and Harry would not be sharing a bedroom. Harry soon confirmed that theirs would be a marriage in name only. He did not want to touch her, did not really want to see her—except when they were out in public together. As he explained, "Love of women is a sealed book to me. I have not wanted it, or sought it, and I never shall."[4]

This is the best endorsement in the world for sleeping with someone *before* you marry them.

As far as records show, Harry kept his promise, and the two never consummated their marriage. If Harry Lehr had love affairs, they were (most likely) with men. He wrote blissfully about his time with his best friend, Tom Wanamaker, claiming, "His company is like a draught of wine to me."[5] Tom had helped him initially settle in New York, providing an apartment which he was "only too pleased to loan...to anyone as amusing as Harry."[6] Tom was, of course, married himself. Later, Harry would have a similarly close relationship with Charles Greenough, a fellow resident of Newport, who was also married. To top it all off, hanging in his bedroom, Harry had a prized picture of the notoriously promiscuous playboy Robert Gould Shaw II, in which Robert appeared entirely nude. So very nude that we can't include that picture in this book, but you can look it up.

To be clear: This was completely normal, as there are many gay people in this, and every, period. The difference is, of course, that people were not encouraged to openly discuss their sexuality back then, and so, societally acceptable platonic marriages were arranged to save face. Harry knew all about this. Shortly after telling her they would never be having sex, Harry informed his new bride, "How many men in New York, how many among our own friends, have entered their wives' rooms on their wedding night with exactly my state of mind but they prefer hypocrisy to the truth?"[7] Though homosexual acts at the time were illegal—and people convicted of practicing sodomy could be punished with jail time[8]—gay culture still thrived and was hardly a secret.

It's a wholly untrue notion that gay men existed entirely in shamed isolation in New York City during this period. They did not. This was an era when saloons or "resorts" filled with gay men—like Paresis Hall, Little Bucks, and the Black Rabbit—peppered the Bowery. Moreover, during the 1890s, women were beginning to take an interest in the demimonde as well. Middle-class women of the period recalled that "it was considered very smart to go slumming."[9] On these "slumming" expeditions, young people of both genders would visit various resorts in the Bowery to be pleasurably shocked and, at least a bit, titillated. Many would go to dance halls where "fairies" (men powdered, rouged, and often dressed in drag) were employed to sing and dance and sit in booths teasing big spenders. In his book *Gay New York*, author George Chauncey explains that "the fairies' presence made such clubs a mandatory stop for New Yorkers slumming."[10] And it wasn't like the papers were keeping these clubs hush-hush either. *The Herald* even explicitly reported in 1892 that these establishments were "a matter of common talk among men who are bent on taking in the town and making a night of it."[11]

Prior to their nuptials, Harry may have thought that Elizabeth would have suspected he was gay. There were many New Yorkers who would have realized this without him having to spell it out for them.

Unfortunately, Elizabeth was not apparently among them.

When Harry delicately attempted to explain to Elizabeth that he was not "animal" or "emotional" in his relations with women, she simply replied, "I thought all men were."[12] She seemed truly bewildered as to what he was attempting to convey.

This naivete is somewhat understandable because lawmakers, politicians, and moralists of this era had conspired to ensure that Elizabeth—and other upper-class women like her—would *not* know about different sexualities. Poorer people growing up in different circumstances might have been exposed to all manner of predilections early in life. Middle-class people might have examined the poorer areas of town for fun. Poorer people might have even had to ply their trade at the very clubs that those middle-class people frequented. But sexual matters were rarely discussed around women of Elizabeth's social station. Indeed, one of the distinguishing characteristics of the upper crust was that their daughters would be kept sheltered from any of the baser facts of life prior to their marriage. In her own memoir, Elizabeth recounted that when she'd asked her mother what to expect on her wedding night:

> Her mother responded with open contempt: "You've seen enough pictures and statues in your life," she said. "Haven't you noticed that men are…made differently from women?" When her daughter shyly indicated that she had noticed, Lucretia Jones decided that the case was closed. "Then for heaven's sake," she said, "don't ask me any more silly questions. You can't be as stupid as you pretend."

THE AUTHOR WOULD LATER CLAIM THAT THIS LACK OF EDUCATION "DID more than anything to falsify and misdirect my whole life."[13]

Harry expected a certain degree of sophistication and understanding from his wife. After all, she was a widow and already had a child. But Elizabeth, like so many women of her class, had grown up with an intensely religious mother. She remembered a childhood in which Queen Victoria was considered the ideal and "in the midst of a fast-changing New York social world, where already the old standards enjoyed by a Puritan ancestry were slipping farther and farther into the past, [mother] remained unshaken."[14] Divorced people were not even allowed into Elizabeth's childhood homes. This pretty much meant that Elizabeth was frightened to even consider divorcing her, *at best*, trickster of a husband (though this makes him sound more like Rumpelstiltskin than a gold digger who convinced a woman to marry him under wildly false pretenses).

And it wasn't just Elizabeth who was in the dark. The Comstock Act of 1873 had forbidden the distribution of literature or tracts containing information about reproduction. Nothing could be mailed or printed that might "deprave and corrupt those whose minds are open to such immoral influences, and into whose hands publication of this sort may fall."[15] This meant that children, especially those who eventually grew up into women like Elizabeth, were expected to remain cozily sheltered. Over time, this sort of state-sanctioned ignorance led to outrage, and by 1902, newspaper editorials remarked angrily upon the hypocrisy of the Comstock laws, claiming, "When people seek to marry, they are supposed to be old enough to desire information about sex as well as other responsibilities. They are children no longer." The same article speculated that "the time will come when the laws of sex and procreation are introduced into the common school curriculum...the heresy of one age becomes the gospel of the next, in spite of inquisitions and Comstock agencies."[16] This would eventually come to pass (at least, in some parts of the country), but American society still had a long way to go back at the end of the nineteenth century.

And so, Elizabeth had grown up with expectations that her marriage would consist of not just companionship in the world, but at home too. Alas, Harry continued to push her away, telling her in no uncertain terms: "For God's sake leave me alone. Do not come near me except when we are in public, or you will force me to repeat to you the brutal truth that you are actually repulsive to me."[17]

It's important to note here another crucial detail: Elizabeth Wharton Drexel Lehr was by no means repulsive. She was a knockout by any standard. Truly what you imagine a beautiful woman looking like in a movie version of this period. You might sift through picture after picture of "renowned beauties" of the era thinking, "Huh, really? Well, dental care was terrible, I guess, but I'm sure she was charming in person," whereas the second you spotted a picture of Elizabeth, you'd immediately say, "Put her on the cover of *Vogue* tomorrow." This is not to say that her beauty (or money) was the only thing that mattered, just that his rejection was (in all likelihood) probably one of the only times she'd been turned away by a man in her life. The fact that it was her husband, no less, undoubtedly would've made it worse.

Inevitably, Elizabeth would find her marriage to be little more than a "cruel farce."[18] It was quite obvious that Harry was only interested in her money. After their wedding, he told her that he could not possibly go on selling wine, boldly stating, "I am giving up a perfectly good livelihood because I love you far more than my career... and you will have to supply me with all that I am losing."[19]

Of course, Harry's unkindness to Elizabeth was reserved for their private interactions. In public, he called her "darling" and praised her extravagantly. But when people were not looking, their dynamic was quite different. While Harry seemed to regard Mamie as a peer and best friend, he clearly considered his wife to be more like a shoddily attired ATM. Yes, in addition to calling her repulsive, Harry also had the nerve to critique her sense of style. Elizabeth would later recall regularly going to church with him and seeing "his eyes half closed, his lips moving in the appearance of prayer, only pausing to hiss at me, 'What a perfect fright you are looking! Why on earth did you put on those shoes?'"[20]

Keenly aware of her friend's situation, Alva Vanderbilt offered to help Elizabeth obtain a divorce. But Elizabeth, a devout Catholic, declined. To this, Alva sighed and remarked, "You are the old-fashioned woman, Bessie. I am the woman of the future."[21] This proved to be true, as Alva not only divorced her own husband but also immersed herself in the burgeoning suffragette movement. Elizabeth and Harry, on the other hand, remained quite miserably married for twenty-eight years, parted only by his death.

Meanwhile, Mamie was blissfully ignorant of Elizabeth's misery, though she knew Harry Lehr was gay. While Harry's wife found her husband's sexual orientation to be a "heartbreaking realization," Mamie Fish happily informed her own husband that he did not need to worry about her spending so much time with this man as he was "just one of us girls." In a time when homosexuality was criminalized, Harry's orientation actually proved to be an advantage regarding his relationship with women like Mamie and, consequently, his social status. He knew that his sexless relationships with women were "the secret to my success. Love affairs are fatal to ambition. I have seen the shore strewn with the wrecks of people who have given way to their passions.... I'm running no such risks. My position is not stable enough for that."[22] As a result, "the men saw in him a sort of watchdog who would keep their wives amused and therefore out of mischief."[23]

It must have been a relief to Harry that, with Mamie, he could be his queer self without feeling guilty. He was happy to spend all morning with Mamie at the dressmaker, advising her on the most flattering attire or the latest fashions. Likewise, he spared no expense when it came to his own outfits, and he sometimes expressed disappointment that he had not been born a woman, because the clothing was so much better. Still, he missed no opportunity to show off his own unique sense of style. One paper observed that for the upcoming Newport season, "Harry had provided himself with a particularly cute bathing suit of his own designing with which to ravish the eyes of the 400. The vest will be cut decollete in order to expose the whiteness of his snowy neck, and the trunks abbreviated so as not to deprive his admirers of a full view of his shapely limbs, which will be modestly encased in sunken hose."[24]

He was also open to flaunting his feminine side. *The Saint Paul Globe* described him as "such a ladylike person,"[25] and he once went to a masquerade ball in drag dressed as "a prominent soubrette."[26] He was pictured knitting—a very feminine hobby—with another dowager, Mrs. George Gould. To modern readers, everything he did would read as gay. This caused a minor scandal, though it did not appear to faze Mamie, who truly did not care whether he was gay or feminine or any way at all, really—as long as he was consistently hilarious.

And he really did make her laugh.

Not so long before, Ward McAllister had lovingly, and quite sincerely, referred to Mrs. Astor as his "Mystic Rose." Harry joked at one party that if he had to come up with a similar floral name for Mamie, it would be "Climbing Rose." She replied that in that case, she would call him a "Mari-gold."[27] Marry...gold. Like a gold digger, a thing we all call our best friends.

The world of Mrs. Astor seemed to be disappearing into the past, as people found that her "stately dinners lacked spice."[28]

Not so at Harry's dinners with Mamie. Soon, people were abuzz, swapping stories about the "informal dinners given by Mrs. Stuyvesant Fish, leader of the gayest set, often frowned upon by older, more staid society matrons for her unconventionality, when the whole table would be convulsed with laughter at the sallies of Harry Lehr and his hostess."[29] It was understood that "Mrs. Astor was dignified. Mrs. Fish was flip. Mrs. Astor gave conventional balls. Mrs. Fish staged unconventional routs."[30] It was glaringly apparent that if you were invited to Mrs. Fish's dinner the same night Mrs. Astor was having one, you'd have a better time at Mamie's.

And if a more conservative set did not take kindly to this sort of silliness and debauchery, then Harry and Mamie would force it upon them. One Newport hostess informed Mamie that she simply could not invite the two of them to a dinner she was hosting, despite the fact that she had invited Mamie's husband and Harry's wife, sighing as she said, "Very sorry, my dear... but I can't have you and Harry Lehr at this party of mine. You make too much noise."[31]

Of course, it *was* true that the pair were famously noisy, always joking and laughing extremely loudly. Mamie, remember, had been known to start screaming about horse-drawn carriage accidents if she wanted to create a commotion. They both liked to gasp and pretend to faint at auction houses.

In this case, the hostess wanted to celebrate a serious musical performance at her home, and she was worried Mamie and Harry would distract the rest of her guests. Unbothered, Mamie replied, "Well, let me tell you, sweet pet, that unless we are invited, there won't be any party. Harry and I will tell everyone that your cook has developed smallpox."[32]

That is insane, and it's nice to think they would not have actually done it. But the hostess wasn't sure.

It will surprise no one that Mamie and Harry were subsequently invited. The hostess apparently felt that Mamie and Harry heckling their musicians was less offensive than the threat of salacious smallpox rumors. Acquiescing to respectability, Mamie and Harry agreed to stay out on the terrace during the musical performance, but for a long time afterward Mamie took a great deal of pleasure in telling people that she and Harry were considered "disturbing elements."[33]

And yet, society during these years wanted to be disturbed. It had sat too long on uncomfortable divans. Now things might be less wholesome, but that meant they were a great deal spicier. And Mamie's future exploits would mean that chroniclers would soon refer not to Mrs. Astor's Four Hundred, but to the Fish-Astor Four Hundred.[34]

CHAPTER 12

Conquering New York society wasn't enough for Mamie. Decades earlier, Ward McAllister had established Newport as the place to be. Now, Mamie needed to throw parties there that put his hyper-elaborate picnics to shame. But she rented a plain, rather small house by the seaside. If Mamie was to become the queen of society, this would never do—she needed a castle of her own. And they looked, but nothing on the market had everything she wanted.

So Mamie and Stuyvesant decided to build a dream home of their own.

This was hardly a novel idea. During this period, Newport was increasingly dotted with elaborate mansions. These residences popping up everywhere were intended to be lived in, sure, but more than that, they were meant to absolutely stupefy guests with their grandeur.

In recounting this period, Louis Auchincloss, the historian and chronicler of the upper classes, remarked that "new society," which is to say society no longer bound by the rules of Mrs. Astor and Ward McAllister, "understood it was not enough to go regularly to church, to give generously to the poor, to maintain the strictest moral standards and set an example in one's speech and decorum. No, one had to provide some bread and circuses, too."

In other words: These houses were built to *entertain*.

Thank God Mrs. Fish knew a thing or two about the circus.

Marble House, for example, had been a gift from William to Alva Vanderbilt for her thirty-ninth birthday in 1892. The beaux arts–style palace was inspired by the Petit Trianon in Versailles, Marie Antoinette's "rustic" cottage. It was constructed of five hundred thousand cubic feet of white marble, and it cost $11 million ($371 million today). Marble House famously boasted a Gothic room for Alva and William's revered collection of medieval art, which was nearly overshadowed by its stunning arched stained glass windows. In the ballroom, the mirrors, sculptures, and walls were all covered in gold.[1] As the Society of Architectural Historians noted, "We are left to imagine what effect the light from scores of candles in the two huge chandeliers would have had on such a shimmering setting."[2] It was the perfect home for what Mark Twain would call the Gilded Age, though Alva Vanderbilt didn't live in it long.

By 1895, just as she'd suggested to her pal, Elizabeth, Alva divorced her husband and left Marble House behind. This meant that—just as Elizabeth had feared—there were drawing rooms in which she might not be received. Unless of course, she married another equally rich man.

So she did just that. Alva promptly married the banker Oliver Belmont and moved to a new mansion, Belcourt Castle. The plans for that estate, completed in 1894, were inspired by the hunting lodge at Versailles. A fanatic equestrian, Oliver had nearly the entire first floor of the house taken up by stables so that he could visit his horses—and, later, his expensive automobiles—whenever the mood struck him. The horses in their stalls, each with a gold nameplate, were given pure white sheets to sleep under. In a less convenient detail, there was no in-house kitchen. Belmont was greatly afraid of fire (and what it might do to the horses), so the meals had to be delivered from town. Like Marble House, the castle was a wedding gift to Alva from her new husband. She promptly remodeled it, and a banquet hall for human use was added to the first floor. She soon turned it into a perfect space for entertaining.

Not to be outdone by either his brother or his ex-sister-in-law's new husband, Cornelius Vanderbilt II completed The Breakers in 1895. Like Marble House, it was a mammoth undertaking, three years in the making—and the result was iconic. To this day, people still debate whether Marble House or The Breakers best exemplifies the indulgences of the wealthy Newport set during this period. Rather than the French style employed at Marble House, The Breakers was styled after Genoa's Palazzo Doria-Tursi. Cornelius Vanderbilt was nearly as afraid of fire as Oliver Belmont, as his last house had burned to the ground. So, The Breakers was built out of steel, brick, and limestone, ensuring that it was a perfect mix of the most modern materials with a classical style. The Great Hall was inspired by Roman courtyards and had a ceiling fifty feet high. The entire place was built to make you feel like you were in an almost otherworldly, infinite palace. It was twenty-four thousand square feet large and contained forty-eight bedrooms. And, in what was still a new innovation during these years, it was fully electrified so that it beamed like a fairy palace to those who approached.

To set herself further apart from these contemporary castles, Mamie Fish wanted a uniquely American-style house.

Crossways, as it was called, was designed by a local architect, Dudley Newton. The home, painted white and looking like something you might see in a culturally reductive film about the old South, was built between two roads running through the town (hence, the name). The long road led up to four magnificent columns beneath a pointed room, and behind the house there were magnificent views of the ocean. It was said to be an "ideal spot for a summer seaside home…and its fair mistress, already christened 'Diana of the Crossways' rules over it with…conscious pride."[3] The *San Francisco Examiner* added that Crossways had "such a commanding site and seems to scream out of the landscape 'Here I am.'"[4] The fact that it had been built "with pine instead of stone, as originally planned, and the decorations are inconspicuous"[5] was rarely mentioned. However, it does explain how the Fish had been able to construct their home for only $100,000 ($3.7 million today)—a large sum of money, to be sure, just not as jaw-dropping an amount as what their contemporaries would have spent. Then again, Mamie often lamented that she never had as much money as most of her friends and claimed that the Fish wealth never exceeded more than $3 million.

In spite of its considerably cheaper price tag, Mamie had no patience for those who refused to acknowledge Crossways as a landmark. In her mind, it was *the* definitive destination for anyone who wanted to party, and she expected everyone to talk about it accordingly. When one young snob dismissively asked Mamie the name of her place—was it Crosspatch? He couldn't remember—Mamie snapped back, "It's a patch you'll never cross."[6]

Crossways was, by any normal standard, a spectacular house. But if you were comparing the colonial home to The Breakers, it was downright cozy. The relatively understated nature seemed to prevail in everything except her British butler named Morton, who turned out to be a rather disastrous choice of employee. Morton claimed that he'd developed "through much aristocratic service a fine taste in wine." As it turned out, he really, *really* enjoyed consuming wine as well as pouring it, and this trait didn't serve him well.

One afternoon, when Mamie invited eighteen friends over for lunch, Morton burst into the room drunkenly shouting, "I suppose that because you happen to be Mrs. Stuyvesant Fish, you think you can drive up and down the Avenue inviting who you like to the house. Well, let me tell you, you can't. Sixteen is my limit and if you ask any more, they go hungry!"[7]

Mamie, understandably, felt that because she *was*, indeed, Mrs. Stuyvesant Fish and it *was* her house, she could invite as many people as she wished. Her house was designed for entertaining. The butler fumed and, according to *The New York Times*, "a stormy scene ensued in which the butler was ordered from the house, but refused to go, and became abusive."[8] After barricading himself in his room, Mrs. Fish finally called the police, and they had to break down the door to remove him. The next day, as Mrs. Fish prepared to host a dinner party, she was shocked to find that Morton had dismantled all the dinnerware. Mamie's friend, Elizabeth Drexel Lehr, recounted that "with amazing ingenuity, he unscrewed the whole of the gold dinner service into three hundred separate pieces and mixed them in one heap on the dining room floor, so that they resembled a jigsaw puzzle."[9]

Ironically, this seemed like the kind of prank Mamie Fish would have pulled had their roles been reversed. There must have been some part of her that gazed at the golden jumble and admired his style. Still, Mamie was left to figure out how to deal with the consequences of Morton's meltdown on her own, and she decided that the future help at Crossways would be much more down-to-earth.

And she would certainly need a great deal of help if she wanted to carry out all the festivities she'd been dreaming about for years. During the time it took to build Crossways, Mamie often talked about her plans to liven up Newport. She'd already developed quite the reputation as "one of the most positive, if not popular, young matrons of New York society."[10] Now, she was also known as someone who declared war on the old guard, complaining that the Newport Four Hundred were old-fashioned and "dull."[11] And she knew intrinsically that if you're going to make such a claim, you need to throw truly epic parties that illuminate how they *should* be held instead.

On July 16, 1898, about a year after work on Crossways had been completed, Mamie and Stuyvesant began entertaining modestly with a simple dinner for forty. If you're thinking to yourself that forty people still sounds like a *lot* for a dinner party, just know that the estate's dining room had been built to accommodate eighty (though it would later be expanded to seat two hundred). From the start, the couple intended to host regular Sunday night dinners with a sizable guest list. The food was said to be terrific. So was the wine. People claimed that the Fish's "cook was a genius" and the "cellar was a noted one."

However, there was one big problem. Mamie did not especially like the drawn-out, multicourse meals that were de rigueur. Under Ward McAllister, dinners (which, remember, should never feature two courses with brown sauce—the *horror!*) dragged on for hours. She did not want to be stuck talking to whoever was seated next to her for hours on end, and she was surprised that anyone would enjoy this. Since Mamie could not abide these lugubrious affairs, she vowed that she would always serve dinner in under an hour. And she somehow managed to pull this off, though she did occasionally take this stance to an extreme. Once, when an eight-course dinner was served in half an hour, "guests had to hold down their plates with one hand while they ate with the other to keep servants from whisking dishes away as soon as they arrived."[12]

But decadent as these dinners might have been, they were a mere precursor for the extravagant housewarming that Mamie intended to take place on July 30, 1898.

CHAPTER 13

W(HILE MAMIE HAD BEEN PREPARING FOR SOCIAL BATTLE, OTHER members of the Fish family were dealing with the tragedy of quite another sort of conflict.

Hamilton Fish, Mamie's nephew, had always been considered a black sheep by his family. But he seemed to have found his calling by joining the Rough Riders, a group of volunteer cavalrymen commanded by Teddy Roosevelt fighting for independence in Cuba.

At the Battle of Las Guasimas, however, Hamilton was the first of the Rough Riders to die.[1] He was shot directly through the head, shouted, "I'm shot, I think,"[2] and then expired.

The Globe newspaper visited his parents following word of his death and found them sobbing and staring at a framed photograph of Hamilton from his college days. Rarely did people glimpse wealthy families at their most emotional. Clemence was reported asking if, perhaps, there was a chance that the information might be wrong. Her husband had to keep telling her it was not. Nicholas spoke warmly of the friends who had been killed alongside

Hamilton. He talked about how his son loved his life as a soldier and how he knew Uncle Sam needed him.

"I know he died like a soldier," Clemence added. "But it seems like a sin to send such young fellows into a deadly ambush, when there is hardly a living chance." Mrs. Fish, *The Globe* reported, "could not speak of her son without weeping."[3]

The intimacy of these details—and the genuine, relatable heartbreak on the part of his parents in an age where parent-child bonds were considered increasingly important—turned Hamilton's death into a national tragedy.

Hamilton had been buried "at the crossways of Las Guasimas."[4] All the public seemed to mourn him, as he was transformed from a wastrel into a national hero. "America hadn't been used to the thought of death in Cuba,"[5] reported *The Brooklyn Daily Eagle*. "This was war. Hamilton Fish's death brought the ghastly knowledge into hundreds of houses in New York from which mothers had sent carefully reared sons to fight."[6]

The battle that killed Hamilton took place on June 24. By the 26th, New York was in mourning for him. It was reported that "the swell young men in society are wearing crepe on their arms in memory of Hamilton Fish."[7] By the 30th, the newspapers were teeming with accounts of his death.

That also happened to be the same time Mamie was busy planning to welcome guests to her new home.

EVERYONE THOUGHT THAT MAMIE WOULD CANCEL THE HOUSEWARMING. After all, the Fish would be in mourning for their nephew, who was now seen as a beloved war hero. *Brooklyn Life* reported on July 16 that "owing to the tragic death of their nephew, Mr. Hamilton Fish Jr., it is hardly probable that Mr. and Mrs. Fish will entertain much this season."[8]

Brooklyn Life could not have been more wrong. To Mamie's mind: The party *must* go on.

The fact that she didn't cancel shocked some people. As *The Brooklyn Daily Eagle* noted, "Many thought it was cruel. Many thought it was in bad taste. Society argued the case for weeks. Much was said on both sides."[9] But shocked though they may have been, society still showed up for the event.

Of course, there were numerous reasons they might have attended in addition to general excitement. For one, the fact that Mamie was known to have a sharp tongue meant that some would have been afraid to get on her bad side and potentially suffer her wrath in the future if they skipped the fete. Others, though, might have been desperate to see the interior of Crossways, and more still likely wanted to stay on the list for any future parties that might be held there.

Whatever their reasons, on the night of the housewarming at Crossways, "beams of light poured from every window, handsome equipages rolled up to the doors, from which alighted men and women in rich costumes who thronged the house, which was decorated with flowers and whose treasures were lavishly displayed."[10] The flowers in front of as well as inside the house were gorgeously in bloom. Women showed off their jewels to one another. Everyone marveled at the spectacular view of the ocean. They drank glass after glass of champagne. The orchestra played on while the rich and beautiful danced until dawn. Afterward, the housewarming at Crossways was described in the papers as "one of the most spectacular balls in American life."[11]

This decadence in the face of the war that so many of their countrymen were fighting in caused one paper to assert, "Dead in Cuba, dancing and dining in Newport... Which appeals most to the consideration of Americans?"[12]

This particular line of criticism wasn't anything new—and it hasn't gone away since. After all, Truman Capote's Black and White Ball took place sixty years after Mamie's housewarming, and people still expressed fury then that anyone could celebrate when young men were being sent to Vietnam. However, it's essential to keep in mind that the United States has been in some sort of conflict for approximately 93 percent of its history. The problem is not that dancing is more of a focus in American life than mourning those who've died in war. It is that if you want to wait for a time when the United States is completely at peace to have a party, you'll be waiting a very long time.

The critical difference in Mamie's case was not that she was having a ball when men were dying in Cuba. No, the real cause for alarm among traditionalists was that one of those men—really, in the public view, the most famously mourned man of this particular conflict—was her own nephew. The *Valley Spirit* newspaper was aghast that "any loyal American can approve the merry making by members of a prominent family at a time when the last sad rites were being performed over the body of a fellow member."[13]

Indeed, Nicholas and Clemence Fish were (very understandably!) distraught over their son's death. Hamilton's mother, who had been especially close to her son, was inconsolable, unable "to overcome her grief at her great loss." The two had been "completely wrapped up in each other, and she never could see that he had the slightest fault so dear was her love for him." And Mamie's willingness to party in the face of their despair was, in their eyes, infuriating.

By this point, Clemence had also been upset for years that Mamie had outshone her socially, especially as she was married to the eldest son of the Fish family. While Mamie was gaining acclaim for being a wild card who threw magnificent parties, Clemence was left to give "excerpts from Wagner with Wagnerian tenors" at her home while "Mrs. Stuyvesant Fish reigned at Newport" and was "generally spectacular."[14]

God, Clemence hated her based on that alone. She didn't sign up to be constantly outdone by a woman who kept making fun of her maiden name.

And that wasn't the only grudge Clemence held. Nicholas and Hamilton were both known to have been heavy drinkers, to Clemence's chagrin, and Nicholas was not faithful. Meanwhile, it was no secret that Mamie's husband, Stuyvesant, was completely faithful and generous as far as she was concerned. To make matters worse, earlier in the same year, Clemence's father had been declared by a judge to be incompetent to manage his affairs, which meant that she was now dealing with a drunken, philandering husband and a father with dementia while grieving a dead son.

All in all, it hadn't been one of Clemence's better years. And now, Mamie was too busy partying and shooting off little quips in her enormous new house to even acknowledge that Hamilton was dead. If their relationship had been lukewarm before, following Mamie's housewarming it was positively frosty.

It is likely that today many people would have canceled the housewarming. Not due to any notions about respectability that have held over from the nineteenth century, but because a nephew dying is far more important than any party you might have scheduled, barring, perhaps, a wedding. It's also worth noting that, fortunately, twenty-five-year-olds die less frequently nowadays than they did one hundred years ago. And parties carry less cultural cache.

But things were much different for women back in 1898, even for those as intelligent and funny and—frankly—ruthless as Mamie. Women in many states couldn't even own property, and if they worked, their wages were turned over immediately to their husbands. There were women who earned medical degrees, or were successful authors, but these women were extraordinarily few. When women did work, they earned far less than men. Spousal abuse was still legal until the 1920s, given the notion that husbands should have power over their wives. For someone of Mamie's class, social power was one of the very few ways a woman could achieve any kind of influence. From that perspective, refusing to cancel a party at that time might be better compared to a corporate executive today still going to work despite hearing of their nephew's death. Still questionable, but comprehensible.

Ignoring her in-laws' seething disdain, Mamie kept on partying.

On August 8, Mamie hosted a grand celebration for 110 guests to formally introduce her seventeen-year-old debutante daughter, Marian. According to reports, "At the height of the dance a donkey came rushing into the room, causing a scattering of guests to places of safety. It was soon seen that the little animal... was laden with cotillion favors."[15] The donkey was delightfully dressed for the occasion, decked out in garlands of flowers, with tinkling bells around his harness and with his hooves painted gold. According to *The New York Times*, the donkey also delivered favors to attendees, including "baskets of flowers tied with silk ribbon, wooden rakes, bows and arrows."[16] The party was later referred to not as Marian's Coming Out Party, but as Mamie's "Donkey Party." Marian herself didn't seem upset by this—though if she'd been upset about being outshone by a donkey that would have been understandable. Mamie was delighted that people responded so well. Already, the residents of Newport were buzzing about whether anyone would be able to one-up her originality.

Almost immediately, someone did: Mamie herself. Within two days— hardly enough time for many of us to have cleaned up the house—she hosted a dinner party where attendees were entertained by circus performers. A mandolin club provided the music and "a troupe of gymnasts gave a clever exhibition in the hallway, which was heartily applauded by all the guests."[17] It was as if she'd brought Cirque du Soleil into her own home.

She also began helping her friends throw their own grand celebrations. At a party hosted by Alva Belmont, Mrs. Fish helped her receive her guests (perhaps as a signal to show that she did not care that Alva *had* gotten a divorce). That party at Belcourt was held under an outside tent and featured fortune tellers and variety shows—novelties so typically Mamie that everyone would have seen it as being as much her party as Alva's.

Within one month Mamie hosted again, this time to commemorate the opening of her barn. As expected, she went all out. The attendees were ferried over to the barn in hay-filled open wagons where they found Mrs. Fish dressed as a dairymaid, standing next to a scarecrow she had borrowed from a local farm for the occasion. The barn was lit up with electric lamps, scarecrows with "illuminated heads," and hundreds of carved, glittering jack-o'-lanterns. The stalls of the stable were fitted up as "flirtation booths"[18] where people could discreetly canoodle. The guests were called to dinner by ringing cowbells, and they could even ride a hay cart from the barn to the main house "if they felt so disposed." Once they arrived, they would see Shetland ponies, fetchingly garbed in red harnesses, prancing about in the ballroom.

But that wasn't all. A "golden tree" had also been wheeled into the ballroom. On that tree were "small, wooden cages containing live young chickens, goslings, and Belgian rabbits,"[19] which the guests were encouraged to pet and cuddle to their heart's delight and take home if they wished. Puppies were also available as party favors, though they were, naturally, too heavy to suspend in cages from the tree. Still, guests were encouraged to pet and cuddle them as much as they liked.

You have to admit: This sounds *so much more fun* than a stodgy, three-hour dinner. Who among us would not want to go to a party filled with puppies?

On top of everything else, attendees were also encouraged to dress in rustic attire. Whereas once, at Alva Vanderbilt's costume balls, "all had to be kings and queens and courtiers,"[20] now at Mamie's barn party they donned rustic attire. "For the reason that the entertainment was given in a stable," the *Fall River Daily Herald* reported, "silks, satins, velvets, laces and jewels were discarded, and in their place plain calicoes, muslins and chintzes were worn, while the somber evening dress of the men gave way to costumes of chefs and of New England farmers."[21] Women, meanwhile, dressed as flower girls and shepherdesses.

Partygoers were laden with so many gifts that they might have paid for a small farm, including "sun hats trimmed with sunflowers and goldenrod," gilded scythes and horseshoes, and carriage bells they could ring. Guests waved monogrammed pitchforks festooned with flowers, and milk pails trimmed with red ribbons and painted with Stuyvesant's initials were handed out. Women were also given huge whips to wield, while men donned tiny crops—perhaps a cheeky way of demonstrating who Mamie felt held the real power in relationships (though it must be said that her own marriage, one based on genuine affection and mutual admiration, was quite rare at the time). At the end of the evening, guests received photo frames—silver for the women, leather for the men. Now that people were being photographed, they might want to include a picture from the evening as well.

If there was any concession to the familial tragedy, it was merely that during the cotillion, "the stars and stripes were prominent."[22]

Despite Mamie's desires for a traditionally American, non-European home, she was not overly invested in American affairs. She may have eschewed Marie Antoinette memorabilia, but nothing is more reminiscent of Le Petit Trianon at Versailles than some of the wealthiest people in the country dressing up as farmers and dairymaids while cuddling little ducklings. But her events also contained rare new glimpses of frivolity and fun in a society that had a habit of taking itself very seriously. To look at pictures of Alva Vanderbilt's housewarming, for example, was to see people very beautifully posed, conscious of their wealth, position, and glamour. At Crossways, people were allowed to laugh, to relax, to forget about their wealth and power for a few hours—a privilege that, up to the point, had largely only been afforded to men and women frequenting brothels, music halls, or other "low-class" arenas of entertainment.

The New York Times raved about how Mrs. Fish "entertains so originally and pleasing[ly]" and that anyone attending her parties "might as well now make up their minds to have a good time or stay home."[23]

This was one of the first times that guests were told they had better make merry at parties. More was more. And as the summer season drew to a close, Mamie retreated with ample time to devise new novelties for the coming year.

CHAPTER 14

$\mathcal{I}$N May 1899, *THE KANSAS CITY TIMES* REPORTED THAT MRS. FISH would be engaged in "the fight of her life" for social supremacy during the Newport summer. Mrs. Bertha Potter Palmer, the wife of a Chicago millionaire, was returning from Europe, and much to everyone's excitement, her friend, the Russian Prince Cantacuzène, was coming to visit. And it wasn't just Mrs. Palmer; the second wife of William K. Vanderbilt (Anne Harriman) and Mrs. Hermann Oelrichs had also expressed ambitions to become the new queens of Newport society. However, what made Bertha Palmer especially threatening to Mamie was the fact that she and her niece, Miss Julia Grant, would be returning stateside not merely with a prince but "with wonderful wardrobes made abroad."[1]

Mamie Fish took the idea that people might lose interest in her to heart. Her dressmakers began "turning out for her a summer wardrobe that in beauty of design and artistic finish has never yet been equaled in the annals of American society."[2] These would not be the elegant, subdued gowns of yesteryear; these were extreme and daring dresses, designed to ensure that all eyes would remain steadfastly fixed on Mamie. One evening at the casino, she turned heads clad in "a bright scarlet spangled gown . . . cut with the fashionable eel skin skirt, a long train and slightly low corsage . . . the serpentine lines of the scintillating, brilliantly colored garment made Mrs. Fish look as if she was clothed in flame." It was considered "the most original, unique, daring, becoming, expensive, sensational novelty of the season." People gasped at how the spangles were "counterfeiting fish scales."[3] Or, as one person amusingly declared, "There comes Mamie, dressed like a salamander."[4] Although the dress cost a whopping $2,500 ($95,000 today), it was money well spent for the way it burnished Mamie's reputation.

It was also good business for the Newport Casino, where she wore it. Many people who merely wanted to visit Newport could not attend the dances there. However, for one dollar[5] they could stand in the galleries, see what everyone wore, and *pass judgment*. If you cannot see the appeal of this, allow me to direct you to any number of reality television programs and their viewers.

Even as her new fashions grabbed the attention of everyone in Newport, it was still her parties that aroused the greatest anticipation.

Back in February, she had invited people to a "Reversible Dance," with the idea that everyone in attendance had to wear their clothing back to front. She declared that "people should look as if their heads were on the wrong way round."[6]

In her New York home, which was in the process of being completed, she hosted a combination Valentine's Day Dance/Mardi Gras Ball. In honor of Valentine's Day, a temporary "post office" was installed where guests could drop off letters to other attendees. Once in the house, "little boys representing cupids in [tights] and wings and quivers of arrows and a little silk drapery, came from the post office, and handed to each guest a letter with his or her name on it. These contained handsome and satirical and witty valentines."[7]

As for the Mardi Gras aspect, she transformed her ballroom into a "Satanic Flower Garden" where all the flowers were designed to resemble fire, and the words "Mardi Gras" were illuminated with electric lights and flowers in an archway. Letters were also given out to guests in the spirit of

Mardi Gras, which meant that, unlike the charming Valentine's Day ones, these were "letters from hell."[8] Sadly, the content of these letters has not survived, so it's hard to determine whether the notes sent by Satan were spicier than those from Cupid. Guests were also given—in what was quickly becoming a Fish decorating mainstay—tiny pitchforks as party favors.

When they tired of these entertainments, guests could watch ballerinas perform a "flower dance" in which each dancer represented a different bloom. In a display that guests found especially dazzling, "their skirts were illuminated with tiny electric lights, arranged with a small battery, and the flashing and dying away of these fires were most weird and effective."[9] This already outdoes any Valentine's Day party the average reader might attend, where the most you can hope for are heart-shaped cookies and maybe some fun garlands, but then Mrs. Fish unleashed *doves*. A supper was served at three in the morning, after which guests headed home with baskets filled to the brim with pink and red roses, "in which tiny batteries were concealed so as they could be lighted by electricity."[10]

People absolutely loved electricity during this period. They got excited every time they saw an electrified house. We should honestly be more dazzled by it today!

It is heartbreaking that these parties took place before the age of Instagram. Everything Mamie did appeared to positively sparkle—and she would have *dominated* social media.

Especially during 1899, when her travels would have enthralled people.

Because that was the summer when Mamie decided to chase a bear.

GIVEN ACCESS TO THE RAILROAD BY HER HUSBAND, MAMIE HOPPED ON A private train car in the summer of 1899 with Stuyvesant, some of her best friends—a mix of men and women—and her daughter, Marian, to spend a few weeks hunting in Yellowstone. They'd originally planned to go to Alaska, but Yellowstone proved to be a more manageable destination.

The most notable of those compatriots, and one of the women Mamie appeared to genuinely respect, was Greta Pomeroy. If Mamie Fish had hobbies in her youth, they would have been confined to a domestic sphere—things like needlework, painting, or music. But women's interests were changing and broadening. You did not have to just sit and play the harp anymore.

Greta's hobby, for example, was shooting things.

By this time, it had become known as "the latest fad of society," and it was said that "women of New York City are just as well armed nowadays as the men, and some of them can shoot just as well."[11] Eager to capitalize on the new market, jewelry stores started stocking gold and silver revolvers, some of them inlaid with mother of pearl, just for the ladies. Greta spent a great deal of time practicing shooting with Marian, who was also known as "a handy one with the revolver."

When Greta joined in the Yellowstone hunt, she did not intend to be a mere spectator. Initially, she had been urged by men in the party to stay behind as they stalked the bear, since there was always the risk of an attack. Greta "laughed at their fears to scorn and showed by her calm and determined manner that she was as fit to meet the bear as any of them."[12]

Before long, the party started pursuing a bear with three cubs through the mountains. When they caught up to it, the bear proceeded to kill the party's hunting dogs in a fury. After what was described as a "short but perilous pursuit"[13] with a speed that shocked the rest of her party, there "rang out Miss Pomeroy's rifle and the angry bear, with bloodshot eyes and foaming mouth, dropped dead in her tracks."[14] Greta reportedly killed it with a single shot. Mamie joined everyone in congratulating Miss Pomeroy with "peculiar heartiness"—but she also vowed that the next time there was a bear hunt, *she* was going to be the one to kill the animal.

When the Fish arrived back in Newport, they found the town positively atwitter over the ball the Palmers were preparing for Prince Cantacuzène. It was rumored that he might even have his wedding at the couple's home. But still, Mamie didn't appear worried, and people started dreaming up all the possible parties she might host, wondering if "she will draw upon Europe, and even the Orient, for surprises before Fall."[15]

Instead, Mamie pursued new adventures.

Mamie loved her reputation as a woman who lived on the cutting edge of society. Her house was modern, her parties were modern—should not her mode of transportation also be modern? The *Savannah Morning News* declared that "the fashionable summer girl of 1899 is an automobile girl... the fad is direct from Paris, where grande dames have taken it up, along with pretty nearly everybody else who could afford it."[16] It is fascinating to envision a year of women just driving around in cars in ball gowns and shooting at things. Throughout France and Germany, increasingly intricate motorcars, like those by Renault and Opel, were being produced. However, the average automobile at this time cost as much as a working man's yearly salary, so the list of people who could afford the conveyance was still somewhat limited.

The Wichita Eagle noted that "the expense of the automobile as a fad would appall most indulgent fathers... even among Newport millionaires automobiles are not distributed broadcast in the family without a few minute's deliberation."[17] Nonetheless, the wealthy men of Newport could not get enough of them. Wealthy horse enthusiasts Oliver Belmont, Joseph Widener, and Foxhall Keene all began driving automobiles, but it was still a somewhat risky hobby. Keene's automobile appeared fine. However, when Mr. Belmont took his out, the spokes came off the wheel. Mr. Widener mixed up the accelerator and brakes and promptly crashed. Like Toonces, the driving cat, even though they could drive, it didn't mean that they could drive *well*.

Mamie probably figured she could do no worse when a demonstrator of a new electric automobile came to Newport and suggested that she take it for a whirl. And so, she and Greta Pomeroy—truly her best friend that summer—set out on a driving lesson. *The Boston Globe* reported that "it was her intention to stick closely to the drives and crosswalks, but the automobile saw a stone wall and made for it head on. The automobile won and a large section of the wall fell with a thud."[18] But Mrs. Fish seemingly found plowing into a stone wall very exciting and *did not stop driving*. She gave up on roads and proceeded to drive through a bush, positively giddy about the way this was going.

Her excursion came to an end when she finally crashed into the steps of her villa. The villa survived. So did Mamie, in good spirits. Mamie stumbled out of the wreckage, laughing wildly and shouting, "Whom the gods love, they punish."[19]

No one before or since has ever been so happy to be in a car accident.

Greta was presumably less pleased, although she also emerged unscathed and left the car. The fact that she was not thrown out of the car was surprising to many, and her skill on a horse was credited. Had she not been so good a rider, a reporter from *The Boston Globe* supposed, "she would not have been able to keep her seat during this up-to-date steeplechase."[20]

The demonstrator of the car, after witnessing this escapade, told Mrs. Fish to try once more. And, ever the optimist, Mamie imagined she might just need more practice. So she bravely got into the car again, at which point she successfully took it out onto Bellevue Avenue. Unfortunately, just as she was doing so, a man in a straw hat—minding his own business, going about his day—foolishly tried to cross the street. Mamie tried to pull the lever to stop the car, but instead she jerked it over and immediately ran over the man. "Fortunately," *The Marion Star* reported, "it was a very light car and Mrs. Fish was a tiny woman—no damage was done."[21]

Embarrassed, Mamie attempted to right herself and yanked the lever backward to reverse. In doing so she ran over this poor man again just as he was getting up. By this point Mrs. Fish was beginning to panic and pulled on the lever one more time—*running over the man for a third time.* The man, in what seems like a very intelligent response, stopped trying to get up and rolled to the side. "He balefully regarded Mrs. Fish and she balefully regarded him. Neither, to at least his lasting credit, said a word."[22]

Other than the way the drive ended, Mamie claimed that she had "enjoyed the afternoon immensely."[23] Though she wasn't the only woman interested in driving, Mrs. Fish was, predictably, credited with "starting the [automobile] craze here."[24] She and other female driving enthusiasts, like Mrs. Hermann Oelrichs, even began talking about whether they could organize "an automobile parade."[25]

No word from the man she ran over three times about that.

Eventually, after a series of adventures, new experiences, and near man-slaughter, Mamie found the time to throw her own parties again. While her rival, Bertha Potter, conducted formal affairs to introduce royalty, Mrs. Fish focused on more rustic entertainments. She hosted a "flower ball"[26] where all the women would appear dressed as flowers, and the men wore green dress suits. Mamie's daughter, Marian, was seen "in a halo of youth, beauty, and plump money bags."[27]

Mamie's energy—for bear hunting, for crashing automobiles, and for parties—was inexhaustible. People wondered when she slept. One day, a cab driver in Newport reported seeing her "looking as fresh, as crisp and well rested as your everyday woman after eight hours of undisturbed slumber." The driver remarked to the *St. Louis Post-Dispatch* reporter, "Look at her . . . ain't it a caution; her party never gave way an inch till 3 o'clock in the morning. Look at me, hardly able to hold me head up and all I done was sit outside. . . . But you'll see her around the casino bright and early tomorrow morning. Lord knows how they stand it; it beats me out."[28] When an Englishman was told this, according to *The Salt Lake Herald*, "he flatly refused to believe that a grown daughter could call the slight, vivacious little lady mother."[29]

(This is extremely inspiring, until you realize Mamie was thirty-six years old. This is approximately the age of the characters in the original television show *Sex and the City*.)

Regardless of how old she might have looked, or how much sleep she may or may not have gotten, her zest for life was captivating. "Without being a great beauty, she is irresistible," quipped a reporter. "Her friends say it is because, 'Mamie Fish has a sharp tongue, but a heart of gold.'" The reporter continued, "Her enemies believe she is a witch" but "everybody knows she is always ready to do or dare anything 'just for fun.'"[30]

Doing things for fun seemed to be her self-appointed job during these years. Her festive summer eventually culminated in September, when her many friends in Newport attempted to throw her a surprise party. *The New York Herald* reported that a group had been busily planning it, but "they were not half as secretive as they should be."[31] As such, Mrs. Fish quickly found out what her friends were up to. Playing her part, Mamie allowed herself to be taken out to an early dinner on the intended night. But when her twenty friends—including Mrs. Ogden Mills, Evelyn Burden, Nathaniel Thayer, and Harry Lehr—arrived to set up, they found a party already arranged. As they walked into Crossways with streamers ready to hang, "the preparations for a cotillion were visible, and to cap it all there was a small army of men getting ready to spread a banner."[32] In the end, Mrs. Fish had arranged her *own* surprise party, secure in the conviction that she could do it better than any of her friends.

Her friends knew, at least, that this was the kind of prank they could expect from her.

As had become de rigueur for Mrs. Fish, her unsurprising surprise party "was novel in almost every way." Mabel Slocum, who was said to be the most beautiful girl of the season and had been informed of Mamie's plan in advance, was costumed as a Dresden figurine "with very full skirts, woven of dainty buds and blossoms over a wire framework. The hat was of the shepherdess order, in baby colors." She was charged with distributing the party favors, which included "chattering parrots"[33]—a not-so-subtle suggestion from Mamie to converse more quietly in the future if friends wanted to actually surprise her. A golden tree was hung with fishbowls holding goldfish for the guests to take home—both to remind people of Mamie's surname and perhaps also to indicate that Newport was a kind of fishbowl, where everyone always knew everyone else's business. Guests also went home with floral sashes and badges after a maypole dance.

It was a summer full of notable parties. W. K. Vanderbilt hosted one at the golf club, which was filled for the occasion with flowers and electrified elements. Others were held on yachts.

By the end of the season, though, Newport society remained in thrall to Mrs. Fish.

Even those thousands spent on her wardrobe appeared to have paid off. "The cobwebby, half shawl, half fichu adopted by Mrs. Stuyvesant Fish at the beginning of the season has been picked up by every feminine creature capable of wielding it," noted the *Journal*.[34]

She was now a reigning style queen, a party queen, and a home inspiration icon.

Brooklyn Life reported that "with a new and spacious villa of her own planning at her disposal, Mrs. Fish has become the acknowledged leader of a new movement that has novelty as its watchword."[35] In the years to come, *The New York Times* would claim that to be a success in Newport, which was filled with "wild people who spend their time giving monkey and dog dinners" you needed to "determine from your experience what convention teaches is the right thing to do, and then do the precise opposite."[36]

Mamie was determined to defy convention at every turn. She had a coterie of both male and female friends at a time when many men were supposed to treat women as essentially decorative objects. Certainly, a group of people who were so sequestered by society as to know nothing about sex weren't a group of people you spent a lot of time joking around with. You just kind of admired them, like you would a lovely flower you could occasionally kiss. But Mamie transcended the limits of her sex, with men claiming that she was "a good fellow." She was known to "have a fund of anecdotes, always knows the latest and raciest gossip, and no one can tell as a store that 'is the limit' as well as she."[37]

She even employed a male secretary. When one woman, who was visiting her and in need of help with her correspondence, mentioned that she had looked all over the house and "couldn't find the girl," Mrs. Fish wryly replied, "Have you looked under the secretary, dear?"[38]

Mrs. Astor would *never*.

The group of people that Mamie felt were good company was quite a bit smaller than Mrs. Astor's circle, because she demanded her friends not only be monied but also funny and creative.

So the Four Hundred was said to have been overthrown and replaced by a new, especially smart set of one hundred run by Mamie. In 1899, *The Baltimore Sun* asserted that "there must be no fad or fashion that is a year old. That would be commonplace. Nothing must be commonplace. It must be bold, original, and daring. Piazza dinners...vegetable parties, costume balls, cake walks, dinner service without servants where the guests serve themselves, and bachelor luncheons, with only one hostess, like the brilliant Mrs. Stuyvesant Fish."[39] Granted, not many of these events sound wildly daring today—a potluck where guests serve themselves, for example, is pretty standard fare—but these ideas were largely pioneered in high society by Mrs. Fish. *The Baltimore Sun* declared that, of this new generation of society's upper class, Mamie was "the most daring, courageous and invincible."[40]

And Mamie wasn't overly humble about it either; she herself proclaimed that when it came to daring entertainments, "I am the limit."

As the old Oscar Wilde saying goes, "Imitation is the sincerest form of flattery," and as her celebrity rose, so did the number of people in Newport who tried to imitate Mamie's style in one way or another. Society women were tired of following Mrs. Vincent Astor's example of conforming perfectly to social rules and expectations, remaining discreet, tasteful, flawless. Instead, women began displaying their *own* quirks, talents, and passions with pride.

Inspired by Mamie's daring, Mrs. John Jacob Astor, an amateur ballerina, convinced women in Newport to take up ballet. *The Baltimore Sun* reported that, in her glamorous ballroom, "a class was formed. And the ladies, costumed in the regulation ballet skirts and full tights, learned the steps the premieres trip so lightly on the opera bouffe stage."[41] Meanwhile, Mrs. Arthur Kemp swanned around town in a tiara "made like a bird of paradise in precious stones." And Sarah and Eleanor Hewitt, who had just founded the Cooper Union Museum for the Arts of Decoration in 1897, were the hosts of the "vegetable party." You might, understandably, think that this was a party where vegetarian dishes were served. It was not. It was much weirder. It was a party where everyone *dressed up as* vegetables. Mrs. Harry McVickar, an amateur actress, created a sensation at the party when she arrived as an onion.

All this to say: Mamie had, consciously or not, empowered the women around her with the freedom to be a little weird.

Admittedly, these were still wealthy white women. And they were still expected to remain attractive—on very little sleep from all those night-long parties—well into their dotage and spend thousands upon thousands of dollars on clothes. But pushing back against the constraints of an age that had, until recently, demanded perfect, unceasing elegance and respectability of them must have been, if not an act of true liberation, at least a delightful step in the right direction.

CHAPTER 15

Now that she'd conquered the Newport scene, Mamie was determined to bring her newly cultivated brand of merriment to New York City, where a new house for her and Stuyvesant had been under construction for the past several years. For the job, she hired Stanford White, the era's preeminent architect who had already designed the Vanderbilt and Morgan mansions. This home would not be in the American style Mamie had embraced in Newport, as Stanford White was known for his ornate, beaux arts designs. (In six years, White would be killed by the jealous husband of his love interest, Evelyn Nesbit, while watching a rooftop premiere of *Mamzelle Champagne* at, quite ironically, the theater of Madison Square Garden, which he'd originally designed.) Initially, Mamie and Stanford estimated that the townhouse at 25 East 78th Street near Madison Avenue could be built for a relatively thrifty $250,000 ($9.3 million today). Like anyone else who has tried to build or renovate a house, they exceeded their budget immediately, and costs kept rising until the house surpassed "the million mark."[1]

The result was a magnificent five-story Italianate home that would become famous in New York society. Indeed, Italian influence infiltrated

every corner of the not-so-humble abode; the home's furniture and decorations were imported directly from Italy, and the spacious rooms held
Venetian mirrors framed with gold. The place was "filled with painting and
statuary, rich in marble and gilt, and with a great hall patterned off the hall
of the Doge."[2] The *San Francisco Examiner* added that "the prevailing tone
is yellow, with decorations in gold. Old gold brocade, with a crimson background, lines the walls, and the hangings are of crimson velvet picked out
with gold threads."[3] There was an elaborate marble staircase in the center,
featuring what were said to be "splendidly carved balustrades" that were "a
marvel of Venetian reproduction."[4] According to *The New York Times*, that
stairway led to "a Gothic-style bedroom with period furniture" while the
other bedrooms featured ivory decor.

The townhouse wasn't just pretty either; it also promised entertainment. Mamie had a stage erected in the dining room, but it was not a stage
intended merely for people who might want to sing a song after dinner. It
was designed to cater to professionals. The setup "was complete in every
detail, the upper, side and footlights being electric, and the scenery fresh
and painted…the curtain which draped at both sides when drawn up was
of crimson velvet, and the proscenium arch was handsomely painted, and, in
the center, over the stage, was the crest of the Fish family."[5]

Though Mamie spent a fortune on the Gothic master bedroom alone, she
never actually slept in it. In truth, she found it disturbing. Instead, as the
newspaper *Reveille* noted, "she preferred the cozier atmosphere of an adja-
cent dressing room." The Gothic bedroom, they supposed, "had been for
public exhibition—like everything else in Mamie Fish's amazing and exotic
life."[6]

Mrs. Fish had held her Valentine's Day/Mardi Gras Ball in the unfinished
house the prior year, but by January 2, 1900, the house was fully complete,
and Mamie was, at last, ready to christen her new home. To start things off,
she sent out invitations promising three evenings of entertainment to be held
on the Saturdays of January 13, 20, and 27. Between these entertainments,
Mrs. Fish spent the month of January hosting other smaller affairs like "a
dinner of 36 courses"[7]—hopefully not one of her dinners famously served

in an hour, because it seems really hard to eat even a bite-sized course in a minute and a half—as well as musical evenings for friends.

The first Saturday event was a musical reception where guests could settle in to hear some of the finest soloists of the day: British cellist Leo Stern, the contralto Ernestine Schumann-Heink, and Mackenzie Gordon from the Metropolitan Opera. Being able to listen to any one of these performers, let alone all three, would be considered a treat. But then, Mrs. Fish had famously been known to talk through such performances—even ones held at her own home. She had never appreciated music the way some of her acquaintances did, though she acknowledged and enabled this appreciation. Hosting musical receptions as a way of introducing the new house to society was probably more for the enjoyment of her peers than it was for her own, anyway.

The next Saturday's entertainment was thoroughly Mamie—and it was as daring as the first evening was traditional. On January 20, Mamie staged a vaudeville for the elite of New York. Vaudeville entertainments, which featured a variety of singers, jugglers, comedians, and anyone else who had a talent that might entertain the general public, had been growing in popularity since the 1880s.

What was particularly unusual was that Mamie's vaudeville would be one where the members of the audience would all be utterly roasted. The performance was called "Little Puddle, Big Fish."[8] Guests entered the Fish home to find posters on the walls proclaiming, "Vaudeville Tonight, but Not Tomorrow," "Beware of Speculators," and "Tickets Purchased on the Sidewalk of No Avail." The vaudeville itself focused on a story about a male gold digger (of the Yukon variety) coming to New York. It included jokes about all the families in attendance—extending, for instance, to the unreliable quality of their streetcars, or their reputations as spendthrifts. The vaudeville also featured a dancing pony, trained dogs, clowns, and acrobats. After the show concluded, Harry Lehr "announced that there would be a change of bill at Fish's weekly, and that subscription sale of seats would open next week."[9]

Everyone attended this performance, including the über traditionalist Mrs. William Astor. Not so very long ago, people had been shocked to dine out in public, and now everyone was being entertained by dancing horses. People applauded Mamie—yet again!—for offering an evening that could "vary the traditional monotony."[10]

For the last party in the series, held on January 27, Mrs. Fish reverted to more traditional entertainment. She gave a cotillion, where dances were led by Elisha Dyer Jr., one of the foremost dance leaders in the city. There was a pastoral theme, and the "extremely pretty"[11] party favors included flowerpots filled with artificial flowers, watering cans, shepherd crooks, pipes, and gunmetal picture frames. In only a month, the Kodak Brownie camera would be released, allowing amateur photographers to take pictures and fill those frames to their heart's content—making photography more prevalent, though simultaneously less of a status symbol.

Once again, this party was attended by New York's elite. Mrs. Astor showed up at this event too, before hosting her own annual ball on January 29. This one does seem like it would have been more the conventional speed favored by the older guard of society.

In the weeks and months to come, Mamie threw more and more inspired affairs—though not all of them were executed as flawlessly as she'd planned. She hosted a cakewalk where white mice intended to serve as party favors escaped, scuttling across the floor to the excitement and terror of the guests. And that Reversible Dance she hadn't been able to manage the year prior? This year, people *begged* for the experience. They could not lace up their clothing in reverse fast enough. So she gave a "Looking Backwards" party, where everyone had to wear their clothing back to front, which was regarded as "excruciatingly funny."[12]

The fact that these balls were beloved when Mamie threw them didn't mean they worked as well when other people did—and other people were trying to, even those who'd never met Mrs. Fish. Terre Haute, Indiana, got "[its] first imitation of the ball hosted by Mrs. Fish." This one was thrown by a Mrs. Strong and featured people dressing in eccentric rustic costumes. It was described by *The Indianapolis Journal* as "grotesque" and "caricaturing the real thing."[13]

Poor Mrs. Strong!

If you wished to see "the real thing" in action, you could watch Mamie close out the Newport season that summer with her "Harvest Ball." No sooner were the invitations sent out than the ball, which was estimated to cost $18,000 ($676,000 today), was the "talk of the smart set."[14] The grounds of Crossways, generally covered with flower beds and rolling lawns, now featured hay bales and scarecrows in honor of the autumnal season to come. In the middle of the lawn were "three yoke of oxen quietly resting after their hard day's toil at hauling in all the material for the farmyard scene."[15] The house itself was filled with thousands of sunflowers and poppies, and sheaves of corn and wheat were tied with red ribbons. Beehives were carefully stacked in such a manner as to avoid any bees getting loose upon the guests.

The guests themselves were clothed in farmer-inspired costumes. You could see more than one of the wealthiest women in America garbed as a dairymaid. Harry Lehr showed up dressed as a peasant, pushing about a massive wheelbarrow filled with pumpkins and potatoes and "trying to do his prettiest to carry out the character that he'd assumed."[16] The 110 guests dined on wooden benches, eating soup on a tablecloth made of potato sacks. Party favors included "silver and gold animals, particularly roosters, hens, and young chickens, with mechanical devices, which on pressing the button, emitted characteristic notes."[17]

Wearing a golden gown, the hostess supreme appeared "holding a shepherd's crook, of course, for all her guests were lambs of the social flock, and she had long been recognized as its shepherdess."[18] In turn, the guests brought themed offerings to Mamie, such as "some useful domestic animal or product of the harvest. She was given pigs, ducks, geese, chickens, and even Angora cats"[19] to be placed "all at the feet of 'Good Queen Mamie,'" reported the *Fall River Daily Herald*, "as she will now be called for all time."[20]

It's worth noting that Good Queen Mamie, inspired by the party where this had happened by accident, released white mice at this event in order to send the female guests scattering and screaming, because while she was a good queen, she was also a *very* mischievous queen—and one of her favorite bits was making people scramble.

CHAPTER 16

$\mathcal{M}$AMIE REALLY DID EXERT A QUEENLY POWER OVER THE CITIZENRY of Newport, but she used it in a benevolent fashion, at least when it came to Mrs. George Gould.

Mrs. Gould—née Edith Kingdon—was a new addition to Newport society. In 1885, she married George Jay Gould, the son of Jay Gould, a railroad magnate and the head of one of the wealthiest families in town. She was known to be pretty, bright, charming, and generally delightful. She had been an actress before her marriage—"an allegation," according to *The Philadelphia Times*, "that could not be and was not denied."[1]

Back then, being an actress afforded women more freedom—to travel, to live alone, to earn money—than was average. An actress could exist in a world relatively free from male oversight. Her father, for instance, would likely not be around to police her suitors. This meant that many people assumed that actresses were having a *ton* of premarital sex. Some were (good for them!). Some were not (good for them too!).

For her part, Mrs. Gould made absolutely no excuses for her comparably "wild past." She even turned her coach house into a theater, where she presented the first production of "The Twilight of the God" by Edith Wharton in January 1900, with herself cast in one of the central roles (naturally). Garish though it might've seemed to some of the more traditionally minded folks, the Goulds' friends appreciated this entertainment—some might have been primed by the stage they'd seen in Mamie's house—and Edith was said to be "a vision of loveliness. The applause was long and vigorous, and it was some minutes before the action of the play could go on... from beginning to end Mrs. Gould was constantly interrupted by applause. Mr. George Gould beamed with delight at the praise meted out to his wife."[2]

Everyone in their close circle seemed thrilled by George's marriage to a talented actress, Mrs. Fish most of all. Mrs. Fish attended the theatrical entertainment and led the dance hosted by the Goulds afterward with her friend Elisa Dyer Jr. This public acknowledgment was said to have secured Mrs. Gould's acceptance in society, as by that point, Mrs. Fish "represent[ed] society with a big S."[3] It didn't hurt that the post-theatrical party was one after Mrs. Fish's own heart; a man dressed as Santa Claus rolled a giant snowball into the ballroom that a ballerina jumped out of, and all the women were given gold bonbon boxes as party favors.

Mrs. Fish adored Mrs. Gould. Whenever they were at the opera, Mrs. Gould sat with Greta Pomeroy and Mrs. Fish, exchanging "a symphony of smiles."[4] Many others in their circle were similarly delighted to have a new, talented, interesting person with whom to talk. In their eyes, knowing an actress was a big plus.

It was over these years that Mrs. Fish began to gain more female friends. Prior to this, most of her quirks—her love of pranks and her willingness to make fun of those close to her—had been associated with men (like Harry). That was changing. More unconventional women were beginning to enter their social sphere. Not so long ago, Mrs. Astor had been disgusted by the idea of people meeting Adelaide Ristori precisely *because* she was an actress. Now, Mrs. Fish spent her evenings gossiping with one in cozy intimacy.

Not everyone was as welcoming, though. Plenty of people in Newport were still convinced Mrs. Gould should be treated like a prostitute.

So intense was this readily assumed notion that actresses would sleep with wealthy theatergoers, that when recounting the meeting between Mr. Gould and the former Miss Kingdon, the papers had to explicitly note that *nothing physical* happened between her and Mr. Gould before marriage. They told everyone this when recounting their love story. According to reports, when Mr. Gould asked the owner of the theater at which Miss Kingdon worked to introduce the two of them, the theater owner replied, indignantly, "No, I won't introduce you to Miss Kingdon. We don't want any foolishness about this theater." Mr. Gould replied that his intentions were extremely pure, and the theater owner relented, but not before declaring, "Edith Kingdon is a lady, every inch of her."[5]

So much for existing in a world without male oversight. The public could be reassured that the theater owner was gallantly playing the role of her father.

Even so, many of the residents of Newport still had their doubts. And they simply couldn't stomach mingling with a woman who had grown up in a poor family and had taken to life on the stage before having a *maybe* (doubtfully) chaste romance with a millionaire.

"To permit the entrance of Mrs. Gould [into Newport society] was, of course, to relax the heretofore stringent and almost inflexible rule laid down by Mrs. Astor, former head of American society, whose husband was the possessor of millions inherited from a grandfather who peddled clocks, bought fur, and sold pianos,"[6] *The Philadelphia Times* archly remarked. No one could list any reasons that they, personally, thought Edith was especially objectionable—she seemed, by all accounts, to be a very nice person—but nevertheless, when the Belmonts gave a dinner at which the Goulds were guests, the Vanderbilts refused to attend, purely out of principle. Mrs. Oelrichs joined Mrs. Vanderbilt in opposition.

Edith's husband, George, a railroad executive, did not fully understand what was happening. He'd done everything right. He'd told everyone that he had not even *thought* about sex with his wife before marriage. He'd given the impression that he'd marched into that theater with an engagement ring in his pocket. He didn't seem to understand why everyone wasn't getting on board. After all, he was also a millionaire, used to having people do what he wanted.

But the women of Newport could not be commanded as easily as his employees. This was their world, not his. Indeed, according to *The St. Paul Globe*, George "did not realize the importance of society as compared with that of railroads. The world, viewed from the Newport aspect, could easily get along without railroads, but without society, never."[7]

Mamie, however, realized precisely what was happening and took the Vanderbilt and Oelrichs' refusals to dine—or even be seen with—Edith Gould as a personal affront. Before long, "the pro-Gould element, as represented by Mrs. Stuyvesant Fish"[8] was actively fighting for Edith's inclusion in the upper echelons of society.

In her quest, Mamie enlisted, as she often did, Harry Lehr to reach out to the Vanderbilts and Oelrichs. He determined that Mrs. Vanderbilt was only rejecting the Goulds because she heard that Mrs. Oelrichs (to whom she was related by marriage) disliked Mrs. Fish. When he approached Mrs. Oelrichs directly, she said that she only disliked Mrs. Fish because Mrs. Fish disliked *her*.

Look, it's very possible they didn't want to hang out with Mrs. Gould because they thought she was a tawdry slut, but were unwilling to say so. But, given that this was the story they were going with, the situation was resolved when Mrs. Fish held a dinner for everyone at her house.

Then, in 1908, when Edith Gould returned to the professional stage, the Vanderbilts were in the audience for her first performance, proving that they'd come full circle.

Mamie proceeded to throw herself headlong into friendships with actresses, including vaudeville comedienne Marie Dressler. Their friendship began when, during a New York theatrical performance, Miss Dressler whacked Mrs. Fish on the head with a leek. At the time, performances were still rowdy enough that theatergoers were known to throw rotten tomatoes at the actors if they were displeased. One of Miss Dressler's comic bits hinged on the fact that she was willing to throw produce back at the audience if they displeased her. Mrs. Fish subsequently asked her to perform at one of her parties, and Miss Dressler offered to do it for free.

"Very well," Mamie replied firmly, "you may come to my party, but you may not appear."

Marie would attend as a guest, only with no expectation to sing for her supper. And so, she and Mamie became friends.

Mamie never missed an opportunity to lavish gifts on her new pal. At another party, Marie recalled Mamie saying goodnight and declaring, "Here's a souvenir of the evening." The souvenir was a gold pocketbook filled with more gold. Another time, Mamie removed a jeweled bracelet from her wrist that Marie had much admired and gave it to Marie, claiming she never wore it anymore. "You wear it," she told Marie. To which Marie later claimed, "And I did! Indeed, I didn't wear gloves for a month."[9]

As she had with Edith, Mamie took Marie with her to Newport and introduced her to society where, by Mamie's account, she had a wonderful time. As people whizzed by them on Newport roads in automobiles shouting "Bonjour!" with an elegant French flourish, she would yell back "Hoi polloi!"—or "the common people!" in Latin. Marie herself acknowledged that she was accepted largely because of Mamie's influence, though reporters said her success in fashionable circles was due to the fact that "she was as unabashed when facing the aristocrats of wealth, fashion and brains as when facing an audience in the theater. Her wit and humor sparkled as brightly and as spontaneously in the one situation as the other."[10] In this regard, Marie Dressler sounds more Mamie's equal than most of the dowagers of Newport. For her part, Marie said of Mamie, "I always admired her, first for her brains and then because under her somewhat gruff exterior there was a protective instinct. She always tried to hide her soft spot, but it was there."[11]

Actresses like Marie Dressler and Edith Gould weren't the only newcomers to society Mamie championed around 1900. Another would be James Henry Smith, a forty-five-year-old broker who, rather unexpectedly, inherited $50 million from his uncle, instantly making him the richest bachelor in America. Before 1901, he was known merely as "J. H. Smith, broker," but once he started to feel the heat of the limelight, he quickly earned the nickname "Silent James" (due to his shyness around the press). He had been raised middle-class and worked as a railroad director at a time when "railroad directors are more plentiful than blackbirds on Wall Street."[12] After his extraordinarily lucky windfall, Mr. Smith explained, "I am not a public man. I decline to become a public man. I wish to deny my identity. The seclusion of poverty is a blessing."[13]

Mrs. Stuyvesant Fish took him under her wing and began to disabuse him of the notion of the merits of poverty. Before long, Mr. Smith was spending a massive amount ($15,250 plus $8,000 for the party favors) on a ball at the fashionable New York restaurant Sherry's. Naturally, Mamie and Alva Vanderbilt assisted with the planning.

Only 150 people were invited to this exclusive event, including the Astors, the Oelrichs, the Goelets, and of course, Mr. and Mrs. George Gould (who was apparently "gorgeous in rich red velvet").[14] The ball was held on Valentine's Day 1901, and the banquet room was "entirely transformed into a bower of roses." The walls were covered with lattice work and rose vines. Thousands upon thousands of roses hung from the ceiling. A six-foot rose tree was mounted on each of the eleven tables, with the branches carefully pruned to begin at two feet, so the diners could still see one another without obstruction, "and at the same times, enjoy the exquisite shelter of a rose bower."[15] The trees were trimmed with electric fairy lights—an absolute must at upscale parties by now—and the menus were shaped to resemble valentines. Guests enjoyed a meal of turtle soup, beef, Virginia ham, fresh mushrooms, and fried hominy. There was a story that the party favors were covered in jewels, but this was, disappointingly, false. Instead, there were matchboxes made of mere silver, inscribed with the date of the dance, and women were also given perfume bottles and wands festooned with flowers. The ball and dinner were said to be "one of the most beautiful entertainments that has ever been given in New York, not so much for the lavishness or prodigality of expenditure as for the taste and the perfection of every detail."[16]

It wasn't a secret that James had spent a small fortune on the event. The *San Francisco Examiner* noted that "Uncle George, from whom James Henry inherited his wealth, did not spend as much in a year as the nephew spent in an hour at the ball."[17] But this was, now, in the new century, what a man with this kind of wealth was expected to do. A social profile was an asset; you were not merely supposed to be good at making money, you were supposed to be good at spending it too.

"The mysterious Mr. Smith" was soon being profiled at length by papers like the *San Francisco Examiner*. His hobbies were said to be collecting rare books, yachting, opera, horseback riding, and billiards. These choices may be surprising given that many of these hobbies take time to develop skills, and he had only recently acquired enough money to pursue them. It's possible that he just listed the hobbies he thought a very rich man might, or even should, have. With that in mind, it makes sense that this profile of him also noted, "His aspirations: to be the leader of society and the arbiter of fashion."[18]

Before long, word of Mr. Smith spread across the country. In March of 1901, he traveled in the Fish private railroad car to San Francisco. He was immediately approached by reporters, and he "assumed a startled air and beat a hasty retreat." Apparently, "he ha[d] a perfect horror of sketch artists."[19] Alas, for all his newly assumed rich-person hobbies and mannerisms, he never did develop "the art of conversation"[20] and remained as socially awkward as ever.

It soon became clear that Mamie was organizing James Henry's entire social life. He built a house in Tuxedo, a village in upstate New York, "and had Mrs. Fish engineer his house parties. He took a box at the horse show, and Mrs. Fish asked the guests, and generally succeeded in having toasts of the town among them."

But they showed up, largely, because they knew Mrs. Fish would throw a great party. They did not show up to try to lob conversational starters about rare books at Mr. Smith while he sat there silently.

Indeed, James Henry did not plan an entertainment on his own until 1904, and it was a total disaster. He planned a musical evening at home featuring artists including the acclaimed tenor Enrico Caruso. Unfortunately, he scheduled his event on the same night as the opera, so his guests did not show up until midnight. This was common. Unfortunately, rather than being greeted by a feast, Mr. Smith began the preparations for the meal *when* the guests started arriving (truly something you learn not to do after you have your first friend group over for dinner in your twenties). Supper was then not served until two in the morning. Many of the guests, already tired, left before the food had even been laid out. Mr. Smith grew increasingly miserable and "several of those who were there noticed his chagrin as he glanced over the supper rooms and saw the many empty tables."[21]

He tried once more to host an event without Mrs. Fish's help, but the outcome was much the same. Consequently, he swore that he would never entertain again. This wasn't as socially destructive for him as it might have been for a woman in his position; after all, he still had a great deal of money, and a house not only in New York but also a beautiful townhouse in London. Papers may have said he wanted to dominate the society set, but for a man in that era, there were plenty of other areas to exert his ambition. He could remain just as much of a catch without ever being charming or imaginative, or even serving dinner at an appropriate time, because he was an absurdly rich man. And if he really wanted to throw great parties, he could simply marry a great hostess. Which he did. In 1906, he married Annie Stewart, a divorcée and the former wife of William Rhinelander Stewart, who was known as "one of the most beautiful and notable hostesses of the fashionable world."[22]

Problem solved.

It is interesting to ponder why Mamie was so invested in helping Mr. Smith. There was little personal benefit in friendship with this taciturn but socially ambitious man. She was wealthy on her own, so she did not need to rely on him for money. She could plan and host her own much-lauded parties rather than doing so for someone else. She did not even attempt to marry this extremely eligible bachelor to one of her closest friends.

Instead, papers speculated she'd "helped Mr. Smith for the amusement or éclat or diversion of the moment."[23] This made a lot of sense, as the people whom Mamie wished to launch in society—people like Mrs. Gould and Mr. Smith—were never the wellborn children of Knickerbocker royalty. In fact, she had very little interest in such people and would be actively dismissive of them later in life. She did not like introducing people who were *easy* to present to society; she liked launching people who were challenging. Plus, doing so provided her with friends who were unusual and might have been livelier than those who followed in more traditional footsteps. It also served as a reminder of how much social power Mamie had accrued. If she said someone was to be accepted, then they would be.

Others were aware of her influence and tried to use it to their advantage. Around the turn of the century, the swindler "Count" Gregory wanted to play a prank. He and a friend, George Law, were discussing whether someone could pass as a millionaire without the proper background. Law was presumably not aware of his friend's own unsavory background—Gregory's title was fake. Law insisted that pretty much anyone could pass as a millionaire if he had the right clothing, but his friend pushed back, declaring, "any man who has not had some training, or even breeding, will betray himself at a club or in a drawing room."[24]

Shortly afterward—and it should be noted that you have to take his word for this—a vagrant came up to the table where they were drinking, begging for cash. The millionaires seated with them sent him away, but Law offered to buy him a drink. Shortly after, Law remarked, annoyed, "Those millionaires were too good to have a drink with this tramp this morning—but by heaven I bet they'll be glad to accept his hospitality before I am through."[25] He asked the beggar if he'd like to play a trick on the millionaires, for which George Law would buy him a new suit. The man happily agreed, and Law purchased him "an afternoon suit, an expensive overcoat, a correct hat and complete outfit of underclothes, shirt, collar, tie and even an ebony cane." He was then given a shave and $200 to spend liberally, and the two went their separate ways, with a plan to reconvene later.

Later in the day, Law pretended to "meet" the vagrant anew and introduced him as an old friend who'd just returned from abroad. Meeting the millionaires gathered, the vagrant immediately asked if he could buy everyone a drink, grandly remarking that "champagne is my only beverage." Those who had rejected him earlier were now positively thrilled to drink with him, none the wiser. Everything went so well—as it often does when you're drinking free champagne—that he was invited to one of Mrs. Stuyvesant Fish's parties the next night. The man agreed with great relish, noting that he'd "had such a delightful evening the night before."[26]

To a modern-day reader, it might feel wrong to use another person as a prop to prove a sartorial point, but it does bear mentioning that this man appeared to be having the time of his life, and immediately began referring to the millionaires as "old chap[s]."[27]

"To present the man at one of her social functions," declared Count Gregory, who seemed to be observing this escapade with great delight, "would be an achievement which would settle beyond question whether clothes are the hallmark of gentility."[28] This is the plot of *My Fair Lady* if the protagonist were Eliza Doolitle's dad. Before Mrs. Fish's party, the Count coached him a bit on the kind of small talk he could expect. The man took this advice very much to heart, and Count Gregory noted that he "had thrown aside his meek, slouching, beggar ways, and had taken on the airs of a snob to a considerable degree and seemed to enjoy ordering servants and clerks around with an air of impatience."[29]

To his new friends' delight, the man (who, at this point, rapidly sounds as though he was becoming insufferable) was warmly greeted by Mrs. Fish. At this particular event, the Princess of Hohenstein was in attendance, and apparently the vagrant "bowed with a very becoming grace and said something to her which caused the Princess to flush." Later, he and the princess were seen walking arm in arm into the conservatory "to seek out a secluded corner where they engaged in a most animated tete-a-tete."

George Law and Count Gregory recalled being flabbergasted that the princess appeared to genuinely like the man, and Law, remarking that "it will be a tragedy for my wife if Mrs. Fish discovers the truth,"[30] handed the vagrant one hundred dollars and told him that the joke was over. They should have gone full *Trading Places* and allowed him to run a railroad, but sadly that movie had not come out yet. The man agreed, so George Law and Count Gregory were astonished when, a few weeks later, they saw him again at a fashionable charity ball, still hovering around the princess, who, at this point, at least seemed to acknowledge him as an acquaintance.

Ultimately, the fact that this man had been at Mrs. Fish's ball was enough to prove that he had the credentials to mingle and flirt with a princess.

In addition to proving Law and Gregory correct, this episode also illustrates that one's background and reputation no longer mattered as much to people around them. Part of this was likely due to New York's rapid expansion. In 1880, the population of New York was 1,919,000. By 1900, it was 3,802,000. And by 1910, it would be 6,230,000.[31] It was no longer possible to know where *everyone* at a party had come from—even if you wanted to. You had to simply rely on the assumption that if people were at a party hosted by a person as eminent as Mrs. Fish, then they belonged there. It's a bit of a shame that the vagrant's origin was never revealed to Mamie, as she might have fully stewarded his rise in society.

But she was also quickly finding that retaining her well-earned social power was a challenge in and of itself.

Planning and hosting a constant round of entertainments was extremely time-consuming. Now around the turn of the century, at the apex of her power as a "lady of leisure," Mamie's life may have been luxurious, but it was also anything but leisurely. In New York City, her days began at 9:00 a.m. and did not end until 3:00 a.m. She was so famously busy that even *The Evening World* reported on her schedule, claiming that she was "probably the 'hardest working' woman in New York—that is to say, she is as much the 'leader' in society as any woman to whom that term may be applied."[32]

A typical day in the life of Mamie might have looked like this: She'd wake up around 9:00 a.m. and have breakfast at 10:00 a.m. She would then lay out her housekeeper's duties for the day and "gave an audience to the decorator or caterer in regard to a proposed fete or entertainment." Afterward, at 11:00 a.m., she'd read through all the mail sent to her, and she "answered all letters calling for that formality." After this, her maid would dress her, and she would go for a ride through the park, where she would see, be seen, and wave to her friends. At 1:00 p.m., she might visit her dressmaker to be fitted and discuss plans for upcoming outfits or costumes she might need. This would take approximately an hour, after which she would drive through the park again. (Visiting the park twice may seem a bit much, but this was a very typical afternoon pastime. Plus, given the amount of time she was spending at her dressmaker, she had a lot of finery to show off.)

At 3:30 p.m., Mamie would make social calls. Though this might have been partly for pleasure, it was also a way to establish who was in and who was out of society, as it had been for Mrs. Astor and Mrs. Vanderbilt. Women aspiring to earn a higher position in New York's elite circles were subtly, or not so subtly, vying to have Mamie Fish visit them, have tea, eat cookies, and chat for an hour. It behooved you to have a cook who made *really good* cookies, though it probably behooved you more to have a husband who ran a really important railroad. Mamie was obligated to visit not only women whose company she enjoyed but also those who were new to New York and whose more significant friends, or business associates of Stuyvesant, had urged her to see them. Whether these would've been great fun for Mamie or torturously boring probably depended on the day.

At 5:00 p.m., Mamie would return home and take a nap until 6:00 p.m., which *The Evening World* jokingly described as "the one little oasis in the desert of the social routine." Then, she would be roused for "the ordeal of dressing…for the real work of the day is just begun."[33] Mrs. Fish and her maid might consult on which dress would be most appropriate for dinner, and which undergarments would be necessary. Preparations would take about an hour, whereupon she would go to her host's home. Despite the rising popularity of restaurants like Delmonico's, dinners for those of Mamie's stature were still almost always served at a private house. That dinner would likely last until 9:00 p.m., at which point the participants would move on en masse to a ball, the theater, or an opera. If the night's entertainment was a cotillion, it would begin around midnight, and "one must be on hand promptly, especially if she is to 'lead' [the dance], and Mrs. Fish often does." And so, the *Evening World* claimed, "on goes the dance, and the small talk between, till well into the wee small hours."[34]

Around 3:00 a.m., Mamie would finally fall into her bed, only to begin approximately the same schedule again the next day.

And the day after.

And the day after that.

CHAPTER 17

*M*AMIE WAS EXALTED. EVERY PARTY SHE THREW DAZZLED. EVERY-one loved her.

But her happiness at her peak popularity was short-lived.

As a very clever person who was now receiving absolutely no pushback, Mamie Fish was quite simply growing bored. The more popular she became, the surlier she became. She found many of the people she entertained to be tedious, and she resented that they did not show any semblance of the originality for which she was renowned in their own entertainments. Mamie had always been brusque, but now she was known for it. Indeed, to be mocked by her became a part of her appeal, the way today fans of certain performers are excited to be heckled by them.

Frederick Townsend Martin, a writer and "millionaire with a mission," recalled Mamie once complaining, "Don't you get bored dining out night after night? What's the use of it?"

Martin replied, "The use of it is that we can get fresh thoughts from one another."[1] Mamie dismissed him as being a moralizing fool.

Later, on a separate occasion, Martin revealed that he had given a speech to benefit the blind and that, at its end, he'd asked his audience if they'd prefer to be deaf or blind.

"What was the verdict?" Mamie wondered.

"They were unanimous in deciding in favor of blindness," he replied.

"What?" Mamie shot back. "After hearing you talk for an hour?"[2]

Like many people, Martin was delighted to be the butt of one of Mamie's jokes, but Mamie's animosity toward him feels more real. She was not just roasting a friend; she really did seem to think some of her acquaintances were stupid.

Not everyone was so enamored by her and her retorts. One nameless society beauty was less fond of Mamie's wit. This lady scented all her stationery with expensive perfume, assuming it would make people think pleasantly of her. Mamie hated this habit, which she found pretentious, and wrote back to the woman that she "had to have a butler stand in a strong draught to read it."[3]

Even if Mamie behaved badly, even if she told people they were boring, her position in society was not threatened. Mamie might have always wanted that kind of power, might have even felt a bit of security in it, but she now found there wasn't much sport in it. No matter what she said to people, they just giggled obligingly.

Frustrated, she tried to get herself out of the doldrums by planning another bear hunt. It had thrilled her the previous year, and this time, she hoped that she would be the one to take down a bear.

And so, on May 26, 1900, Mamie assembled a party to head out West. *The Idaho Statesman* declared, "Mrs. Stuyvesant Fish, conqueror of the 400, is out for her first bear,"[4] while the *San Francisco Examiner* headlined that "Mrs. Stuyvesant Fish Goes Gunning for Grizzlies."[5]

At long last, here was something that could actually pose a challenge for Mamie once again!

Alongside her friends Moncure Robinson, Henry Clews Jr., Mrs. Hermann Oelrichs, Addison Grant, James de Wolf Cutting, and Greta Pomeroy—who had established her prowess as a hunter—Mamie and company departed from Grand Central Station in three special train cars on Mr. Fish's railroad line, the Illinois Central Railroad. With them, they carried "weapons of all kind, including rifles and shotguns, with which to slay the wild beasts of the Rockies, also fishing rods, and a copious wine cellar."[6] The journey to the Pacific coast would likely take about three weeks. The fact that a voyage across the country could now be undertaken in such time appealed to more people than just Mrs. Fish. That same year, the Illinois Central Railroad had made the largest order for equipment—1,500 new freight cars—that had yet been placed by any railroad in America. Stuyvesant claimed that they would be adding 3,700 cars to the line before the end of the year.

Intentionally or not, this bear hunt was also a fantastic promotion for her husband's business. All the most glamorous people were traveling across the country. The American West, with its beauty and new possibilities, was opening up—and people were keen to explore. City dwellers could now see places where the "region is swarming with bears of all kinds, panthers, and other big game. There are still bears wandering about who have passed a long lifetime killing men and cattle and have baffled all efforts to trap or shoot them."[7] The fact that you could go out and see dangerous animals that might kill you was actually seen as an incentive, as it can only be to people who have spent most of their lives in considerable physical safety.

Meanwhile, people in New York mourned that "Mrs. Stuyvesant Fish was a straw at which the hopes of a June Season clutched vainly. Mrs. Fish is a social barometer, and the very fact of her taking a large party in three special cars across the Rockies at this time of year is an indication that for the next two months society will be here, there, and everywhere."[8]

In 1899, it had been taken as an abdication of her role in a social battle when Mamie went off bear hunting. Now, with virtually no competition left, her absence indicated that society itself might as well not exist.

With nothing to distract them at home, those who were not traveling with the Fish were reported to be intensely invested in her escapades, and they were divided into two classes: "those who hope that Mrs. Fish will get the bear, and those who hope that the bear will...not be caught."[9] Most felt that the bear should be more scared of Mamie than she should be of it. As the *San Francisco Examiner* predicted, "She will meet the bear with the same high courage that she had displayed in dealing with rival society leaders, obstinate dressmakers, impertinent butlers and others whom she has vanquished on many a well-contested field."[10]

By June 28, 1900, the party arrived in Chicago. They planned to move on to Milwaukee, Wisconsin, and then St. Paul, Minnesota, after which they would take the Canadian Pacific Railroad all the way to the Pacific coast. Stuyvesant had intentionally not attempted to make a precise schedule, as he declared, "I want to go anywhere fancy may suggest."[11] Ultimately, his own fancy did not take him farther than Chicago, as he was called away on business, but the rest of the group traveled on to Vancouver, British Columbia. Throughout the trip, they would leave the train cars behind them for a time and ride, on horseback, into the wilderness in search of game.

By July 18, the party returned to Newport. By the end of their trip, they had given up on hunting and turned instead to fishing. Mamie "made a record by capturing the largest trout ever caught on a pacific slope."[12] This accomplishment was sufficient to make *The Philadelphia Times*, but still, it was no grizzly bear.

This may have disappointed her. Mrs. Fish was used to getting what she aimed for, and the absence of a grizzly trophy must have gnawed at her somewhat. But before long, at Crossways, she would turn her attention to a different kind of animal entirely.

CHAPTER 18

IN 1901, AS MAMIE WAS READYING HERSELF FOR HER NEWPORT SEASON, a male friend complained, "Women of today prefer dogs to men for their boudoir pets."[1] Mamie looked askance, feeling, perhaps, that if women did not want men in their beds, the problem lay not with the women or the dogs, but with the men. She mused that if men were on the way out, she'd have to rethink her party invitations. And so, the seed was planted for what would become one of Mamie's most well-known parties: a dinner for dogs.

Specifically, this was "a dinner at which each man should appear with a dog's head on and at which the ladies should be free to select for their partners the particular kind of dog they were fond of."[2] Men were said to have tried desperately to determine the favorite breeds of the prettiest society women in advance so they could don the appropriate mask.

Presumably these moguls disguised as pugs would also be allowed to breathe heavily, beg for attention, and stare up at women with doggish adoration.

Honestly, this sounds like a lot of fun, especially if you were a woman used to competing for male attention in Newport society.

Harry Lehr—a man who never wanted to be in *any* woman's bed—quickly stepped in to help, agreeing to hold the affair on the veranda of his summer house. One hundred invitations in total were sent to Newport's finest, with the ladies explicitly instructed to bring their "dearest pups." They did mean dogs, in that regard, not male friends. The dinner itself was presented in a traditional style, with candelabras on the table and five butlers serving the esteemed guests. "Mighty Atom,"[3] Harry Lehr's own Pomeranian, was given a place of honor at the table, and all the rest of the pets in attendance were seated next to their mistresses.

Did the dogs wear tails on top of their tails? Of course they did. They'd dressed for the occasion and had napkins fastened around their necks as they sat at the table. This may have displeased Mamie Fish, as it would cover the $15,000 diamond collar her own dog was sporting. There was a rumor that the dogs were served foie gras, but Elizabeth Lehr recounted that "the dinner was served on the veranda, leaves from an ordinary dining-table placed on trestles about a foot high. The menu was stewed liver and rice, fricassee of bones, and shredded dog biscuit."[4] Guests of both species ate with gusto; at least one dog fell asleep on its plate and had to be carried home in its owner's arms. The event was declared "just the loveliest thing of the season" and to be such a "sweet innovation."[5]

Mrs. Fish, never one to let any of her guests succumb to lassitude and loveliness, introduced (human) guests into the room following the dinner, and the activities devolved into joyful pandemonium for everyone. But when the human guests and overfed dogs awoke the next day, they found that the newspapers had a very different perspective on this event.

Journalists thought the excess was absolutely abysmal and would lead to the downfall of civilization. *The Standard Union* worried that if people grew tired of regular dinners, they would also grow tired of their spouses. They remarked, "It is the weakness and futility of idleness that leads to half-men and half-women that you and I—yes, you and I—couldn't afford to waste our time on. That leads to dog dinners and the divorces. It will lead, if it has not led already to the degenerate and the parasitic."[6] To this, the *Austin Daily Herald* added, "Could there be anything more ridiculous than this 'dog dinner?'...As Tennyson put it, here are people glowing with health and boundless wealth, yet sickening of some vague disease, they know so ill how to deal with time, they must play such pranks as these."[7]

Mamie was surprised; her most extravagant parties for humans had never before been met with this level of rage and fury.

Newspapers piled on, claiming that "the hostess who gave the feast and those who abetted her in it have far less sense than the dogs that ate the costly viands. There is absolutely no excuse for this unwarranted, ostentatious display of wealth. It arouses resentment in the minds of the hungry poor."[8] *The American Eagle* sniffed at the dog dinner too, asserting that "for people who like that sort of thing, that is just about the sort of thing they would like." It exhorted the working man to think about why they were upholding a system that "provides dinner of courses for ugly pugs, and leaves your sweet babies only skim milk."[9]

To a modern person accustomed to over-the-top "dog weddings" (yes, this is an actual thing you can find on Google), a party for people's pets may seem genuinely harmless. Indeed, it might've seemed strange that such an innocent party could arouse so much ire. Some attendees, such as Elizabeth Lehr, suspected that the resentment toward this particular party could be traced back to one journalist. As Harry and Mrs. Fish were setting up the party, they'd noticed that "under the trees a young man waited, holding a little dog tied to a string, a paper ruffle round its neck. Harry Lehr, not recognizing him as one of the guests, went to question him, ascertained that he was a newspaper reporter, and had him put out of the garden."[10]

Although they initially congratulated themselves on ousting him, this action was exceedingly stupid of Lehr. Stunt journalism was all the rage during the period, and while this may not quite have been on par with Nellie Bly going undercover in a mental institution to chronicle the maltreatment of its patients, a reporter sneaking into the party with their dog would doubtless have made for an interesting—likely even funny and positive—piece, mostly focused on a dog having a nice afternoon.

However, the outrage here probably stemmed from more than just one displeased reporter. He may have left with his tail between his legs, but no individual could incite dozens of papers around the country to decry such an event. *The Purcell Register* may have come closer to touching on the actual source of public irritation when it noted, "The dinner cost hundreds of dollars. At the same time there were thousands of human beings in New York on the verge of starvation.... we say this is a civilized, Christian country, and yet we sometimes wonder what breeds anarchy and socialism."[11]

The political climate in the country was changing yet again around the turn of the twentieth century, and many different aspects of American life were leading the general public toward socialism, including income disparity. The Socialist Party of America was formed in 1901 and attracted members for this very reason. While Mamie Fish's dog was wearing thousands of dollars in diamonds, the average American's annual salary was only about $380 ($12,820 today). The cities were teeming with tenements, run-down buildings that packed families one on top of the other as industrialization boomed. Meanwhile, workers had few, if any, protections. Novels like Upton Sinclair's *The Jungle*, written slightly after this period in 1906, showcased the horrible conditions workers were subjected to as they labored, often ill, for ten to twelve hours a day in factories filled with the stench of rotten meat (which was then mixed with sawdust and sold).

Everyone would very understandably be jealous of the dogs eating foie gras.

There was no recourse if you *were* upset to take out your frustrations on your employer. The Clayton Act, legalizing strikes and boycotts, would not be passed until 1914. This meant that if workers did try to go on strike, they could be mercilessly beaten or killed.

Reading about the Dog Dinner in light of these strained circumstances was different from reading about one of Caroline Astor's parties. Lina's events were, frankly, more relatable to the average American. She doubtless spent as much on them as Mamie—anyone who has planned a wedding knows those floral arrangements get very expensive—but her entertainments essentially consisted of friends gathering at her home and dancing. It was not inconceivable that the average worker would have done something similar at a friend's or family member's wedding. It *was* inconceivable that, if they had the money for food, they would spend it on dogs.

The people in Newport, however, adopted a time-honored approach to class warfare: pretending that it was simply not happening.

Harry Lehr and his set embraced this denial with gusto. Elizabeth, Harry's wife, observed that not only was everyone undeterred by the negative press, but they were finally inspired to host ever more outrageous parties of their own. After the Dog's Dinner, "everyone wanted to give a party whose keynote was originality, not extravagance." This led to the financier Henry Clews hosting a "servants' ball" where Newport's millionaires were expected to arrive dressed as servants. "When the evening of the party arrived no one had the courage to face their servants dressed in what appeared to be clothes purloined from their own wardrobe, with the result that the Park was thronged with maids and menservants who had been given an unexpected evening off."[12]

It's bizarre that none of these attendees thought a "wouldn't it be funny to pretend to be poor" party might be ill-timed, especially amid all this class discontent. But these "servants' ball" parties weren't uncommon. By 1905, they'd become popular enough that in the book *Bright Ideas for Entertaining*, Mrs. Herbert B. Linscott recommended them as a potential theme, saying that you could serve milk and mush in tin cups alongside a "come in your rags" dress code. The invitations might even read "There is a-goin to bee lots of phun for every boddy" and that a woman must "leave her poodle dorg at hum."[13]

No fricassee for dogs at those parties, clearly.

Other fetes, though extravagant, were mercifully less focused on "mocking poor people." Nancy Leeds—who later became the Princess of Greece through marriage—gave a party where she took the guests by boat to a surprise destination that turned out to be an "amusement park [that] had been reserved for the afternoon at an enormous cost."[14] Attendees were taken to the park by yacht and spent the day on "switch-backs, water-chutes and in different sideshows" before being ferried back to Newport for dinner.

Meanwhile, the socialite Mrs. Hermann Oelrichs "transported the whole Russian ballet from New York to entertain"[15] her guests. Paul Rainey, the coal heir, began traveling with an orchestra that regularly performed on his yacht. When he arrived at one of Mrs. Fish's parties, he declared, "I have brought my music with me. I hope you don't mind?" Mrs. Fish replied, "Of course I'm delighted, but I never knew you sang"[16] and was—in a rare instance for her—surprised to see a full band emerge behind him.

Again, these were fairly harmless, clever parties. There's not really much about amusement parks to provoke ire, unless you positively hate clowns and are furious to have an unplanned day spent among clowns (very fair).

Yet the newspapers raged on. The *Los Angeles Times* seethed that Americans should "Take the case of Newport, where the vulgarist [*sic*] rich are oftenest on show. The best that they can do in the way of fun is to have a number of vaudeville performers come in" despite the fact that they were "a group of very rich people, who have had the means to enable them to devote their lives to good things, if only they chose." The reporter sighed, "It must be that among the women of the 400 there are bright or even intellectual women. How lonesome they must be."[17] Or perhaps, they speculated, these same women were engaged in immoral affairs!

Newspapers could gripe all they wanted, but the vaudeville performers were still going to dance.

The *Los Angeles Times*'s greatest complaint wasn't related to the entertainment itself, but rather focused on the fact that this desire for frivolity was now spreading to other classes. Mamie Fish's example "had its effect upon the town," they dolefully reported. "The girls dress too richly, better than they can afford…and [are] also trying to have the same kind of scandalous fun which characterizes, and is supposed to interest, those inferior persons who are supposed to be so very superior."[18]

The problem wasn't parties.

Well, except for the making-fun-of-poor-people parties. Those were tasteless.

But the economy, or the moral state of the world, is not made worse by someone hiring a ballet troupe to perform. If anything, it seems like good financial news for that ballet troupe.

The greater problem, which newspapers had more trouble addressing, was massive income inequality that kept factory workers starving while they processed rancid meat *and* people at the other end of the spectrum were rich enough to put jewels on their canines. That is a societal problem. But it was a lot easier for people to get upset with people having parties—especially women having parties—than it was to rage against those women's husbands who were ensuring that their workers were kept without the free time or the means to make merry themselves. It's more satisfying to say that you're opposed to partying because rich people do it—and it is, somehow, therefore immoral—than to do the necessary work to create a more equitable society, wherein everyone can enjoy themselves.

As for Mrs. Fish, her attention was, rather sadly, not yet preoccupied with the workers of the nation. Instead, she'd be turning her focus to aristocrats of another nation.

CHAPTER 19

*D*ESPITE SOME NEGATIVE PRESS, MRS. FISH REMAINED UNPERTURBED. In a world where entertainment was currency, she was richer than a king. And for all her heart and hard work, she had a right to fancy herself more significant to society than, for instance, the Grand Duke Boris of Russia, whose impending arrival was the talk of Newport in the summer of 1902.

In August 1902, the twenty-seven-year-old duke, who was known primarily for crashing automobiles and playing polo, made his way at last to America. Stateside, he disembarked with a staggering ninety-four trunks, which contained, among other items, dozens of serge suits and gold bracelets (presumably to give away as gifts). It wasn't unlike him to throw money around. During his travels, he'd been introduced to the game of poker and immediately lost $2,000 ($74,000 today) in one sitting. Given that his net worth was estimated to be $10 million ($368 million today), the loss may have even seemed modest.

The principal beneficiaries of Boris's money were the showgirls of the age. Grand Duke Boris *loved* women and spent most of his time in America pursuing chorus girls, attending so many performances featuring scantily clad actresses that the *Philadelphia Ledger* wondered if, in traveling to America, "he was seeking information for the Russian censor."[1] And these women were practically served to him on a platter. Reportedly, "he suggested he liked blondes and the blondes were promptly forthcoming."[2] In Chicago, he drank wine from a showgirl's shoe, prompting the *New York Mail and Express* to uncharitably remark that "he must have wanted a big drink"[3] and the *St. Louis Globe-Democrat* to say that if he drank out of a slipper that enormous, he'd get "beastly drunk."

It's unclear why the papers decided women from Chicago were big-footed beasts. No one had learned anything from Ward McAllister's mockery of Chicago, clearly!

Boris was not exactly eloquent about his preferences either. When asked about his visit, he declared, "I like American girls because when you meet a pretty one, she is really pretty."[4] As illuminating as this may be, it also gives the impression that Russian women were merely a stack of snakes wrapped up in a ball gown. However, he seemed to be having such a good time on his adventure that the *Baltimore American* noted, "It is to be hoped that the Grand Duke Boris will not write a book of his experiences in the United States when he goes home. If he does, we will have a tide of princely emigration setting towards these shores which will sorely tax our social resources."[5]

Not everyone was charmed by the fun-loving duke. The First Lady, Edith Roosevelt, refused to dine with him when he visited the White House, as she considered him to be extremely immoral. Mamie Fish was also less than impressed, though she was less shocked by his behavior than Mrs. Roosevelt. She just continued to harbor the low-level skepticism regarding aristocrats— considering them gold-digging and needlessly pompous—that she'd had for her entire life.

By September 1, the Grand Duke arrived in Newport. He and his party were originally slated to stay at a hotel, but they were promptly "rescued"[6] by Mrs. Ogden Goelet, who offered to let them stay in her mansion, Ochre Court.

This was less of an attempt to be kind to visitors than, as viewers of the HBO series *The Gilded Age* know, an attempt to enhance her own social status—something Mary Goelet was always eager to do. It was well-known that her husband was a man of simple tastes and "a quiet home life with his wife and their two children, Robert and Mary, would have been to his liking."[7] Mrs. Goelet, however, did not feel the same way. Like her husband, she loved yachting, and they owned an $800,000 yacht that they used to flit among Newport, New York, London, the Isle of Wight, and the Riviera. She wanted desperately to be accepted in both American and European society. As such, she arranged a debutante ball for her daughter to be held in London in 1897.

She was positively salivating at the idea of the young, eligible duke staying with her in Newport. Like many an eager mother, this was her ideal summer scenario.

Soon, however, the duke and his friends were being feted not only by the Goelets but also by the Vanderbilts. The duke was having the time of his life. He was delighted by Newport, claiming, "I have never even dreamt of such luxury as I have seen in Newport. Is this really your America or have I landed on an enchanted island? Such an outpouring of riches! It is like walking on gold. We have nothing to equal it in Russia."

Many of the residents in Newport were fully inclined to love him as much as he loved them. One night, he was the guest of honor at a dinner party hosted by Mrs. Richard Gambrill. Everything was off to an excellent start as he settled down to a glass of Sancerre. But then—horror of horrors—the butler proceeded to serve soup to Mrs. Gambrill *before serving it to the duke*. According to the *San Francisco Examiner*, "This was so astonishing a breach of Russian imperial etiquette that the Grand Duke, making some trifling excuse, rose from the table and regretted that he was obliged to go."[8]

The duke was correct about the order of service. At formal dinner parties, the first person to begin the meal is typically the guest of honor. If there is no guest of honor, the host. Sure. But the essence of being a well-brought-up person is not so much following etiquette precisely, but trying to make everyone around you feel comfortable. If someone awkwardly picks up a finger bowl and drinks from it, you pick it up and drink from it too. The idea that manners could be used to facilitate kindness and not as a cudgel with which to scold people, Ward McAllister style, was beginning to catch on. Everyone knew the duke was technically correct, and everyone also agreed he could have been polite about it. After all, this felt a bit uptight for a man who was happy to drink liquor out of a chorine's shoe.

His friend Baron Greaves would later deny the occurrence, protesting that the duke would not have been offended by such a matter. True or not, people began to grumble that "he expects to be treated with the same groveling humility here which is naturally given to the imperial family in autocratic Russia."[9]

All of this happened as Mrs. Fish was in a particularly patriotic phase of her life. Only recently, she'd hosted an all-American "Peace Ball" replicating the one held in 1789 at Mount Vernon. Crossways was lit up for the occasion with 150 electric lights flashing the year "1789" above the entrance, and guests passed by portraits of George and Martha Washington and Mount Vernon on the grounds. Inside, the walls were draped with American flags, and pictures of Revolutionary War heroes garlanded with laurel hung about the ballroom.

She'd also invited all the diplomats in Newport—people like Charles Hoage, secretary of the Legation of Norway and Sweden; the Baron Ritter von Grünstein, secretary of the German Embassy; and Baron Max von Oppenheim of the Spanish Legation at Cairo. She was so intent on creating an authentic, early American feel that she demanded all the men attending shave their mustaches in advance, so as to better embody the period. This basically meant that the men of Newport who were attached to their mustaches were forced to choose between "the lady or the mustache?"[10] Many essentially begged Mrs. Fish to please let them pretend to be an *eccentric* early American who, for wilderness pioneer reasons, had a mustache. Mrs. Fish finally relented on the mustaches, though the men did dutifully agree to wear colonial costumes, including knee breeches, buckles, and stockings. The women, meanwhile, wore "their hair powdered and their cheeks exhibited an extra touch of red just as those of the pretty girls of 123 years ago used to."[11] Cherry trees, like the ones George Washington declined to chop down, were given out as favors, as were lanterns, matchboxes embroidered in gold, and miniature portraits of George and Martha Washington. Harry Lehr, as always, made an appearance, dressed to the nines as a member of the court of King Louis XV, to general laughter. The Duchess of Marlborough, Consuelo (Alva Vanderbilt's daughter), also attended this party, apparently leaving any tensions regarding the revolution long in the past.

Overall, the ball was considered "her most successful function."[12] And none of these dignitaries made a fuss when they were served their soup.

Not long after this ball, Mamie Fish was invited to go boating on the governor of the New York Hospital Commodore Gerry's yacht, the *Electra*. Baron Greaves, a friend and traveling companion to the Grand Duke, was also invited on the outing. During this trip, Mamie attempted what was, for her, polite conversation. She approached the baron and, with a laugh, declared, "Baron Greaves, I know the secret of the Grand Duke's visit to Newport."

The baron, who was at least initially amused, replied, "You are very clever, Madame. I did not know there was a secret."

Mrs. Fish drew herself up to her full height. "Why, of course, he is here to marry Miss Goelet." Mrs. Fish was referring to Mrs. Ogden Goelet's twenty-four-year-old, famously beautiful daughter, Mary. Again, Mrs. Goelet, who was making sure to pull out all the stops for the duke's visit, would have been *thrilled* if this happened.

The baron was horrified. "No, Madam," he replied. "Please do not say such a—pardon me—stupid thing. You must know that His Highness cannot marry one not of royal blood." (Also, it bears noting, he did love blondes, and Mary Goelet was a brunette.)

Mrs. Fish, who had never shown much partiality to Mary Goelet in the past, was outraged *as an American*. "But you know she is one of our greatest catches?" she insisted.

The baron was not swayed and asked her to drop the matter.

"Oh, nonsense, Baron Greaves," she huffed. "You know it as well as I do: he's here to catch a rich girl. You know he is a very dissipated young man and he must manage somehow to pay his debts."[13] Remember, despite his gambling losses and frivolous spending, the Grand Duke was still estimated to be worth $10 million, so it's unlikely that this was truly the case. But if she meant to be insulting, she succeeded.

And again, by this point in her life, whenever she tossed out an insult, most people chuckled and assumed it was just Mamie being Mamie.

The baron, however, did not.

Instead, he stalked away from Mrs. Fish, mouth open and utterly aghast.

Mrs. Fish later claimed (quite lamely) that she was just trying to make conversation, but "the more Mrs. Fish thought the matter over the more she resented his indignation."[14] First of all, titled nobility *did* marry Americans. In only 1895, Alva Vanderbilt's daughter, Consuelo, had married the Duke of Marlborough. She was visiting Newport that very summer, and when she left, she was said to take with her "the adulations of Newport, her title, and 53 trunks."[15] Consuelo was considered to be a triumphant American success story. After all, "it is but a shot time, measured even by human events since her respected great-grandfather pulled a sturdy oar on his ferryboat," noted *The Oregon Daily Journal*. "Commodore's rich, red blood charged through three generations until it became royal purple."[16]

If Consuelo Vanderbilt was proof of anything, it was that Americans could marry whoever they damn well wanted. What made the Grand Duke think that he was so much better than the residents of Newport? Why did his friend, a baron, get to turn his back to Mamie in disgust? Offended, Mrs. Fish struck back in the only way she could: by refusing to send the baron an invitation to the dinner party she intended to end the Newport season.

Duke Boris, himself, had been very much looking forward to the dinner. He was so excited when he heard about it, he exclaimed, "Of course we must go! Delightful woman, Mrs. Fish." After all, her parties were exactly the kind of events that would appeal to someone who would not hesitate to drink champagne from a shoe.

The baron replied, a bit awkwardly, that he had not been invited. When the duke pressed him as to why, the baron relayed his conversation with Mrs. Fish. After hearing that his reputation had been impugned, the Grand Duke was "furiously indignant."[17] He was shocked that he had "been painted as a dissolute fortune hunter" and "begged Mrs. Goelet to take some action which should vindicate him, making it clear to the fashionable world of Newport that Mrs. Goelet, at least, did not endorse Mrs. Fish's view."[18]

The Goelets reportedly already had their own issues with Mrs. Fish. According to Elizabeth Lehr, the family had been enraged by Mamie's refusal to invite Mrs. Goelet's special friend (a term which could mean anything from her lover to her gay best friend), the "manly beauty" James Cutting, to her parties. When Mrs. Goelet pressed her on this decision, saying that if Mrs. Fish needed more men in attendance Jimmie could happily fill in, Mrs. Fish replied, "I will not have Jimmie Cutting if I am reduced to the Training Station for men," referring to the naval training school nearby. So Mrs. Goelet was, if not enthusiastic about all-out war with the social queen of Newport, at least not averse to it.

And so, Mrs. Goelet hastily sent out invitations for a party celebrating the Grand Duke, intentionally planned for the exact same time as Mrs. Fish's final party of the season.

This was, predictably, awkward for many who were invited to both events. If they accepted one invitation, they knew they would make an enemy of the other woman. The only logical thing to do would have been to decline the invitations to both parties and perhaps flee the town for a weekend. Which, honestly, considering the amount of packing you had to do every time you traveled anywhere, sounds like it would've been a huge hassle for everyone.

Well aware that this had become an awkward situation, Mamie went to Harry Lehr for comfort. She bemoaned that people in Newport were "uniformly stupid" and "crazy about dukes and things."[19] Lehr's wife, Elizabeth, recalled her frazzled friend saying, "You have to get me out of this, Lamb, you must do something." Lehr replied, "The only thing you can do is to turn the whole thing into a joke. You must make people laugh so much that they will not be quite sure of what has really happened."[20]

Lehr had never been fond of Mrs. Goelet, nor she of him. It was well known that Mrs. Goelet "detested his effeminate manners."[21] Meanwhile, Harry had joked on the beach at Newport upon seeing their yacht that the

Goelets had "gone to the European pawnshops...to purchase a battered ducal coronet for [their daughter] Mary."[22] It might have been regarded as a great success when Alva Vanderbilt married her daughter off to a duke, but the Goelets' blatantly obvious attempts to marry their daughter into the foreign aristocracy had begun to seem embarrassing. When Mrs. Goelet heard about Harry's joke, her hatred to him moved from "vague homophobia" to "a very specific hatred of Harry Lehr."

Indifferent to Mrs. Goelet's feelings, Harry and Mamie hatched a plan to get society back on their side.

Soon afterward, Mamie Fish sent out invitations announcing that if the Grand Duke of Russia would be at Mrs. Goelet's party, the Czar of Russia would attend her own.

This seemed unlikely because Czar Nicholas II was currently fully occupied doing an exceptionally poor job ruling Russia. Nevertheless, Newport society—whether out of guileless belief, or curiosity, or the simple terror of earning Mrs. Fish's enmity—flocked to Mrs. Fish's event. None of the guests, including Senator Chauncey Depew, Pierpont Morgan, and Lord Charles Beresford, abandoned her, but rather gathered in hushed anticipation.

A duke was one thing. A *czar* was quite another.

When minutes passed, and the guests had not yet welcomed royalty, Mrs. Fish turned to Alice Drexel, who loved to brag about her experience in European court circles.

"Dear Cousin Alice, do help me," asked Mrs. Fish. "You are so familiar with court etiquette, and I am so afraid I will not be equal to the occasion. Will you go out to the porte-cochere and receive his Imperial Majesty?"[23]

Alice returned with "His Imperial Majesty, the Emperor of Russia"... who turned out to be Harry Lehr, sporting a tinfoil crown and holding a scepter. He was garbed in Mrs. Fish's emerald green opera cloak, turned inside out to better resemble the royal robe.

People caught onto the joke nearly immediately. "The ladies nearest the entrance, in varying degrees of hesitance, sank in a court curtsey, only to recover themselves with shrieks of laughter when they realized they were paying homage to Harry Lehr!... The whole room rippled with merriment as in his royal robes he made a solemn circuit on the arm of his hostess, pausing here and there to talk to people, in exact imitation of a stately royal progress."[24] He proceeded to behave with all the grandiosity of "a monarch in a comic opera."[25] Throughout the dinner, hostess and guests alike kept up the ruse, with Mamie peppering him with questions like "Would your majesty prefer to drink your wine out of a slipper?"[26]

Meanwhile, Harry demanded that he must be served food before anyone else—just like a true royal. Each time a plate was laid down, he checked to ensure that he had been served first. At the end of the evening, the Hungarian band in attendance played "God Save the Czar," and the rest of the guests stood while Harry Lehr remained seated, "listening to the stirring music that was being played in his honor."[27]

The general bubble of worship surrounding foreign royalty had been humorously but definitively punctured, like an overfilled balloon popped by Harry Lehr's scepter. However, by the time the hangovers started to set in the next morning, attendees once again worried about whether there would be social consequences or general criticism of Mamie Fish's party.

This time, there were no repercussions at all, as the Grand Duke had seemingly rediscovered his sense of humor. While walking along the beach the following day, he encountered Harry Lehr and his wife. He called them over and, with a laugh, declared, "I hear you represented the Emperor last night...I only wish I had been there to see it. It must have been most amusing. Our party was poisonous. We shall have to call you King Lehr in the future!"[28]

Like many of her passing obsessions, Mamie's patriotism faded with time. Later that winter, she commissioned a coat of imperial Russian sable "long enough to cover all but my French heels."[29] It would be lined with white and gold silk and modeled off one worn by Marie Antoinette. So much for stars and stripes.

Much to Mrs. Fish's chagrin, and her mother's delight, Mary Goelet, the brunette beauty whose possible alliance with the duke horrified Baron Greaves, did marry a nobleman the following year, though it ended up being

Henry Innes-Ker, the Eighth Duke of Roxburghe, and not Grand Duke Boris. Mrs. Fish would later say that she thought the marriage was "folly. They paid down $2,000,000 to do it. Of course, the Duke is not as bad as some foreigners, who have married American girls, for he has some money, about $60,000 a year. But that is not much for people in his station. I think it very foolish."[30] It may have been, though it was at least reported that "due to the Goelet millions, that Roxburghe coronet is no longer battered."[31]

Within the next couple of years, that groveling spirit ascribed to autocratic Russia would crumble just as unexamined reverence for royals did in America. In 1917, Grand Duke Boris was imprisoned during the Russian Revolution, but, amazingly, he succeeded in fleeing the country. After all that fuss about how he had to marry someone of his exalted status, he ended up marrying his longtime mistress—a chorus girl. The couple settled quietly in France, where they raised his wife's niece and were said to be very much in love.

Truly a win for the chorus girls of the world.

CHAPTER 20

$\mathcal{T}$HE ABSENCE OF PHYSICAL DANGERS IN THE FORM OF REVOLUTION may have been a relief, but it did not mean that New York's wealthiest were protected from tragedy.

While Mamie and the rest of her set partied, Clemence Fish's mourning period continued. It was well-known throughout the city that Clemence had still not recovered from Hamilton's death in Cuba. She never ceased to wear black and "worshipped the memory of her boy."[1] The years since had been remarkably unkind to her. Shortly after Hamilton's death, her father passed away after his battle with dementia. After that, she had stopped entertaining. The merriment that Hamilton and his outgoing friends had brought to their home was gone. No one came to dinner. Certainly, no one danced the night away there.

If Clemence found any comfort, it was in her work bringing music to the poor following her son's death. Having studied under the German composer Richard Wagner, she believed in the uplifting power of music, but also understood that there were "hundreds who dearly loved good music without the price to pay for it."[2] So she assembled musicians to come to her house and play for those less fortunate. She also offered lessons to girls from poorer families. Slowly, as she sat and played, she emerged slightly from her despair.

The same could not be said of her husband, Nicholas. He, too, "brooded constantly over the death of Ham, as he invariably called the boy."[3] Though he and his wife grieved very differently, both had been undone by the loss of their child. *The Washington Post* reported that, since Hamilton's death, "his father's life appeared to his friends to be of little value to him, and everybody in his circle of friends had observed the stunned and disconsolate condition of the once brilliant, dashing and amiable Nicholas Fish."[4] Nicholas wanted no gentle comforts and had absolutely no patience for his wife's retreat into a quiet life of charity work.

Unable to bear staying at home in their darkened mansion, Nicholas plunged himself into the world, hoping to find at least distraction in the less savory streets of New York. He spent the nights prowling through bars, drinking and carousing, hoping to—at least for some hours—escape the memories of his loss. The names, titles, and reputations of those he spent time with were of no importance; anyone who would drink with him was good enough. He was reportedly seen "in very queer company a number of times."[5] This did not mean "queer" in terms of sexual orientation so much as it meant "poor people."

So, it was not atypical when, one day in September 1902, he wandered into the Ehrhard Brothers Saloon with "two women known in the neighborhood." Those women were largely assumed to have been prostitutes, and while they may have been sexually interested in Nicholas, just as likely they were simply happy to encounter a man willing to buy them a drink. Mrs. Nellie Casey, the wife of a piano player, and Mrs. Libbie Phillips, a divorcée who managed a boarding house, were all too happy to clink their beers as Mr. Fish drank whiskey alongside them.

After four rounds, the trio was joined by the formidable Thomas J. Sharkey. Sandy-haired and burly, Sharkey was a Brooklyn native who had grown up in the neighborhood of Red Hook. Nellie and Libbie both knew him and waved him over to the table, where they sat making small talk for some time. Nicholas, very drunk by this point, kept trying to make conversation with Mrs. Phillips while Sharkey was talking to her, shouting over him at times. When Mrs. Phillips told Nicholas that she and Mr. Sharkey were talking, Mr. Fish exclaimed that Sharkey "had no business to interfere with his party."[6] Sharkey claimed that Mr. Fish became increasingly furious. "He referred to the fact that I had not been buying any drinks, and as I was about broke I could not 'make good.' He kept abusing me, telling me to go away, and called me a 'bum' and 'a loafer' and a lot of other unpleasant things."[7]

When he ran out of cash, Nicholas (who had bought all the drinks) "announced that he would have to draw a check."[8] Unaware that this was one of the richest men in the city, and mad at having been called a bum, Sharkey questioned his ability to use a check to pay for drinks in the bar. "Why would the bartender accept a check? Who the—are you to draw a check?" he shot back, continuing, "Who would cash it for you?"[9] At this point, a red-faced Mr. Fish leaped to his feet. Mr. Sharkey reached awkwardly across the width of the table and slapped Nicholas in the face. It was a glancing, light blow, but Nicholas fell down nonetheless.

Mrs. Casey, understandably upset by the whole debacle, immediately and sensibly exited the bar. Around the same time, a waiter rushed over and attempted to eject the remaining three. Mr. Fish initially refused, but finally, haltingly, rose to his feet and began to exit. Mr. Sharkey attempted to pounce on him as he left. Mrs. Phillips grabbed Sharkey and tried to restrain him, but with no success.

Soon, the two men were brawling again. Sharkey struck Nicholas in the face. Mr. Fish replied, tragically, "If my son Ham were here, he'd whip you."[10] When Nicholas struggled to his feet, Sharkey hit him once more. Nicholas fell through the saloon doors and onto the pavement, where he remained unconscious.

After fleeing in the direction of Sixth Avenue, Sharkey was quickly caught by law enforcement. He attempted to clear himself, recalling the events somewhat differently to police officers. He told them that he knew both the women beforehand, and that "after we had been talking half an hour I said to the women, 'well, it's time to get a move on.' The banker...was not in favor of adopting my suggestion, and he dug into me in the ribs with his elbow and called me names." From his perspective, Sharkey claimed that he was nonplussed by this behavior and responded calmly. In his words: "I got up and left the saloon. As I was going out, I saw the banker run out another door and fall down on the pavement."[11]

Two passersby saw Nicholas sprawled in the street and attempted to revive him but found the task impossible. They called a patrolman who, as soon as he discovered Nicholas's identity, immediately summoned an ambulance to take him to Roosevelt Hospital, where he then lapsed into a coma. Clemence rushed from their home in Tuxedo Park and begged the doctors to perform an operation to save him—but there was nothing they could do.

Nicholas passed away at 3:25 a.m. on September 16, 1902. He was fifty-five years old.

This was the third beloved man in her life that Clemence had lost in four years. She left the hospital, alone, bereft, and the sole administrator of the family's fortune of approximately $275,000 (about $10 million today).[12]

The doctors testified that Nicholas had indeed been killed by a blow. If, the coroner declared, he had fallen on the pavement as Sharkey claimed, his skull would have been fractured (which it was not). Sharkey was later found guilty of manslaughter and sentenced to ten years in prison. Of course, none of this helped heal the sorrow that, once again, Clemence was forced to endure. She was prostrate with grief and almost incoherent upon her return from the hospital. A doctor began caring for her, mostly out of the fear that she might pose a danger to herself. All day long, carriages came to her door filled with friends who were eager to offer their condolences, but nothing could soothe Clemence's heart, now shattered beyond repair.

Newspapers were not overly kind regarding Nicholas's death, and promptly began comparing his unsavory demise to his son's more heroic one. *The New York Times* noted that, in a bit of irony, Hamilton was always getting into scrapes "very much on the order of the one in which his father lost his life."[13] Here, at last, "was the death for her husband that thousands had feared for her son."[14] People suspected that Clemence "knew all about her son's vagaries and possibly may have known something of the weaknesses of her husband."[15]

And the rest of society? Well, they waited, eagerly, to see what quips—if any—Mamie would make about the death. They knew that Nicholas's passing would be mourned by the larger family, "except for this one branch," by which they meant Mamie. It was widely acknowledged that the sisters-in-law had not spoken since the party Mamie held following Hamilton's death; or rather, that Clemence had absolutely refused to speak to Mamie. The *Los Angeles Times* even attempted to goad Mamie into one of her famous jabs, pointing out that Nicholas's branch of the Fish family was "not a type of the new rich, who paint Newport red…who don't know what to do with their money."

Mamie, however, did not take the bait.

In an abrupt and unexpected turn, Mamie came to her sister-in-law's aid without any hesitation. As soon as she heard the news, she ordered her Newport house closed. By 1:00 p.m. the next day, she was on her way to New York to comfort Clemence.

Perhaps her compassion related to the fact that Clemence was now involved in a scandal. Mamie had spent so much of her life sneering at formal, proper society, which she certainly associated with the elder Fish couple. But now, the whole Fish family found themselves in a story that scandalized people far more than any party Mamie could throw. For the first time, the elegant, Wagner-trained Clemence really needed her support. People wondered, considering her brother-in-law's death, "Would Mrs. Fish give a ball or a dinner? She did neither. She came in all haste to the other woman's side."[16] While she'd refuse to cancel festivities following Hamilton's death, now "Mrs. Stuyvesant Fish ceased her New York season, cancelled her engagements, and announced she will be in retirement from this winter's gayety."[17]

And Clemence was grateful for her in-laws' rather forceful demeanor. As soon as they arrived, Stuyvesant took over the handling of the press, answering all their questions about the funeral plans. He appeared calm and patient, until a reporter thrust his camera forward and attempted to take a picture of the grieving family. At this, "Mr. Fish snatched the camera from the reporter's hands and smashed it to bits." When it was explained to him that a camera cost sixty-five dollars ($2,300 today), perhaps remembering his younger days of walking to work for fear of spending his limited funds on the trolley, he was apologetic and wrote the managing editor at the journalist's paper, offering to cover the bill and replace the camera. However, he also warned that if that reporter came near him again, "he would be thrashed."[18]

Reporters learned, at least for a while, to keep their distance.

CHAPTER 21

$\mathcal{S}$ HORTLY FOLLOWING NICHOLAS'S DEATH, THE FISH CAME INTO POSSES-
sion of Glenclyffe. In 1893, after Stuyvesant's father, Hamilton, passed
away, his estate went to Nicholas and Clemence. However, now all on her
own, Clemence found it unwieldy to manage. There were rumors that the
sprawling estate would be sold but, whether for lack of interest from buyers
or a change of heart due to emotional attachment, it had remained in the
family.

The country estate in Garrison, New York, always affectionately called
"the farm" by the family, was first built in the 1850s for Eugene Dutilh, a silk
importer and banker. It was constructed by Charles Vaux and modeled after
a house that Dutilh "had seen and liked in the South." In 1861, he relocated
to England in light of the Civil War—all those houses becoming charred
ruins made the South, and America as a whole, *much* less appealing—at
which time the estate was purchased by Hamilton Fish for $30,000 (about
$1.7 million today).

The house and its considerable grounds, overlooking a stunning view of
the Hudson River, were a source of great pride for Stuyvesant's late father. In

one instance, when his gardener became ill, Hamilton took over the landscaping himself. He did it extremely well, taking great pleasure in the quality of his roses that year, which far outshone his neighbors' flowers. Hamilton was also quite generous with his harvest, as it was said that "he grew enough apples and small fruits to be liberal to his neighbors" and "he cut enough hickory wood for the fireplaces in Stuyvesant Square."[1]

His grandson, Stuyvesant Jr., recalled that, despite his wealth and prestige, Hamilton truly loved living the life of a farmer. He "walked, drove, blistered his hands with a pitchfork, and talked with the stream of visitors. When the day's work was done, he delighted to sit on the south piazza enjoying the resplendent view down the river in the rich sunset light and watching the 'Mary Powell' [a steamboat] as she throbbed northward to Albany. On the north piazza hung a thermometer which he made it a rule to examine thrice daily, the last time just before going to bed; and he neatly entered the temperatures in red and black ink in large volumes."[2] He invited friends like Ulysses S. Grant to join in on this pastime with him; Grant even planted a tree at Glenclyffe two years before he became president.[3]

It was this house that held Stuyvesant's happiest memories. He would forever preserve his childhood bedroom as it was, even though it had no running water. In his eyes, it served as an example of American progress over a matter of mere decades. "None of the maids will sleep in it," he claimed. "It's not good enough for them; yet I spent some of the happiest hours of my life here."

He also fondly recalled how, during his college years, he'd invite his friends up to stay at the estate on the weekends. They spent one night learning poker, and in church the next morning, the passage being read was "And Ephraim went out with a full hand." As a full hand often refers to poker, the men assembled spent the time whispering jokes about "what a chump Ephraim must have been."[4]

When Mamie and Stuyvesant took over ownership of the house decades later, they found it well-appointed. Glenclyffe was already very large, containing twenty-one rooms in total. There were five bedrooms and six bathrooms, a library, a dining room, a living room, three rooms for servants, and a billiards room, as well as stables and a guesthouse. But it wasn't particularly attractive. According to Stuyvesant Jr.'s records, "The house at Glenclyffe was never beautiful. Like 'Topsy' it just grew. After each 'reconstruction' (addition), it became more hideous." The grounds were lovely, though. Visitors approaching would roll up in their carriages through woods and beside a pond full of water lilies. Though her husband's eyes were tinted with nostalgia and affection, Mamie, her softer energies exhausted by being nice after her brother-in-law's murder, was completely capable of looking a gift horse in the mouth—and immediately proclaimed the home too small.

Reader: It was initially sixteen thousand square feet.

For some perspective, the average 1,600-square-foot home in the Garrison, New York, area currently costs $800,000. Many people apparently find that to be a satisfactory size.

By the time Mamie was finished with her renovations, however, the house would be doubled in size to thirty-two thousand square feet. She added a new modern kitchen. She expanded the back hall and staircase. She built a new ballroom. The final house contained fifteen bedrooms, all luxurious, and the stables expanded to house up to twenty-five carriages.

Mamie's bedroom was especially notable. She decorated it so that everything was varying shades of pink—basically Barbiecore long before Barbie. The dancer Irene Castle, who visited, did not appreciate the feminine fancy on full display and remarked that "the house was fantastically costly and far too dressy with its masses of gilt and old rose and paintings and velvet portieres. It bustled with manservants in striped pants and short pea jackets covered with braid."[5]

Irene Castle had fantastic taste—she was known for being one of the chicest flappers of the twenties—but her taste and Mamie's belonged to *very* different eras.

The only room Mamie did not overhaul was the library, which was her husband's domain. It was fully stocked with Hamilton's many leather-bound volumes, largely nonfiction. Quite often, Stuyvesant would enter the house to find Mamie's friends already there en masse and exclaim, "It seems I am giving a party. Well, I hope you are all enjoying yourselves!" before retreating to his books.

Here at the magnificently updated Glenclyffe manor, Mamie was able to entertain in earnest, hosting up to three hundred people at a time. It was perfect for seasons other than the summer, which she spent in Newport. In the spring, she hosted lawn parties, where guests were transported through the grounds by oxcart. At Halloween, she hosted a party for her friends and a party for the servants (though that one was held in the stables). But as much as she busied herself, none of this planning and decorating and partying was quite enough to offset Mrs. Fish's boredom, and her increasing desire to get into quarrels with people.

Her next intended target would be significantly grander than a duke, and much more beloved in the eyes of Americans.

CHAPTER 22

$\mathcal{B}$Y 1903, MAMIE'S PENCHANT FOR CREATIVE EXCESS HAD FINALLY rubbed off on other ambitious hostesses, which was all well and good—until her events were outshone.

In March 1903, the "American Horse King" C. K. G. Billings transformed Sherry's Ballroom, a Fifth Avenue restaurant favored by the Four Hundred, into a beautiful forest with $10,000 worth of plants and a floor that had been borrowed from Barnum and Bailey's circus. Even more amazing than the foliage, thirty-six horses were galloping about, which was fitting, as Billings wanted to celebrate his new $200,000 stable on 196th Street. A seven-course dinner was served to guests, who ate on horseback. In the words of historian Grace Meyer, Billings "reached uncharted heights in planning for the discomfort of his guests."[1] Admittedly, sitting—if not riding around—on a horse while trying to gobble down food sounds, if not uncomfortable, at least challenging, even if small tables were attached to each guest's saddle. The menu also boasted items like turtle soup and caviar, which are both delicious *and* easily spilled (though there were other less challenging offerings too, like rack of lamb and guinea hen. But if you're committed to eating on horseback, hell, you might as well go for the caviar). The fact that anyone was able to hold on to the 1898 vintage champagne that Billings provided is a marvel. Billings himself only drank ginger ale.

In the end, it did not really matter if this dinner was conducive to anyone enjoying the actual meal. What mattered was that it was spectacularly unique and gave the upscale guests something to talk about for weeks if not months afterward. They would treasure those memories much more than the silver horseshoe souvenirs. After years of attending Mamie's increasingly creative gatherings, New York's elite were coming to expect, in Mamie's words, "something besides dinner."

Look, Mamie could have been enjoying this. She'd wanted a more interesting world with more amusements. And now, that world existed.

For much of their lives, Stuyvesant Fish had been a friend to Theodore Roosevelt. Stuyvesant later said that he had known the president "since he was a toddler so high."[2] Now fully grown, the two enjoyed hunting together. The fact that Roosevelt headed the Rough Riders during the Spanish-American War and had been close to Hamilton meant there was another special bond between the families, particularly now that those two branches of the Fish family had reunited.

Theodore Roosevelt's second wife, Edith, had also known Teddy since childhood in New York. One of Teddy's sisters was good friends with Edith, "and the two little girls were often to be seen playing quietly with their dolls, while the future President, in indifferent boy fashion, busied himself in his books at a distant window."[3] Following the death of Roosevelt's first wife, the couple married in 1886. Edith was a studious, well-read woman who was dedicated to the Needlework Guild, which provided clothing to the poor. She famously helped renovate the White House during her tenure as First Lady, and she also met with "the wives of cabinet members to discuss moral standards and the appropriate level of spending on parties."[4]

The White House renovations were well received.

Her morality talks, however, were not.

Telling people not to spend money on parties might have been politically correct, but at a time when people were having horseback caviar dinners, it was also a huge bummer.

Again, the answer perhaps is not to scold people for spending money on parties—you only end up sounding like a killjoy—so much as it is to try to ensure that people of all classes are paid enough to be able to spend some of their money on recreation (though, admittedly, probably not horseback caviar parties. Those *do* seem pretty expensive).

Given her "don't spend too much on parties" stance, it's probably not a big surprise that Mrs. Fish and Mrs. Roosevelt did not have quite the warm relationship that their husbands did. They were very temperamentally different people—Edith an introvert to Mamie's extrovert. They also had very different styles—literally. While Mamie was something of a clotheshorse, Edith was known for re-wearing the same gowns to parties and simply changing the press release description of them.[5]

This could have been seen as evidence of her good sense and thrift.

But not by Mamie.

The feud all started when Mamie made the mistake of publicly remarking, "Mrs. Roosevelt dresses on $300 a year, and she looks it."[6]

She did not say this simply to be mean, although it is a withering put-down. She felt that it was the patriotic duty of First Ladies to promote American designers on the world stage. Mrs. Roosevelt's seeming lack of interest in fashion meant she was not doing this. As Mamie explained to the press, "I think that in dress the American woman imitates Europe too much. American makers build just as handsome and costly gowns as the Parisians. . . . If the wife of the president or some other great lady would start the fashion, every woman in America would soon be wearing gowns of domestic make and the chances are that in a short time the society leaders of Europe would be wearing New York gowns instead of the Parisian creations."[7]

There were some sacred cows on which society agreed that Mrs. Fish could take aim. Any European royal was obviously on the table. For that matter, she could call any rich American an idiot and people would largely be fine with it. The wife of the president, however, was above criticism. *The Independent* was indignant, writing that "We should be sorry to believe that many American citizens are capable of making such comments upon the wife of the President."[8] Another paper wondered, "Wouldn't Mrs. Fish, charitable mortal, kindly hand down to Mrs. Roosevelt, wife of a pauper president, some of the duds that appeared at the monkey show?" Meanwhile, the *Transcript Telegram* sniffed, "There are plenty of fish in the sea as good as Mrs. Stuyvesant Fish."[9]

That isn't even a particularly good insult! It doesn't make sense.

Mamie responded to all the outrage by making a series of even *more* ill-advised comments—among them that she thought that she, personally, ought to go into politics, "for there are many things in the country I want to change. I believe that women could do a tremendous amount of good in politics."[10] That said, she also added that she "did not believe in being too democratic," as she thought some people really were better than others. (In her relatively diplomatic and demure age, Mamie would have been a terrible politician. In the 2020s, her outspoken, vituperative style might have made her a successful one.) At the time, *The Buffalo Times* remarked, "Mrs. Fish expresses a desire to go into politics. If she should, one of the first things to be impressed upon her mind would be the advisability of keeping to herself such opinions as she has expressed."[11]

It was true that Edith Roosevelt, with her homespun dresses, did seem to inhabit a much different realm than Mamie's. Even though Edith had grown up wealthy in New York, her public persona resembled not that of the older generation of New York royalty like Mrs. Astor, but something more akin to the values of a middle-American matron. And this earned her a lot of praise from both the press and the public.

The Piqua Daily Call newspaper in Ohio passionately supported the First Lady, writing, "If Mrs. Roosevelt prefers to be economical and save money for distribution among her children, what is it to Mrs. Fish?... She is known as a woman of good sense, pursuing the even tenor of her way, avoiding the limelight, and shrinking from notoriety. She is known as a woman who does not shrink from maternity, and as a woman who is personally rearing her children instead of transferring that duty to hired help."[12] Mrs. Roosevelt, *The Star* added, was a "purely good and simple American mother."

In the battle of Mamie versus Edith, *The Independent* stressed that Mrs. Fish was the one out of touch. "A fine old aristocrat, who had never been anything else, whose forebears have never been anything else for a millennium or so, has some of the attractive qualities of an ancient vintage or an exceptionally ripe old cheese.... Would be aristocrats who are doomed to live in a democratic society are in no way attractive."[13] *The Charlotte News* opined that, given Mrs. Fish's dress bills, "Mr. Fish could never have been the President of the United States."[14] And in an especially vicious quip (and a low blow, in this humble author's opinion), *The Anaconda Standard* sneered that "were she disposed to retaliate, Mrs. Roosevelt might remark that, while she possesses large wealth, Mrs. Stuyvesant Fish's face is not her fortune."[15]

This marks one of the rare times when Mamie appeared to walk back her comments, declaring weeks later that, in all seriousness, she hated snobbery and that "I am disgusted with this new fad, conservatism. That is aggravated snobbery. I believe men of mental ability—thinkers, artists, and that class—should be invited to our best drawing rooms. Nothing would enliven the present-day dullness as would the presence of brilliant men and women."

In other words, she wanted society to be more democratic, in opposition to her earlier comment.

Mamie then blundered on, "Newport society life is infernally stupid, I'm going into politics. What makes our social life so stupid is that the women do nothing but dress and talk nonsense....American women ought to do something—that's the reason the Lord gave them brains, and I for one, intend to know something about what interests me most, and that is politics."[16]

It is possible that Mamie genuinely wanted to do more than critique the First Lady's dresses. She might well have wanted to critique policies being set in the country. But while Mrs. Fish might be able to boss the men of Newport into dressing up for parties, women still weren't in a position where they were able to exert much real control over anything outside the domestic sphere. (While throwing parties may be a really fun, creative part of the domestic sphere, if you are not being paid for them, it's still just part of being a housewife.)

Even Mrs. Roosevelt, arguably the woman with the most political power in the country, was being judged primarily for her clothing, her selfless (unpaid) volunteer efforts, her home furnishings, and her aptitude as a mother. Here were women who finally had enough free time—something that would not have likely been available to them in a more rural existence—to exert their intellectual as well as creative impulses. But American society was more interested in whether they kept up with the latest trends, and who was having a catfight.

A hundred years later, we're still pretty preoccupied with that when it comes to famous women.

In England, though, conditions were already beginning to change. In 1903, the same year Mamie was lamenting how women were not able to use their brains, the Women's Social and Political Union, a militant branch of the suffragettes, had formed, demanding the right to vote, aligned under the motto "Deeds not words." That stance would inspire acts of civil disobedience, such as trying to storm Parliament, and hunger strikes (women over thirty would gain the right to vote in England in 1917).

In America, meanwhile, women's suffrage was slowly gaining ground among the less privileged classes. In 1903, the Women's Trade Union League was formed stateside to help advance the rights of female workers. Suffrage, they argued, was necessary to improve conditions in the factories where many women labored; without the ability to vote, male politicians could entirely ignore them and avoid suffering any electoral repercussions.

As it was, people treated Mamie's apparent interest in politics as a hilarious joke. Granted, it does not seem like Mrs. Fish would have been sufficiently diplomatic to succeed as a politician, but much of the criticism also carried with it a tinge of misogyny. What would a woman like Mrs. Fish know about politics or anything serious? critics wondered. As *The City Journal* joked, "This female fish might be pardoned for [her] opinions. They are the vaporings of a shallow brain that she cannot help. A lucky money-making husband has been able to seat her upon a pile of gold, and she—poor thing—imagines that the kowtowing of the public is all to herself instead of the gold pedestal."[17]

Mamie spent the Fish money in more ingenious ways than almost anyone else in the period. There are plenty of people in the modern era who are paid to throw parties that are nowhere near as creative as hers were back then. And, given her nearly constant stream of quips, there's little question that, if she was not book-learned, she was at least quick-witted.

Nevertheless, papers would stress, as they often do with married women today, that her only real value lay in what she contributed to her marriage. Women like Mamie were supposed to sit still, be quiet, have children, and look beautifully attired on a very thrifty budget. "Mrs. Roosevelt," *The Star* declared, "is above all things a sane woman. This means much in these latter days when all sorts of degenerate and erratic opinions are being conspicuously aired in print."[18]

Mrs. Fish may have been too outspoken by the standards of the time, but many of her opinions echoed initiatives undertaken long before and long after her. First Ladies have been advised to promote the American fashion industry since as far back as Martha Washington, who was told to wear homespun clothing rather than don pieces made in Britain. A century and a half later, during the Great Depression, Mrs. Hoover was instructed to pose in cotton dresses to help revive the cotton industry. More recently, First Ladies like Michelle Obama have made a point of sporting American designs, particularly in international settings. It's fair to debate whether this should really be a part of their "job," but Mamie was not saying anything about Edith Roosevelt that a fashion columnist wouldn't say today.

In other words, she may have been rude, but Mamie was not insane. Even so, being rude is not a terribly *helpful* quality in the long run, as Mamie was about to discover.

CHAPTER 23

*I*F YOU HAVE READ MUCH OF THIS THINKING, "I ACTUALLY DO NOT LIKE that Mamie constantly says witty but mean things to people," well, this chapter is for you. In 1906, after years of social dominance, the golden pedestal that Mrs. Fish had perched herself upon was starting to topple. And the person shaking the base? None other than railroad executive Edward Henry Harriman.

And it wasn't enough for Harriman to take down Mamie—he wanted to take her husband down with her as well.

Stuyvesant Fish had been the head of the Illinois Central Railroad since 1887. Then, in February 1907, after an unblemished twenty-year record, he was reported by E. H. Harriman, a board member of the Illinois Central Railroad, for misconduct of funds.

Harriman alleged that Stuyvesant had used the Illinois Central Railroad as a personal asset, loaning himself $1 million of its funds ($33.5 million today). *The Baltimore Sun* alleged, "When the loans were first reported, Mr. Harriman said, he smoothed over the difficulty which had arisen, and prevented action by the directors in the interest of the President, and retained him in office, but...Mr. Fish continued to act in the same line."[1] The trouble with Stuyvesant Fish, Harriman explained, "was that he looked upon the Illinois Central as his personal property."[2] Harriman also claimed that he, personally, had loaned Stuyvesant Fish an additional $1.2 million "so that he could take up various obligations." Seemingly, this was to lend credence to the idea that Stuyvesant had debts he needed to pay off, and that he was using the railroad's funds as his personal piggy bank.

Considering this perceived misconduct, E. H. Harriman decided that he had cause to oust Stuyvesant Fish as the president of the Illinois Central Railroad. However, to do so, he would need votes from the majority of the board. This would prove difficult as Stuyvesant Fish, though he may or may not have been misappropriating funds, was generally admired. It was understood that whatever his failings, he was a good head of the railroad, and he was seen as "a railroad executive of the old order, rough and ready in speech, cautious in administration, scrupulously honorable in his engagements, and completely impatient of fallacious economics."[3]

People liked Stuyvesant. But by this point, a lot of people—Edith Roosevelt included—did not like Mamie. And Harriman *despised* her.

Harriman's personal beef with Mamie started way back when Mamie invited his daughter Mary to a summer party in Newport. At the time, the Harriman daughters were trying to make their way in the "smart set."[4] To be invited to one of Mamie's parties was such an exciting honor for the young woman—so exciting that she said virtually nothing the entire time. Unimpressed, Mamie declared her to be dull and that she did not want to see her again.

Poor Mary Harriman!

Mamie didn't seem as though she was being very fair on this one. Mary was an extremely good-hearted person. She was even an *interesting* person. She founded the Junior League for the Promotion of Settlement Movement to help immigrants to the Lower East Side of New York, spending a great amount of time doing volunteer work on Rivington Street. She provided one of her boats as a place where people afflicted by consumption could go to rest. She was a capable equestrian, known for "her daring riding at horse shows," and of the five Harriman children, she was said to be her father's favorite. *The Buffalo Commercial* reported that "She shared his love of horses and cattle, his plain-spoken ways, and capacity for affairs. He took the greatest pride in her executive ability."[5] *The Salt Lake Herald-Republican* described her as being "another half of her father's heart and mind. She knew of and understood all his great projects."[6]

If she lived today, she would likely be running a very effective corporation, though the first heiress that comes to mind who was intensely involved with her family's corporation is Kathe Sackler, and that doesn't exactly bode well. (But what about Lynsi Lavelle Snyder-Ellingson! She is an heiress who runs In-N-Out, a very good burger chain that, to my knowledge, is not a force for evil in the world.) That said, Mary Harriman was not the kind of person who wanted to gossip and steal streetcars. She had been raised to be a serious person. Her mother had worked extremely hard, to the extent that she did not let Mary or any of the other children know how wealthy they were, to stop her from turning "into a frivolous social butterfly."[7] And she succeeded. Mary didn't appear to want to be a social butterfly; instead, she "insisted on going to Barnard College, to study sociology and biology."[8]

Unfortunately, rather late in the game, the Harrimans decided Mary should be a socialite in addition to being a scholar. And Mamie Fish loved funny, frivolous social butterflies. She did not care about biology. She cared a little bit about philanthropy, but nowhere near the way Mary did. She showed no interest in combatting diseases. Therefore, whatever Mary's positive qualities might have been, they were not exciting to Mamie.

After first meeting Mary and finding her boring, Mamie did not deign to invite the Harriman daughters to any of her parties. I personally think Mary would mostly have been fine with this. It's never fun when someone doesn't like you, but she really just wanted to study biology.

However, the rejection crushed the Harriman parents, "who had social ambitions." Like all other young women in New York, the path toward those goals would be advancing in society. As Mamie now reigned over that society absolutely, if she did not care for them, according to the *Daily News*, "the Harrimans' social path was blocked."[9] They could not even appeal to

Mrs. Astor. As Mamie quipped, "You know how old Mrs. Astor is? Well, she's 80. She's more than that, she's 84. The poor old lady has one foot in the grave. You think I'm her rival?"[10]

Mrs. Astor was only seventy-three when Mrs. Fish made this pronouncement and was presumably not thrilled to be described as nearly dead. But the bigger point to be made here is that Mamie was now wildly overconfident about her position. She was used to being fawned over and idolized, but she was *also* not nearly as universally liked as she imagined. Mrs. Astor certainly didn't approve of her. As Mamie was having wild parties, Mrs. Astor lamented that there was now "no society worthwhile" and that "society is a circus." *The Buffalo Sunday Morning News* mourned that Mrs. Astor's one goal was to "maintain the dignity of social life" and that all of Mamie and Harry Lehr's mayhem had begun "the minute her governing hand was withdrawn."[11]

They did not mention the people crying at her parties or the orgies on her husband's yacht, which, frankly, always sounded more fun.

Mr. Harriman might have been furious at Mamie, but he was not motivated to go to war with Stuyvesant simply because of his dislike for her. He was also known to be a wildly ambitious man in his own right. *The Wall Street Journal* declared, "Harriman's ambition was not only to be arbiter of the American railroad field, as much as a private citizen could be arbiter, but to have a railroad around the world."[12] And he was stymied, in some of his ambition, by figures like Stuyvesant Fish.

Harriman knew that his distaste for Mrs. Fish following her dismissal of his absolute favorite child would capture more sympathy and support than revealing his personal ambitions. As such, he went to the homes of the railroad's board members not to talk to the men, but to sit and drink tea with their wives. This was an incredibly smart move. "Harriman, it is alleged, talked pleasantly to the ladies, and induced them to get their husbands to vote against [Stuyvesant Fish] in order to weaken the struggle of Mrs. Fish for society's leadership."[13] Thanks to their father's clever social maneuvering and manipulation, "the Harriman daughters had their revenge."[14] Harriman even sniffed that he had to take action in part because "the Illinois Central was too big a business to be run from a 'cottage' in Newport."[15]

As the vote was announced, New York buzzed with anticipation. *The Billings Gazette* noted, "To the average New Yorker, money is the only thing worth thinking or talking about, and when the Fish and the Harrimans and the Vanderbilts quarrel among themselves over the division of the spoils, New York looks on in reverent awe."[16] All through town, "the clerks in the financial district and even the stenographers and messenger boys have taken sides in the controversy and discuss the matter among themselves, as if their own millions were at stake."[17]

In the end, Stuyvesant lost the vote.

He did not take his ejection well. In one notable rumpus in August 1907, he proceeded to physically attack James T. Harahan, the new president of the railroad. For sixteen years, Harahan had been the vice president in charge of operations of the Illinois Railroad. He was a natural choice for a successor, though Stuyvesant Fish felt he was merely Harriman's puppet. The altercation garnered a lot of attention, but it was not, as was initially reported, the case that Stuyvesant hit him. Instead, a correction was issued that "he merely clutched Mr. Harahan's throat in the grip of his left hand, throttling the President of the Illinois Central till he began to turn blue in the face" at which point he began "to shake him like a terrier worrying a rat."[18]

That's worse!

Trying to choke someone to death is *much worse* than hitting someone!

Unfortunately for Stuyvesant, the incident was witnessed by many of the railroad's board members, including Cornelius Vanderbilt, who tried to calm the men, and Robert Goelet, who ran out of the room as soon as the fight started. None of the other board members intervened, which makes you wonder how fond they were of Mr. Harahan. Afterward, when he had calmed down, Mr. Fish "picked up his hat, nodded pleasantly to the others, and left the room without saying a word."[19] Harahan went immediately to a lawyer but never actually pressed any charges.

It's difficult to say whether Stuyvesant Fish was guilty of financial misconduct, but it does seem reasonable that the head of a railway corporation should *not* try to choke his rivals to death, no matter how upset he is.

But remember "kid scraps"? This was a time when people were extremely okay with acts of violence among men. If anything, they were *happy* about how Stuyvesant behaved. People found it scrappy and charming.

The next day, after what now might be considered attempted murder, the *Los Angeles Times* wrote that "Mr. Fish was in the best of humor. His telephone was busy all day with friends congratulating him and asking him how he whipped Mr. Harahan. Some wanted him to let them know, it was said, when he intended to 'give Mr. Harriman a whirl.'" He had a stack of congratulatory notes from friends littering his desk. He cheerfully declared, "There is more than one way of skinning a skunk" to the reporter.[20]

This might be an understandable reaction if the well-wishers had still wanted to enjoy the social perks of being friends with the Fish. That wasn't the case, though. They just appreciated the violence in and of itself. However, while Stuyvesant came out of the scandal with his reputation intact (if not, in some ways, enhanced), Mamie did not.

For it was Mrs. Fish who was blamed for her husband's professional downfall.

When Stuyvesant was ousted from the board, it was commonly understood that Mamie's "social dictatorship [was] credited with her husband's loss of the presidency."[21]

How quickly you can go from being considered a queen to being viewed as a dictator.

Newspapers argued that "had Mrs. Fish only consented to recognize the daughters of Mr. Harriman, Stuyvesant Fish would still be the head of the big railroad to which he gave the best years of his life."[22] The problem was simply that Mamie had not been nice and had not played by the arbitrary rules and expectations as set for her by society. Never mind that having an exclusive clique of sufficiently prestigious people that others wish to belong to *necessitates* excluding some people. Apparently, Mamie should have found a way to do the impossible: Be exclusive while also remaining entirely welcoming. People who had long dismissed Mamie's parties as entirely frivolous now believed they were so important that they could determine who ran a corporate empire.

Mamie's pedestal was tipping precipitously. Immediately after Stuyvesant's ouster, she hosted a dinner. She wanted to see if the same people who had so reliably flocked to her table in the past would still attend her soirees. And so, she sent invitations to all of New York's great names for a dinner that would be every bit as fun and creative as those of the past.

But for the first time in years, many of these great names were otherwise engaged. As one attendee noted, "Society's biggest people were absent, and conspicuously so. No representatives of the Astors or the Vanderbilts graced the board. Harriman's power was never more strikingly illustrated than by this dinner of Mrs. Fish's. . . . He had his full revenge over Mrs. Fish. Mrs. Fish will never be the society leader of the city."[23]

Meanwhile, Mrs. Harriman was planning "the first step in her social campaign": the construction of a $2 million mansion that would stand directly opposite the Vanderbilt mansion. In April 1907, it was reported that Mrs. Harriman was also (unsurprisingly) eager to purchase a Newport mansion. Until this point, *The Province* declared, "she had always had entrees into the inner circles of the Four Hundred, but she has never figured as a social leader." However, they now felt that "by right of birth, breeding and wealth Mrs. Harriman is well qualified to queen it in society."[24]

Not to spoil things, but Mrs. Harriman had no discernable qualities that would make her excel in this position beyond "a clever and wealthy husband." There were reporters who may have thought that was all it took, but they were about to be extremely disappointed.

CHAPTER 24

$\mathscr{F}$OR A MOMENT, IT SEEMED THAT MRS. FISH HAD FINALLY BEEN pushed off her throne. But those people didn't know Mamie, who was actually sitting at her home in Newport, quietly seething. Mrs. Harriman and her dull daughters would *never* usurp her.

By August 1907, six months after her less-successful-than-usual dinner, Mamie started plotting her return to social eminence. Townspeople speculated whether she would stage a giant ball, even more lavish than those she had in the past. Or perhaps it would be another theatrical entertainment. Whatever the event, it was bound to be spectacular. Her friends claimed that "all the social strategy that can be brought to bear will be used in 'getting even' for the deal in Illinois Central."[1]

In due time, Mamie would regain her place in society not, as she usually did, through the power of entertainment, but through straight-up aristocratic power. For a woman who up until this point had mocked and decried how in thrall to royalty Americans were, it's depressing that she had to resort to this. But she also knew that Americans *were* in thrall to royalty. And as it happened, in August 1907, Prince Wilhelm of Sweden was visiting

Newport, where he would meet President Roosevelt on his cruiser. Mamie Fish invited him to be her esteemed guest. It was a move not so different from when Mrs. Goelet had entertained Grand Duke Boris at her own home five years earlier. Mary Harriman was not going to get to swan about while Mamie entertained an actual prince.

However, Prince Wilhelm was not as giddy and decadent as Grand Duke Boris. He did not drink spirits from the shoes of showgirls during his visit to America. Indeed, there would be no showgirls at all. Prince Wilhelm was already engaged to the Grand Duchess Maria of Russia, a woman described as "unusually pretty for a princess" considering that "the average woman of royal blood is ugly enough to cause the collapse of a scarecrow in a Kansas cornfield."[2]

Heartbreaking that Mamie herself could no longer make these kinds of mean-spirited jabs.

This meant that, unlike Grand Duke Boris, Newport's young socialites would not be vying over him. Nor did William learn how to play poker and lose tens of thousands of dollars on the trip. Instead, the lanky twenty-three-year-old prince was "so anxious to acquire the right American accent and to be conversant with American expressions that for months he has been conversing daily with a well-known teacher of languages."[3] When he finally landed stateside, the prince impressed the Americans as being "a very democratic and good-natured fellow."[4] During his visit to Newport, he attended Methodist church services and chatted with people at the tennis club about the game's growing popularity in Sweden. He also found time to complain bitterly about an $800 dentist bill, which does seem very high. His accessibility and humility bode well for his country's reputation in the foreign press, as American journalists reported that "the Swedish kings and princes have discarded the pomp of royalty as far as possible and live like a cultivated professional family."[5]

His stay also meant that Mamie controlled access to the prince and was able to determine who could meet him or not. She took pleasure in crossing Mrs. Vanderbilt's name off the list, as Cornelius Vanderbilt had supported Harriman. So, too, had Robert Goelet. As such, Mrs. Goelet was "left off the invitation list, although she had been presented at the court of Sweden, knows the royal family, and has frequently visited [them] in Sweden"[6] in a slight that surprised nearly everyone. The *Los Angeles Herald* remarked that "the visit to Newport of a titled foreigner and the Goelet and Vanderbilt villas dark will be something really unique in the social history of the United States."[7] *The Boston Globe* chimed in that the prince would be entertained "in part by descendants of the kin of old Peter Stuyvesant, who destroyed the transient connection of Sweden with the colonial history of the United States by driving the Swedish colonists out of the country in the middle of the seventeenth century."[8]

Mamie, in her all-American house with her all-American parties, surely must have gritted her teeth a bit through having to fawn before the Prince of Sweden. But she also knew it would be worth it.

When it came time for Mamie to host the dinner welcoming the prince to his five-day stay in Newport, she was uncharacteristically serious about it. No subtle, witty jabs at anyone. No *actual* jabs at anyone. No monkeys. Everything would be done in a style of which Mrs. Astor would have approved, showing the Fish to be people of civilized elegance. Only one hundred guests were invited to meet the prince at her estate. As they walked into Crossways, they saw the lawn "brilliantly illuminated and its path outlined with butterfly lantern cups, [while] the Casino orchestra played the Swedish anthem."[9] The tables were festooned with blue hydrangeas and yellow orchids, while the allamandas were crafted to resemble the prince's coat of arms. *The Boston Globe* noted that "if there had been anything more expensive in the way of flowers to be had, no doubt Mrs. Fish would have procured it."[10]

Mrs. Fish received the prince and his entourage with a few sentences in Swedish, a language she had been studying with a tutor precisely for the occasion. We do not know what she said, but the prince replied in English. The dinner was fairly subdued, possibly because the prince, unlike the monkey Jocko, was abstemious and requested everyone entertaining him "not to introduce highballs or champagne at functions at which he is invited."[11] Following the dinner, the prince and Mrs. Fish drove together to a dance being hosted at coal baron Edward Julius Berwind's home, The Elms, and shared the first dance of the evening.

It's unclear what Stuyvesant was doing throughout this. It's possible that he was in his library thinking about how fun it was to hit people.

The dinner was widely considered an absolute victory for Mamie. *The Washington Post* went so far as to call it a victory for America, writing that "the selection of the guests, the faultless gowns of the women, the decorations, the menu belong in the category not only of epicurean but of social triumphs which have given us claim to distinction in that fine art of higher civilization—successful dinner giving."[12] It also sounds like one of the duller, less inventive parties Mamie ever gave. No dogs! No mice released to terrorize everyone! Not even a costume or a fun party favor. However, it was just the kind of respectable, traditional party that Mamie needed to have to dig herself out of social exile, and the public respected her for it.

Whether Prince Wilhelm himself enjoyed this dinner is more questionable. He was not seen as being impressed by all the pomp, including the extremely expensive flowers Mamie procured. One paper noted that given his democratic tastes, "Prince Wilhelm would much prefer a basket of sandwiches, a fish pole, some bait and the glorious privilege of being independent enough to sit on a pier and fish."[13] Maybe! But the party was never *really* about Prince Wilhelm. It was about Mrs. Fish and celebrating her return to the upper echelon of society.

It worked.

By 1908, a year after her husband's very public fall from grace and a lifetime after insulting everyone in her vicinity, *The Journal* gushed, "All the big social leaders of New York's society have been unfailing in their tact and smooth temper. Mrs. Astor always could be depended upon to do the right thing at the right moment...Mrs. Stuyvesant Fish is almost equally the mistress of herself."[14]

I want to shake the writer of this statement, Stuyvesant Fish style, and say, "What the hell are you talking about?" Mamie Fish was 1,000 percent a streetcar-stealing lunatic who ran over a man three times in a single outing. People are not necessarily stoic and calm just because they're rich and powerful. They can be rich and powerful and also be extremely not in control of themselves.

And so it was that the wild, raucous woman known for wreaking general havoc on civil society threw a single pro-Swedish, pro-royal dinner party that wiped any and all of her errors from everyone's mind. For a citizenry that overthrew a king, Americans certainly did—and do—love princes. It is truly an inspiration for everyone who has been a relentless jerk throughout their life, provided, of course, that you can find a Swedish prince to invite to dinner.

CHAPTER 25

SOCIETY WAS RATHER SHOCKED WHEN, IN FEBRUARY 1913, MAMIE FISH announced that she would be supporting the female garment workers of New York in their strike.

Conditions for garment workers were brutal. In a city where the minimum standard of living was nine dollars a week, the female garment workers producing "white goods" like lingerie were only making between four to six dollars a week for a minimum of twelve hours a day working (the equivalent of around $1.50 an hour today). Their wages were often reduced if they arrived even a few minutes late. They hoped to establish a forty-eight-hour workweek, with time and a half for overtime and a wage increase of 20 percent. The workers had been striking for nearly two months with little headway made in their requests for increased pay. The newspaper headlines echoed the surprise of the city when they blared, "This dictatress of the society of New York and Newport has taken up the cause of the striking girl garment makers in New York and will make an investigation with a view to aiding the strikers."[1]

When Mamie saw the conditions under which the women were laboring, she was horrified. She told the *Oakland Tribune*, "Today in the bitter cold weather I saw girls—pretty faced, bright-minded young things, with nothing on but their outer garments. No warm flannels, no underskirts. It's a sin against human nature and future motherhood that these girls are obliged to freeze and starve."[2]

Many of those girls on strike were as young as age fourteen. The journalist Mary Boyle O'Reilly reported that the strike was led by women very much like those Mrs. Fish saw, women "childlike in appearance, or gaunt from the chronic overstrain that gives no time to make flesh, these girls, most of them only two or three years in this country, have learned that they cannot live on the wage to earn which they have given—are giving—their youth."[3] The conditions were so grotesque that garment workers suggested it might be better to be imprisoned than work at the garment factories, because in prison, at least they'd be given bread for free.[4]

More than ten thousand workers would ultimately go on strike, forming angry and overworked mobs. On February 7, 1913, a bomb designed to damage the factories exploded in Williamsburg, Brooklyn. The Associated Press declared that "the explosion wrecked the front of the building and precipitated a panic."[5] The mob subsequently beat a police sergeant and five patrolmen. In retaliation, employers hired strikebreakers to "hammer the crowd."[6] The very young, extremely underfed women were said to "have fought as fiercely as the men."[7] Seven people were arrested, two of whom were girls aged fifteen and sixteen.

Mamie demanded to speak directly with the strikers, doing so the same night that the bomb exploded. Accompanied by social worker and labor organizer Ms. Gertrude Barnum, who was leading the strike, Mamie went to a meeting at Odd Fellows Hall in St. Mark's Square. Ms. Barnum had come from an upper-class family herself (though she had no relation to P. T. Barnum, her father was a successful lawyer), and she introduced Mamie to the strikers, explaining that she was there to support their cause. They received her with great excitement. "The skinny, shabby girls half curtsied when they saw her magnificence step onstage," claimed the

Morning News.[8] The workers rushed to the front seats to get a better view of the socialite who, until this moment, had only been known for her extreme frivolity.

"I am not a socialist or a suffragette," Mamie informed them. "But I sympathize with the cause you are on strike for." She told them that she did not see how the women could live on less than seven dollars a week. A man from the crowd reporting on the event shouted, "How could a *man* support himself and his family on $7 a week?" Mamie fixed a withering glare on him and replied, "I am not thinking of the men now." At this, "the girls cheered, and the mere man said no more."[9]

She continued, "I think you are fighting a just fight and I believe you will win. Anything I can do to bring your conditions before the public, as they should be brought, I will do."[10] Mamie then told the strikers that she had arranged to receive donations for their cause at her home and walked into the audience to talk to the girls. One sixteen-year-old explained to Mamie that she had started work at thirteen, for three dollars a week. She now made seven dollars but had to use it to support her sister and mother. Their carfare and rent alone cost $3.50 a week. Another sixteen-year-old explained to Mrs. Fish that she was only paid $4.50 a week and could not pay her rent since the strike. Mrs. Fish asked to see their living accommodations, giving them a ride in her automobile. There, "she had difficulty in keeping from stumbling while groping her way up the stairs."[11] The dilapidated tenements were so different a world from the glamorous one Mrs. Fish inhabited just miles away. The girls returned to the assembly talking about their exciting car ride, and Mrs. Fish told them to keep up their good spirits because people would be on their side.

Alas, it seems she spoke too soon. In the days to come, even Mrs. Fish would not remain entirely on the young women's side.

Her brief foray into politics was shaken the moment that the president of the New York Association of House Dress and Kimono Manufacturers came to visit her. As he sat in her elegant Fifth Avenue home, he informed Mamie that "he feared that Mrs. Fish had not been told that the manufacturers already had promised an increase in wages to their employees" and that "her influence might unjustly harm their interests and prevent an early settlement of the strike."[12]

Concerned, and admitting that she knew very little about the complex garment industry, Mamie announced to *The New York Times* that "the union and manufacturers would have to settle their difficulties without any interference on her part."[13]

If only she had exercised a bit of the sass she reserved for social interactions here.

That resolve lasted for about a day.

The president left her a copy of the protocols they planned to adopt regarding their workers. When he initially showed them to her, Mrs. Fish agreed with him that it seemed fair. That protocol, regrettably, promised workers an increase of not less than fifty cents but not more than one dollar a week. Given that the cost of living was nine dollars a week, it would *still* not be enough for the workers to survive. Mamie Fish was always clear that she was not much of a reader, but this was very simple math. Maybe the president was speaking too rapidly and she didn't have time to really take in what he was saying.

Later on, once a man was no longer hovering over her head, Mamie looked at the numbers again. When some of the garment workers pointed out the discrepancy, she agreed, exclaiming, "I am opposed to that." She told *The New York Times*, "I think no girl ought to be asked to work for less than $7 or even $8 a week. We ought to have a minimum wage law, and the only solution I can see for this recurrent strike problem is the enactment of such a law." She finally recognized that the difficulties between the strikers and their employers would ultimately have to be worked out by the union, but she wanted people to know that "I feel sorry for the poor girls who must work for less than a living wage, and that my sympathies are only with those girls."[14]

The New York Times noted that she was in a minority here, and that Mrs. Fish's social set did not appear overly inclined to help fund the girls' cause; by and large, their appeals "had not been met with a generous response."[15]

Mrs. Fish found this lack of support unacceptable. Fortunately, forcing people to fork over their money was something that she knew how to do.

If people wanted to be invited to her parties and have her introduce them to influential people, they needed, in turn, to support her cause. This is still perhaps the greatest influence socialites can have in any age. If you are a person with social power, you can use it to make your friends support people that they would never normally interact with.

By February 13, mere days after the bombing, journalists declared that there had been a change in sentiments among the Four Hundred as "Mrs. Fish served notice today on her wealthy friends that she was ready to distribute donations of money to the striking girls." She proceeded to inform the newspapers that the strikers were being held back in part because of "the rich element who do not care how the poor get along" and "the snobbishness of rich people."[16]

For someone who spent most of her life throwing parties that explicitly catered to the über rich, Mamie Fish had never really displayed an overabundance of affection for people of her own class. She empathized with the struggling women instead, insisting to newspapers that "Working girls [would be] happier than wealthy women, if they only had a chance to earn a livelihood." "Happier" is debatable; these women were working twelve- to fourteen-hour days, which was a fearfully demanding schedule by even modern standards. By contrast, wealthy women were dancing the night away at galas and waking up at 10:00 a.m. to put on gowns these women had labored over. However, Mrs. Fish did maintain a hint of her trademark sense of humor about the whole situation, joking the girls were still better off simply because they didn't have to deal with "boresome society people." As Mrs. Fish lamented, "I sometimes think I will have to do all the talking for my guests, they are so bored they dislike even speaking."[17]

This *may* have been a questionably timed joke. However, newspapers certainly did not understand she was joking.

In fact, Mamie appeared to be much nicer to the striking women than to most of the people at her own parties, whom she greeted by dismissively noting that they had "older faces, younger clothes" with each passing year. A photo taken of Mamie later that year stated, "She is perhaps the most prominent society leader in the United States" and that "no photograph of her ever taken perhaps better illustrates her mental attitude towards the world than this."[18] In the picture, Mrs. Fish is glowering to an almost cartoonish extent. Her eyebrows are raised in a position that is both skeptical and despairing. She doesn't look mad at you; she looks *disappointed in you*.

The more interest she took in the outside world, the more irritated she seemed by the world she dominated.

And yet, society fell in line. Shortly after being called out by Mamie Fish, the United Press Association announced that "a score of wealthy women today visited the hall where the striking garment workers held their daily meetings."[19] They promised both financial and moral support, and then proceeded to picket alongside the working girls. "The sight of the beautifully gowned women walking arm in arm with girl strikers drew large crowds, but, ignoring the jibes of the bystanders, they continued on their work."[20] While they were picketing, one girl fainted. She was rushed to the hospital by the society women, where doctors informed them that the girl—who'd been living off a four-dollar weekly salary before the strike—was dying of starvation.

Ms. Barnum, the strike leader, was not as impressed by the society ladies' help as some journalists. In addition to feeling that Mrs. Fish had turned the cause into too much of a spectacle, she argued, "These girls have paid the whole cost for what is sure to be a great social gain. Surely the so-called leisure class of society should carry on the fight now that the resources of the girls are exhausted. This is not philanthropy, but tardy justice. Society is in disgrace for its apathy under conditions which threaten the very lives of the future mothers of the race. It has been left to little girls to make a fight on our streets against the sweatshops. The leisure class should not be outdone by the workers in courage and self-sacrifice."[21]

Society ladies, in Ms. Barnum's eyes, were doing the bare minimum of human decency.

However, there's just one problem with taking the morally correct position: Picketing is miserable. There are no circumstances under which it is fun. Nowadays, you walk in a circle, frequently in unpleasant weather conditions, talking to people you don't know. But back then, women were doing all that *while* other people were physically attacking them or yelling and laughing at them. There were *bombs*. And of course, it's very hard to convince people to participate in your cause under those conditions unless there is something that directly benefits *them*.

In a utopian world, the fortunate would support the less fortunate because it's the right thing to do, as Ms. Barnum suggested. But in the real world, they needed an incentive.

So Mamie Fish gave it to them.

By February 27, the Ladies Garment Workers Union had won their strike. Forty manufacturers agreed to the women's demands. And New York burst into song—literally. *The Wichita American* newspaper reported, "Pianos which have been stored in the meeting houses against rare occasions of use have been opened and are being played by girls, while men and women join with lusty voices in choruses of popular songs."[22]

There is certainly a limit as to how much credit Mrs. Fish should get for this happy resolution. The bulk of the credit should go to the collapsing fourteen-year-olds marching in the cold so they could better feed their families. Mrs. Fish's help was useful but, at times, wavering.

Still, Ms. Barnum's conviction that she did the movement a disservice by better publicizing it doesn't exactly seem correct either. Publicity—especially when it gets you money—is generally good for causes. There's no denying that Mrs. Fish used her own notoriety and position in society to shine a light on a cause she found worthy of such illumination. Even newspapers as far away as Peru reported on Mrs. Fish's interest in the strike, which brought it international attention and increased the pressure to end it faced by higher-ups in the industry.

Nonetheless, Mamie still emerged from the process somewhat downhearted. Though she had at last fulfilled her promise to enter the political realm, and helped secure a great outcome, her help was not appreciated—and her efforts were merely dismissed as a rich woman's posturing.

The woman who did receive good publicity regarding the seamstress strike? Alva Vanderbilt, who claimed that those working girls were her inspiration as an advocate for a woman's right to vote. When *The Montgomery*

Advertiser asked Alva why she took up women's suffrage as her personal cause, opening her estate in 1909 for suffrage symposiums, she explained, "I came of a race who believed in justice. Yet I never went into it so enthusiastically until some years ago when 30,000 girls in the shirt waist factories struck. The conditions under which they worked were awful." She went on to point out that the mayor had no time to meet with those girls because "30,000 girls had not a single vote to give. It is not what women are going to do with the ballot, it is what the ballot will do for the women."[23] It may have hurt Mamie's feelings when Alva, who was being extensively praised for her commitment to the fight, continued, sighing to *The Mongomery Advertiser* that "Of course, the women who have everything they want, do not think much of the needs of these working girls, for if they did they would cry out with one accord for the ballot."[24]

Mamie could not help but feel that she might get some credit for her efforts, and at least her organizational skills, even if she was not a suffragette. But no, everyone rushed to praise Alva Vanderbilt instead.

So, in a very abrupt and spiteful 180-degree turn, Mamie, who had never been a suffragette, decided to come out against women's right to vote. *Hard.*

As always, she would express her stance the only way she knew how: by throwing a party. The 1913 Mother Goose Ball celebrated traditional gender roles. Lest this feel like an unfair attribute to apply to Mother Goose, Mamie made it clear that her ball was an anti-suffrage celebration. She explained that she had chosen the theme because "Mother Goose was a real woman and a real mother with the love of children before anything else."[25]

There are logical flaws with this statement. First and foremost, it bears mentioning that Mother Goose was and is not "a real woman." She's a made-up figure who wears a fun witch's hat in a storybook in which she is often seen *riding a goose.*

Even from the get-go, people were skeptical that Mamie was truly invested in the anti-suffrage cause. "Instead of being looked on as a rebuke to suffragists," stated *The Evening Journal,* "it is viewed by thousands of persons as merely another bid by Mrs. Fish for the position of social arbiter in

New York, in which she has a much more acute interest than in the suffrage question."[26]

This is possible! If Alva Vanderbilt was seen as a wealthy woman invested in progressive causes, then that admirable spot was already taken. If the newspapers needed a socialite to talk about women's rights, they would go to Alva. Mamie likely fancied that by taking the opposite position, she could at least become the darling of conservatives.

The Mother Goose Ball had a special poem written for it, distributed to all the guests, which read:

> *She Never Tried to mold the world*
> *(That Problem superhuman)*
> *She never had a higher aim*
> *Than just to be a woman...*
> *So to her name let praise be sung*
> *More precious than all other*
> *Oh, listen, down the centuries*
> *The Children call her mother.*[27]

Perhaps the most ironic twist of all: Mamie Fish was not particularly renowned for her maternal qualities! Indeed, she had higher—or at least different—aims, and she often dismissed women who were known for their maternal qualities, like Edith Roosevelt, as uninteresting. (Though, admittedly, Mamie dismissed a lot of women who did not share her precise temperament as uninteresting.) Also, she had just finished working to fund and support a large strike *organized by and for women*. Still, Mamie Fish exclaimed, "Suffragettes! I detest them, and my ball is given as a protest to the woman who wants the ballot instead of the things she was created for.... We have too much of sex and suffrage. We have too little of the children, and the word 'mother' sounds old fashioned and prosaic to the growing generation."[28] Mamie's implication here is clearly that a woman's purpose was to bear and tend to her children and provide them with a sense of magic and whimsy.

But Mamie Fish *herself* never actually did this.

Yes, she loved her children—and she certainly spent more time with them than some of the other society ladies at the time—but by and large, her days did not revolve around the needs or desires of her children. She probably spent as much time with them as many working mothers do, but by that logic, her parties and entertainments were her job.

Most suffragettes also had children, and one of the reasons they wanted the right to vote in the first place was to secure them with better schooling and other provisions. A popular postcard from 1915 depicted a group of cartoon babies toddling around while carrying signs that read "Votes for our mothers!"[29] Suffragettes regularly marched with their strollers in parades, both because they were their children's caretakers and because it provided a visual reminder to the general public about their greater goals. The responsibilities of motherhood were at the heart of the suffragette cause.

Mamie either did not know this or refused to acknowledge it. She again declared that her reason "for giving my party is to get back a bit to the good old-fashioned standards of life, which in women must bring them the joy of motherhood and childhood. Mother Goose may help do it, and goodness knows we modern women need help."[30]

After some time, though, Mamie grew bored of the subject. "I have been tired for months of the continual and ceaseless cry of sex and suffrage. Votes for women and the problems of sex have been growing topics of both men and women. I am tired of both."[31]

It bears note that, in 1913, the position that women should focus on motherhood rather than the vote was, generally, unfashionable—even in Mamie's circles. There *were* those who strongly opposed suffrage—for example, saloon and brewery owners were correctly concerned that women would vote to prohibit the purchase of liquor—but these were not generally people Mamie knew. Basically, no one cool was on Mamie's side. Other wealthy women were supporting the movement. And if their husbands were anti-suffrage, they were at least smart enough to stay quiet about it—whether they agreed or not.

After that Mother Goose Ball–inspired poem ran, middle-of-the-road newspapers started publishing choppy, Rudyard Kipling–inspired poems like:

They are hanging Anti-Suffrage
with a judgement calm and cool
For she blocked the path of progress
With her ancient, moss-grown rule.[32]

Remember, too, that Mamie's annoyance also stemmed from a simple desire to have a fun, frivolous time. In a period dominated by politics and the looming threat of war, Mamie told reporters that "in sheer desperation I picked up Mother Goose's melodies from out of my library one day this summer and decided I, too, was getting too morbid and material. I read the jingles until I felt the old fresh enthusiasm coming back. I felt young, and I felt as a child."[33]

Mamie was now sixty years old. Sometimes, people wish to keep everything the way it was in their youth because it allows them to convince themselves they are still young. Her circle may have disagreed with her regarding the right to vote. But they could certainly understand wanting to have fun at a time when the rest of the world seemed very serious indeed.

And so, Newport readied for the ball with almost feverish enthusiasm. As soon as the invitations were received, women rushed to their dressmakers, eager to create the most sumptuous costume. Every woman wanted to be the best-dressed person in fairyland, and these attendees spent approximately $3,000 per person on their gowns and accessories (approximately $88,000 today). All in all, the jewelry worn by these women was appraised at $12 million.

As automobiles rolled up the path to Crossways, they saw the entire lawn covered with "fairy lanterns" hung from bamboo poles. Every bush and tree was covered with tiny lights, with ten thousand lights in the garden alone. It was said to be like "every child's library come to life." One attendee remarked in astonishment that "nothing so quaintly beautiful and fairy-like has ever been seen here before."[34]

Mamie, ever the hostess, appeared dressed as the Queen of the Fairies, "a coronet of diamonds glittered in her coiffeur,"[35] and in her hand, she held a crystal wand that contained an electric bulb she could click on and off, the dream of every child who goes to Disneyland. Her gown was simply spectacular; the "white satin was covered with a cloud of silver spangled net, the shining drapery falling to the end of her court train." Geese roosted on the balconies, while a sculpture of a giant witch riding a goose hung in the hallway. In the ballroom, "scores of flying black cats, with glittering electric eyes, poked their whiskered noses from towering sheaves of wheat or climbed or perched upon the yellow frogs, and similarly gigantic green frogs with iridescent eyes, croaked amid groves of cattails."

If Mrs. Fish had not fully embraced the progressive political times, she had at least welcomed the idea that everything should be electric.

Mrs. Fish introduced various characters like Little Bo Peep, Jack and Jill, and Jack Horner who all danced a quadrille for the guests before falling back "to reveal a witch with her cauldron working with her little devils and casting her evil charms."[36] This may have been a reference to the suffragettes, or it might just have been a fun witch!

Mrs. Goelet had apparently been forgiven at last for her husband's role in the professional downfall of Stuyvesant Fish. She was invited to the ball, along with her husband, and led a live lamb around the ballroom in a tribute to Mary (who had a little lamb). Other guests dressed to the nines as well, though with less impressive props. Mrs. T. Suffern Tailer (Harriet) took to the floor as Miss Muffet in a rose-colored satin and chiffon gown overlayed with a white apron, carrying a bowl of curds (an essential prop, although it seems it might be remarkably unpleasant to ferry about throughout the evening). Mrs. Francis Clark, dressed in white satin covered with crystals, was Goldilocks, with her hair—or an artful wig—braided and hanging down past her knees. Mrs. Fish had even invited men from the nearby naval training academy to help fill out the party; thirty showed up in formal uniforms and "added much to the picturesqueness of the affair."[37] Kind of sad that they did not have costumes, but there are definitely Mother Goose poems about sailors.

The evening concluded with a "dance of the fairies." At its end, balloons rained down on the dancers from every corner of the ballroom. Then, it was announced that "Bluebeard, Jr."—a fictional man famed for killing his many brides—would be presented, and the lights were shut off while tango music played. Spooky *and* sexy.

The whole effect was magical. A reporter at the party mused in *The Morning Journal* that "nothing so quaintly beautiful and fairylike has ever been seen here before."[38]

And no one enjoyed the evening more than Mrs. Fish. "It is good to become like children once in a while," she said. "It is like sweeping the cobwebs off a dark and gloomy ceiling."[39] At the age of sixty, she was once again front-page news, the Fairy Queen spoken about through all the land. As Mrs. Fish gazed out on the party and the great windows overlooking her hydrangea garden where tiny fairy lights twinkled, she gave an uncharacteristically content sigh. She turned to a reporter and said, "My illusion is complete—I would that it could remain always."[40]

But sadly, that was not how the world really was. It was only an illusion, and people were increasingly aware of that.

The times had, yet again, changed by 1913. A war was looming. Social unrest was high. People were expected to pay attention to important issues of the day, not to revert to childhood in a Little Bo Peep costume. One paper wrote of the ball, "Mrs. Fish's Mother Goose Ball made a great hit. A great big fortune went up in all that good time—that dress show, that jewel display, that night of hilarity.... Down in New York City, just a little way from gay Newport, a score of more babies died the night of the Mother Goose ball—died in hell heated tenements, died because there was no money to buy them proper food."[41] The article estimated that the life of a baby could be saved for as little as ten dollars. They did not, admittedly, say how ten dollars could be used to save a baby. And back then, as it still is today, it's very, very hard to convince people to spend their money on strangers rather than on items or experiences that might bring them personal pleasure.

That is why it is useful to have people like Alva Vanderbilt or Mamie Fish threaten to withhold fellow rich folks' pleasure unless they contribute to worthy causes. Though to be able to do that, you first have to create some really pleasurable events that they'd want to attend.

These criticisms did not stop people in the rest of the country from copying Mamie's idea and imitating the ball, even if on a smaller scale. *The Knoxville News-Sentinel* reported, some months later, that their Girls Cotillion Club threw its own "Mother Goose Ball," which was said to be "one of the most fascinating [parties] that Nashville Society has enjoyed for some time."[42] The costumes were about the same—Snow White, Cinderella, and Little Miss Muffet were all in attendance—just without the astronomical price tags.

Mamie initially said that she intended for this party to help people forget "the sordid matter-of-fact business of the world." But, as any of the many naval officers in attendance could have told her, the unvarnished business of the world was not going to be kept from Americans much longer.

CHAPTER 26

*B*Y 1914, EUROPE WAS OFFICIALLY AT WAR. DISCUSSIONS OF SOCIAL-ites' tiffs had been replaced by Newport's newspapers running explanations on "Who's Who in Europe's War," complete with detailed illustrations of various dignitaries (perhaps out of an assumption that you'd want to say hello if you happened to bump into them). And while America would not officially enter World War I until 1917, the fashion industry was deeply impacted by the global divide. Those concerns Mamie Fish expressed in 1903 that "in dress the American woman imitates Europe too much" and that women in America were not "wearing gowns of domestic make"[1] seemed almost prophetic in retrospect.

France was hit the hardest as far as fashion was concerned. Male designers in Paris were no longer creating gowns because they were now in the army. Edna Woolman Chase was the American editor in chief of *Vogue* magazine. It had been founded in 1892 and quickly established itself as a must-read for the socialites in New York, who looked to it for their fashion advice. When she visited Paris in 1914, she found that the "sense of mourning and hopelessness was seeping through the country like a sickness."[2] This was (and still is) a very normal response to a war tearing families and loved ones apart. It was also very bad news for Edna, who had traveled to Paris to report on the new fashions and found...nothing. The department store Wanamaker's ran a report from their buyer that recounted his despair in Paris. "What shall I do?...Have I come three thousand miles for nothing? Shall America have no Paris fashions this autumn? We shall see!"[3]

The prospects appeared bleak. When one woman wondered aloud to a wounded soldier what fashions people would be wearing in the spring, he solemnly replied, "Mourning, Madame. Mourning."[4]

Edna Chase claimed that on her trip to Paris, "I went to the beautiful atelier of Paul Poiret. He was in the blue and scarlet uniform of the French infantry, surrounded by a crowd of weeping women, his devoted helpers. 'I am going to join my regiment' he said calmly, 'an artist is nothing when a soldier is wanted. France needs men today, not artists.'"

To this very patriotic sentiment, Edna stubbornly replied, "But you have nothing ready? No models that I may show to America?"[5]

Oh, Edna. He was going off to war, possibly to *die*. But that clearly did not stop her from focusing on the most pressing priorities at hand: getting clothes to illustrate in the magazine.

It is a shame that Poiret and his sobbing seamstresses could not live long enough to see the cinematic marvel that is *The Devil Wears Prada*.

Rather miserably, Edna returned stateside in defeat because the European designers did, indeed, have nothing ready. However, shortly after, while riding a bus along Fifth Avenue in Manhattan, a stroke of genius occurred to her. Edna suggested that Parisian designers might each make a single piece for a "fashion fete" in New York, which would be worn by models in front of an audience. People could buy tickets to the event, and the proceeds would go to the Committee of Mercy, an organization that aided war widows and orphans. And perhaps most important from Chase's point of view, the whole affair would give *Vogue* something to cover.

Condé Nast, the publisher of *Vogue*, was initially suspicious of the idea. To pique New Yorkers' interest, they would need to find a patroness for such an event, and that seemed unlikely. "You'll never get really smart women interested in this," claimed Nast. "They wouldn't dream of it. Too much to do with trade."[6]

Ms. Chase, however, took this pronouncement as a challenge. She would not only find a society patroness, she would obtain *the* society patroness. And so, Ms. Chase set an appointment to meet Mamie Fish. But when she arrived at Mrs. Fish's home, she was greeted in the beautiful foyer by Mamie's secretary, who informed Edna that Mamie no longer wished to see her, as she did not think the project would be a good fit for her.

This might have been the end of the venture, had Edna Chase not found herself chatting with Mrs. Fish's secretary, who had a very artistic son. *Vogue* was filled with beautiful illustrations and consequently had great need for illustrators. Tenacious Ms. Chase wrote, "I have always believed that any proposition should be considered on intrinsic merit alone, but, if a deal is under one's nose, it is hard not to sniff at it."[7] Ms. Chase agreed to consider his illustrations for *Vogue* and began talking, in an extremely heavy-handed manner, about how very *interesting* it was that the secretary should work in this particular house, a home where the woman in charge could be so helpful to *Vogue*.

Perhaps, they could all help one another.

Perhaps, the secretary could reason with Mamie?

And reason she did. Mamie eventually agreed to meet Ms. Chase that same day, in her rose garden. Ms. Chase immediately began to compliment her effusively, reminding Mamie of how she had once said that "she felt sure American women could be well dressed even without Paris."[8] This was, perhaps, the first time that Mamie had ever been complimented for her comments regarding Edith Roosevelt and how women should be supporting American designers—and she appreciated it. By the time Ms. Chase had finished, Mamie had not only agreed to the project but promised to enlist every socialite in New York to attend. She would begin with the young Mrs. Madeleine Astor (Lina Astor died in 1908), whom, she promised Ms. Chase, "I shall call this minute." Mrs. Fish happily reassured Ms. Chase that "she will certainly be a patroness. So will the others. Can't afford not to."[9]

Mamie's friends, who did indeed have a sense of what they could and couldn't afford, were not nearly as offended by the idea of being in the proximity of the vulgar business of dressmaking as Condé Nast had anticipated. They had come a long way since the days when Mrs. Astor claimed that she would buy carpets for her home from A. T. Stewart, but, as he was a tradesman, she would not allow him to walk on them.

No doubt, the charitable element of the event helped. It was often noted in the papers that the proceeds would go to the "midinettes"—the female seamstresses of Paris, many of whom had lost their husbands to the war. As *The Record* noted somewhat breathily, now "fatherless children were to be brought up, educated, trained to face the vicissitudes of life."[10] The notion that this fete was being hosted in order to raise money and awareness for an extremely good cause meant that it would not face the criticism so often directed toward women's entertainments.

Before long, Mrs. John Jacob Astor, Mrs. William Vanderbilt Jr., and Mrs. Harry Whitney were all on board as patrons. Ms. Chase decided that these women would act as "judges" for the show. That did not mean this was a *Project Runway*–style competition, it merely meant they would be selecting which designers would be allowed to participate. Their advice may have been helpful, but, in truth, Ms. Chase had already selected most of the designers; she simply didn't want to offend those who advertised in *Vogue*. Having the ladies serve as "judges" simply meant Edna could tell subpar designers that while she would love to have them show their work, it wasn't up to her, without those designers canceling their advertisements.

Edna Chase was nothing if not the Anna Wintour of her time.

By the time the show—which ran for three days—was held at the Ritz-Carlton Hotel beginning on November 22, 1914, "the list of patronesses of the occasion, most of whom were present, was practically the roster of New York society."[11] What's more, seated next to them, were all the women who had paid three dollars per ticket to attend, regardless of their social status. As a result, "there were women present in $200 tailor-mades and women in shabby, shoddy, shapeless coats worn every day to and from the factory."[12] Following the show, the patronesses of the event attended dinner with the designers and their staff. In chronicling the event, Edna Woolman Chase recalled, "It came as a small shock, pleasant but unexpected, to the tight little world of society to find themselves mingling with their dressmakers and the dressmaker's models. They felt quite daring."[13]

A hundred years later, this kind of networking with fashion industry members would be one of the main occupations of socialites, but back then it was clearly a first for many.

Women like Mamie were already somewhat familiar with these events. There had been other "fashion fetes" in New York. However, this promised to be the first one where everything shown would "be direct from Paris... all shown for the first time."[14] For the lower- and middle-class women who had found three dollars for tickets, this would likely be their first encounter with haute couture. The wealthy had been visiting Paris for years to shop at featured designers' boutiques, but that was out of reach for most American women, even if they wore copies of French gowns. In 1915, "Americans simply know the great dressmaker by name."[15] Now, they would have a chance to see over one hundred gowns valued at $100,000, all while congratulating themselves that they were doing so in the service of the French Orphans Fund.

People were finding a way to enjoy upscale entertainments without feeling guilty about it. Newspapers weren't going to get mad at you for going to a fashion show when it was to *help the orphans.*

Even better, they would see the clothing modeled by women who were trained to walk for this occasion. Chase wanted to show people that modeling was a proper art and, perhaps, even a potential profession for women. She "taught carefully selected beauties to strut and pivot professionally."[16] The style of walk engineered by Chase for this show in particular is one that models still use today.

The first New York Fashion Week was a spectacular success. The *Lincoln Journal Star* declared that the "fashion fete would make the Queen of Sheba gasp, King Solomon, he of many wives, would go broke."[17] The reporter claimed that he wanted to "[warn] husbands. As you value your bank account, keep your wife away from the fashion fete, you New York husband. But as you value her happiness, take her to see those dresses and hats and evening wraps. Her eyes will be brighter for a week."[18]

The gowns on display were worth as much as $8,000 ($252,000 today)—and that was for "one, apparently simple evening frock."[19] It's infuriating that this gown was not covered in jewels, because it's otherwise impossible to even conceive of how it could cost that much. *The Sun* grudgingly admitted that "our buyers and our merchants may at times do violence to French art standards, but they supply their trade and they have their own triumphs."[20]

When people wondered, in a typically frugal, American way, whether the designs could be replicated at a lower cost, *The Sun* was remarkably brutal about the American public's inclination to cut costs and wondered if the gowns would "stand translation into terms of the cheap prices" or whether they would merely produce a "swarm of feminine folk who trot up and down the Fifth Avenues of the land arrayed in what they fondly believe to be the latest of French fashions interpreted by cheap workmen."[21]

The show did demonstrate that French couture was a cut above its American counterparts, and it ensured that, for some time, every woman who saw the show wanted a genuine Paris gown. Designers like Lanvin, Callot, and Doucet all made pieces for the show. The gowns were universally, timelessly beautiful. You would gladly wear many of these gowns to a ball *tomorrow*. One gown was made of blue velvet with diaphanous white bell sleeves. Another was made entirely of white taffeta with a fluted skirt and a coral ribbon wrapped around the waist. One white-and-black afternoon gown was cut short in the front the better to show off a pair of high white boots, because the shoes are an essential part of the outfit.

However, the most excitement was reserved for a gown designed by Paul Poiret, with his "hit-em-in-the-eye method."[22] It caused a special stir since he had produced nothing in the prior eighteen months during which, in addition to fighting in the war, he'd "designed apparel for the soldiers, having obtained his ideas of their requirements from personal observation and hardship."[23] He had just returned from the front lines before the show, and he told *The Brooklyn Citizen* that "it was a great relief to be able to stop his work under army directions and turn himself loose as it were, in the making of beautiful gowns, something so far removed from trench life."[24] Whatever he designed was "expected to determine the trend of fashion for the remainder of the season."[25]

And he did, in fact, make something that was especially eye-popping by the standards of the time. Poiret gravitated toward shorter, ankle-revealing skirts, with the back of the skirt elevated two inches above the front. The gown he presented at NYFW was considered to be extremely scandalous, the kind that might've caused a ruckus had it been worn in New England rather than Paris. The *Lincoln Journal Star* gasped, the editor clutching her pearls, that "Poiret's gowns have no morals."[26] Which, of course, only made it seem *more* exciting to young women. The entire show "established the French claim to artistic supremacy in the field of dress" and "showed the individual woman of money and taste what could be done with the money and taste."[27]

Most of the gowns on display were overwhelmingly discreet—well-bred women were attending this, no need to make it too scandalous—save, perhaps, for Poiret's. The *Detroit Free Press* remarked that the gowns showed such a modest amount of flesh that some gave the impression that "they had been made first with a high neck and then snipped carelessly from shoulder to shoulder with a pair of scissors." This didn't always have a good effect. One dress was said to have a collar "fastening in the back and fitting well over the chin...that made the wearer look very much as though she were all ready for the electric chair. It was hideous."[28]

In still more demoralizing news, the *Lincoln Journal Star* reporter remarked that "all the gowns I saw yesterday were for distinctly thin women. Not a single garment crossed the stage at the Ritz that would not make the Venus de Milo look like Mother Bunch...the rag and the bone of the vampire jingle summarizes the dressmaker's ideal."[29] Truly a trait that would carry into the fashion shows of the entire twentieth century. Edna Woolman Chase noted, "*Vogue* showed two or three dresses for stout women, but we were so shaken by the experience that they never tried it again."

Regardless, Edna had plenty to write about now. The show's details spanned across eleven pages in *Vogue's* winter issue, with an early advertisement promising readers that "if you missed the Paris Fashion Fete recently held at the Ritz-Carlton, here is an opportunity to review the models at your leisure."[30]

Not everyone took the fete entirely seriously. By December 6, it was being spoofed at a "burlesque fashion fete" where "considerable fun was being had at the expense of the latest styles."[31] There, women and men dressed as animated poppies and harlequins with hundreds of frills. Honestly, this also sounds fun, and it would probably take a comparable amount of work and creativity to make those costumes.

Finally, it seemed, people were learning how to justify having fun without feeling guilty or being shamed for it. At this particular event, no one would point out that children around the world were starving while the rich cavorted—because it was precisely for charity that the show was held in the first place. It was similarly helpful that the event was open to everyone, at least theoretically, if they could afford the cost of a ticket. This approach dramatically shaped large parties going into the new twentieth century. Grand balls would often no longer be given by an individual like Mamie, but instead by an organization in support of a cause (or a socialite looking for a write-off).

Now, a hundred years later, people will happily cavort in black tie alongside dogs, but they'll say they are doing so because they support the ASPCA. And anyone willing to pay the price of admission is welcome.

The era when Mamie Fish could use extravagant balls to determine status in society was nearing an end. That such an ending should be foretold by a party initiated by Mamie herself is, perhaps, only appropriate.

In July, another fashion fete "to alleviate distress and suffering among the refugee and civil population in France"[32] would be given in Newport. Sadly, Mrs. Fish would be unable to attend.

CHAPTER 27

HE NEW YORK FASHION FETE WAS TO BE MAMIE'S LAST GREAT accomplishment. Six months after the triumph at the Ritz-Carlton, in May 1915, Mamie passed away at Glenclyffe.

Naturally, she was in the midst of planning yet another party. She was readying herself, as always, for the social whirl of spring and summer, working on the final preparations for a spring dance to be held a week hence at Glenclyffe, in honor of her sixtieth birthday. She had just sent out nearly two hundred invitations for a weekend of revelry when she suddenly felt ill and suffered a stroke. A doctor was quickly summoned as her children attempted to rush to her home. She died by 10:00 p.m. that evening with Stuyvesant by her side, as he had been for everything.

If there was any question about her position in life, there was not in death. No sooner did she pass away than newspapers as far away as Kansas trumpeted, "Ruler of the 400 Dead."[1]

And though many had mixed opinions of her during her life, New York mourned the loss of such an extraordinary woman. *The Sun* reported that "one of her chief objects in life seemed to be to give pleasure to others.... She had a very kind heart, and it was not only for those to whom she was under social obligation that she was thinking out plans for pleasure, but equally for those whose positions in life were less fortunate."[2] The headline also declared that she was "noted for quiet charity."[3]

This obituary was clearly written by someone who didn't know Mamie well. While it was true that Mamie hosted the NYFW fundraiser and used her platform for good in the case of the seamstresses, Mamie was not actually known for her gentle and soft demeanor, nor for her quiet ways. "Biting wit" would have been a more accurate description. There's something disheartening about the fact that women are necessarily softened into gentle, kind, motherly souls upon their deaths, no matter how funny and strange they might have been in life. *The Boston Daily Globe* at least wrote that she "always delighted in doing things just a little different than her associates and equals."[4]

Now that Mamie's reign was finally over, all those criticisms of her extravagant parties faded away, written off as glamorous examples of a time gone by.

Her son said that a truer description of his mother came from Mrs. Charles Oelrichs, known as Blanche. Recalling Mamie, Blanche had said, "She had the elements of a true comedienne. Her harsh gaiety had the bitter overtone of grotesque disillusionment with herself and everyone else. One knew as one looked at and listened to her that she sensed well the triviality in which she drowned her time, and her brash mirth concealed an ever more exasperated cry at the kind of life that went on around her."[5] After reading this, Mamie's son Stuyvesant noted, "Knowing my mother better than Blanche did, I might change a word here or there, but it is a true picture."[6]

And yet, there is something very sad in this description as well.

If Mamie did not take joy in her life, what was the point of it? Well, even if she did not, many others did. She provided pleasure—a new, more uninhibited kind of pleasure—to so many. She opened society to not only the members of old money but also fashion designers and comediennes and actresses. She endeavored always to find people you might want to chat with over a dinner table rather than just regard in solemn, dignified awe.

That mattered so much that when Stuyvesant died in 1923, a full half of his obituary was about his wife, who "through her own brilliance maintained sway over society." She was remembered as "one of those who protested against the custom of American women sending abroad for all their ideas."[7] Years later, as the appetite for fun returned to America in 1939, she'd be credited with "starting the vogue of stunt soirees."[8] But she also created a new mold of woman, one where creativity and wit could trump breeding, beauty, and solicitude.

As for Stuyvesant himself, that "lucky money-making husband [who] has been able to seat [Mamie] upon a pile of gold" faded into obsolescence almost immediately after his death, if not before. The *Great Falls Tribune* noted that "the death of Stuyvesant Fish of New York the other day would not have excited much interest outside of financial and railroad circles,"[9] save for a provision in his will declaring that no part of his fortune would go to charity.

Whatever happened to that boy in college who thought that money should be intended to help everyone?

He declared that he believed "charitable bequests afford the testator a means of gratifying his vanity at the expense of his heirs."[10] This was hardly a notion in keeping with the sentiments of 1923. As the *Tribune* noted, "The feeling has grown very general in this country during recent years that it is the duty of men who have made great fortunes to use some portion of it for the public good." In death, Stuyvesant, who'd once been so admired for his forward-thinking outlook regarding railroads, had fallen out of step with the times. But then, so had Mamie when it came to the suffragettes. So many people who were once young and cool are destined to slip, somehow without ever noticing it, into old-fogy-dom.

Harry Lehr, the other love of Mamie's life, didn't pass away until 1929—but his later years were far from kind to him. In 1907, he moved to Paris, asserting that New York society was now "ruled entirely by money, and no longer appreciated wit and refined gaiety." Others claimed that he had lost his own sense of humor.

When, in Paris in 1924, a group of "beautiful and young women" unleashed a monkey, a dozen turtles, a rooster, and a young alligator in his apartment (when he was absent), he was horrified. Even though "the only real damage was done by the monkey, who gnawed the parlor curtains asunder,"[11] Lehr was unamused. He could not even pretend to be amused to the press. He declared, "This is shocking vandalism. Some people don't know the difference between fun and bad manners."[12] It is true that unleashing an alligator in someone's apartment is, at best, terrifying hazing and should be illegal. You can't prank people with alligators. But to be fair, it also sounds like the kind of prank that Harry Lehr would have loved as a younger man. The papers were surprised that he did not recognize it as a clever nod to his own days in Newport. But sadly, in his final decade, he felt entirely out of place, and according to Elizabeth, "he would sit for hours at a time in crowded restaurants and bars, trying in a way that was infinitely pathetic to find himself again in a familiar background."[13]

The time when society looked to these people for amusement had come to an end.

Fortunately, Mamie's legacy would endure for some time. In 1924, the *Daily News* reflected on how she "revolutionized the staid rather stupid society of her earlier days in Newport where she enjoyed 'a brilliant leadership.'"[14] The reporter wrote that "up to Mrs. Fish's time society took itself very seriously—so seriously that to be in society at all was more of a bore and a responsibility than a pleasure." In 1926, *The Washington Herald* noted that, following her death and the end of Newport's "circus set," "Newport settled down to a more or less placid existence; so placid, I might add that many hostesses did not feel a Newport season offered sufficient inducements to warrant their opening the great castle-like establishments."

In other words, Mamie died, and *Newport died with her.*

(Not really. Newport is still a wonderful place to visit, especially if you enjoy seeing great castle-like homes and eating lobster rolls, two of the best things a human can do.)

In 1936, *The Pittsburgh Press* stated, "Most of us, if asked to name the society leader of all times, would chorus, 'Mrs. Stuyvesant Fish.'" Two decades after her death, she was considered to be "a trail blazer in this profession."[15] Even as late as 1960, when her grandson was in the process of

getting a divorce, the *San Francisco Examiner* explained why he was important merely by noting, "He is the grandson of the late Mrs. Stuyvesant Fish,
noted leader of New York's 400 half a century ago."[16]

Mrs. Fish was not forgotten.

But the society that Mamie had been so devoted to had all but faded
away. In 1929, the *Daily News* noted that "society is not what it used to
be when Mrs. Stuyvesant Fish and Mrs. W. K. Vanderbilt matched their
wits and their husbands' fortunes for the right to rule."[17] Today, it reported,
"society has arbiters, yes, but no one woman will have the social register so
much under her thumb again."[18]

As for Mamie's children, they had no interest in society whatsoever. Her
daughter, Marian, shunned it as "the very plague," claiming she "had too
much of it as a girl."[19] Her son Stuyvesant retired to Mount Kisco (a bit
north of Manhattan), and another son took up ranching in Carmel, California. By 1942, there was a new Mrs. Stuyvesant Fish, Mamie's daughter-in-
law, who was "an unknown quantity in society" and would remain that way.
How different, the *Pittsburgh Sun-Telegraph* mused, from the Mrs. Stuyvesant Fish of twenty-five years prior who "made or broke social climbers
with a mere nod of [her] head."[20] The new Mrs. Stuyvesant lived in Mount
Kisco and enjoyed fencing, a far cry from her party-throwing, midtown
mansion-owning mother-in-law. And with that generation's lack of interest
in society and spectacle, so did their names slowly fade from the popular
consciousness.

But still, Mamie's name would linger on for some time. Especially in
Newport.

EPILOGUE

*C*ROSSWAYS, THE MANSION THAT HAD DOMINATED NIGHTLIFE IN NEW-port society for so long, was put up for sale by the children and sat on the market for a year following Stuyvesant's death. Partly, the difficulty in a sale lay with finding "the woman who is courageous enough to brace the stares Newport will turn on the matron who announced that she will be the next Chatelaine of Crossways."[1]

It did eventually get purchased by Ella de Peyster Schwartz in September 1926. The *San Francisco Examiner* wondered what Mrs. Fish would make of the sale of her house and noted, "It really is too bad [Mamie] Fish is not here to make one of her classical remarks. It would be snappy and to the point," and they expressed hope that maybe Ella would reopen the house with a Mother Goose Ball in tribute to Mamie.

Everyone who was worried that if they bought that house they'd be compared to Mamie was *right*.

Even if you had never heard her name before picking this book up, Mamie's shadow continues to linger, and not just in Newport. We're apt to believe that history is changed only by very serious people (and namely men). Martin Luther King Jr. Winston Churchill. Men with strong jawlines in military uniforms. And heroes! Progressive heroes fighting for the right causes.

It would be lovely to imagine that Mamie was a progressive hero. She was not. Most people lose that distinction after they run over someone three times in their car. As someone with the benefit of hindsight, gosh, it would have been nice if she had supported the suffragettes.

But the world is changed, too, by people who sought fun and to expand the boundaries of the world to allow for greater amusement. It may have been out of a sheer desire not to be bored, but Mamie changed the makeup of the aspirational class in America.

She made it appealing. And the way she made it appealing was opening it up to more people. Okay, not everyone. Those seamstresses may have gotten a ride in her car, but they did not get invitations to her parties. But comediennes did. And actresses, and the men at the naval academy, and fashion designers, and a lot of other people who "high society" wouldn't have gone near beforehand.

I imagine, in some ways, if you are the kind of person who picks up a book with "glitz" in the title, what she did has touched your life. If your eyes have ever lingered over a magazine spread where actresses mingled with high-society types, that was Mamie. If you've ever been to a themed party, that was her. If you have watched your favorite reality stars from rich families go to a fashion show, well, her again. She made weirdness and glamour compatible. It may have only freed women of a certain class, and it may have only removed the tiniest constraints from them, but that trickled down. She gave people—women in particular—permission to prioritize their enjoyment rather than following a rigid set of social rules.

So, just know that every time you go to a party with a weird theme. Every time you wander into a party that's been decorated like an under-the-sea ball, or a flower-covered greenhouse for Valentine's Day, or even a murder mystery party your friends host, well, Mamie's ghost is floating around there, hoping that you will crack at least a few jokes.

ACKNOWLEDGMENTS

As ever, I owe a great debt to so many people without whom this book would not exist. I am grateful to all my friends for their support, and a few people in particular.

First and foremost, my excellent editor, Carrie Napolitano, who helped me come up with the idea for this book over chocolate martinis. I like to think Mamie would have approved.

For my agent, Anna Sproul-Latimer. Thank you for making something I do for love into something I also make money from. You are so incalculably valuable.

For the entire team at Grand Central Publishing, thank you for copy-editing, designing, fact-checking, marketing, and generally doing the great number of things I have no idea whatsoever how to do.

For my eternal first reader, my mother, Kathleen Wright. Thank you for being willing to say, "This part makes no sense whatsoever," and allowing me to reply, "Well, I'm sorry you hate history" before ultimately taking your note. I love you.

Thank you to my husband, Daniel Kibblesmith, for not only listening to gilded-age facts every time he came home but washing every dish and taking our child to countless playground dates so I could work. You are a true Stuyvesant Fish without all the punching. I love you.

And for my perfect, three-year-old daughter, Madeline, who tried to use my body as a jungle gym whenever I was writing. You were no help whatsoever, and I love you more than anything.

NOTES

Introduction

1. Gail MacColl and Carol McD. Wallace, *To Marry an English Lord: Tales of Wealth and Marriage, Sex and Snobbery in the Gilded Age* (Workman Publishing, 1989), 173.

2. Elizabeth Drexel Lehr, *King Lehr and the Gilded Age* (Applewood Books, 1935), 152.

3. Drexel Lehr, *King Lehr and the Gilded Age*, 152.

4. Helen Harrison, "Society's Next Zany Thrill," *El Paso Times*, December 31, 1939.

5. "Newport Surprised by Mrs. Astor's Interview," *New York Times*, September 20, 1908.

6. Harrison, "Society's Next Zany Thrill."

7. Harrison, "Society's Next Zany Thrill."

8. Drexel Lehr, *King Lehr and the Gilded Age*, 152.

9. Drexel Lehr, *King Lehr and the Gilded Age*, 152.

10. *Los Angeles Evening Post-Record*, July 21, 1902.

11. *Atchison Daily Globe*, November 26, 1906.

12. *Atchison Daily Globe*, November 26, 1906.

13. "Clothes and the Woman," *Boston Evening Transcript*, October 16, 1903.

14. "Query," *Kansas City Star*, November 29, 1903.

15. Arthur T. Vanderbilt II, *Fortune's Children: The Fall of the House of Vanderbilt* (William Morrow, 1989), Kindle loc. 5184 of 12135.

16. Vanderbilt, *Fortune's Children*, Kindle loc. 5184 of 12135.

Chapter 1

1. Nancy Mitford, *Madame de Pompadour* (New York Review of Books, 1954), 6.

2. Gilles Bertrand, "Venice Carnival from the Middle Ages to the Twenty-First Century: A Political Ritual Turned 'Consumer Rite'?," *Journal of Festive Studies* 2, no. 1 (Fall 2020): 85.

3. Jessica Kerwin Jenkins, *Encyclopedia of the Exquisite: An Anecdotal History of Elegant Delights* (Doubleday, 2010), 118.

4. Christopher Klein, "When Massachusetts Banned Christmas," History.com, December 22, 2015, https://www.history.com/news/when-massachusetts-banned-christmas.

5. Kate Van Winkle Keller, *Dance and Its Music in America, 1528–1789* (Pendragon Press, 2007), 309.

6. J. A. R. Pimlott, "Christmas Under the Puritans," *History Today* 10, no. 12, December 1960.

7. Pimlott, "Christmas Under the Puritans."

8. Increase Mather, *The Necessity of Reformation* (John Foster, 1679).

9. Van Winkle Keller, *Dance and Its Music in America, 1528–1789*, 309.

10. H. L. Mencken, *A Book of Prefaces* (Alfred A. Knopf, 1917), 61.

11. "Dancing with General Washington," Mount Vernon Ladies' Association, accessed February 24, 2025, https://www.mountvernon.org/george-washington/colonial-life-today /dancing/.

12. Peter D. Apgar, "Festivals of Colonial America: From Celebration to Revolution," Texas Tech University, December 1995.

13. John Adams, John Adams Diary, 10 August 1769–22 August 1770, Massachusetts Historical Society.

14. "Meschianza," The George Washington Presidential Library at Mount Vernon, https://www.mountvernon.org/library/digitalhistory/digital-encyclopedia/article /meschianza.

15. "Meschianza," The George Washington Presidential Library at Mount Vernon.

16. Lucie Glenn, "A Mis-Kee What?," *Rockland County Journal News*, October 2, 1967.

17. Patrick Glennon "A British General's Big Mistake," *Philadelphia Inquirer*, June 24, 2018.

18. *Newcastle Weekly Courant*, November 19, 1785.

19. Dr. James Thacher, Pluckemin, New Jersey, February 4, 1779.

20. James Tilton to Gunning Bedford Jr., Annapolis, Maryland, December 25, 1783.

21. Jeff Hoyt, "1800–1990: Changes in Urban/Rural U.S. Population," SeniorLiving .Org, updated March 14, 2024, https://www.seniorliving.org/history/1800-1990-changes -urbanrural-us-population/.

22. Kristen Richardson, *The Season: A Social History of the Debutante* (W. W. Norton, 2019), 68.

23. "The Prince in the Metropolis: A Very Great Jam and Very Little Dancing," *New York Times*, October 13, 1860.

24. "The Prince in the Metropolis," *New York Times*.

25. *Baltimore Sun*, October 15, 1860.

26. Ward McCallister, *Society As I Have Found It* (Cassell, 1890), 76.

27. Abram Hill, "The Hamilton Lodge Ball," Schomburg Center for Research in Black Culture, Manuscripts, Archives and Rare Books Division, New York Public Library Digital Collections, August 30, 1939, https://digitalcollections.nypl.org /items/16910cf0-7cf4-0133-46b1-00505686d14e.

28. Timothy J. Gilfoyle, *City of Eros: New York City, Prostitution, and the Commercialization of Sex, 1790–1920* (W. W. Norton, 1992), 162.

29. Founders of the Fifth Avenue Bank, *Forty Years on Fifth Avenue: 1875–1915* (Fifth Avenue Bank, 1915), 16.

30. Tom Miller, "The Lost Brevoort Mansion—Fifth Avenue and 9th Street," *Daytonian in Manhattan* (blog), April 22, 2013, http://daytoninmanhattan.blogspot.com/2013/04 /the-lost-brevoort-mansion-5th-ave-and.html.

31. Madeline Bilis, "When Masked Balls Were Forbidden in Boston," *Boston Magazine*, December 31, 2015.

32. "The Grand Fancy Dress Ball at Newport—Exclusion of Masks," *New York Herald*, September 6, 1850.

33. "Musard and the Paris Masked Balls," *Harper's Weekly*, April 10, 1858.

34. "Society in Fancy Dress: A Glance at Some Brilliant Balls," *New-York Tribune*, March 26, 1883.

Chapter 2

1. Tom Miller, "The 1900 Stuyvesant Fish House—No. 25 East 78th Street," *Daytonian in Manhattan* (blog), February 23, 2012, http://daytoninmanhattan.blogspot.com/2012/02/1900-stuyvesant-fish-house-no-25-east.html.

2. Stuyvesant Fish, *Anthon Genealogy 1600–1914* (Allen County Public Library Genealogy Center, 1942), 8.

3. "Obituary: General William Henry Anthon," *New York Times*, November 9, 1875.

4. Fish, *Anthon Genealogy*, 102.

5. Fish, *Anthon Genealogy*, 103.

6. *Springfield Daily Republican*, September 7, 1858.

7. Fish, *Anthon Genealogy*, 7.

8. *New York Herald*, November 3, 1862.

9. Leslie M. Harris, *In the Shadow of Slavery: African Americans in New York City, 1626–1863* (University of Chicago Press, 2004).

10. *New York Times*, November 9, 1875.

11. US Census Bureau, William Anthon, United States Federal Census, 1860.

12. *New York Times*, February 9, 1856.

13. Nancy Green, "Female Education and School Competition: 1820–1850," *History of Education Quarterly* 18, no. 2 (Summer 1978): 129–142, https://doi.org/10.2307/367796.

14. *Poughkeepsie Journal*, November 17, 1860.

15. Fish, *Anthon Genealogy*, 190.

16. *Brooklyn Union*, July 13, 1867.

17. "Long Island Afoot," *Brooklyn Union*, July 7, 1874.

18. "Married in New York," *San Francisco Chronicle*, July 1, 1896.

Chapter 3

1. *Atchison Daily Globe*, November 26, 1906.

2. Henry Hall, *America's Successful Men of Affairs: An Encyclopedia of Contemporaneous Biography* (New York Tribune, 1895–1896).

3. Fish, *Anthon Genealogy*, 160.

4. Fish, *Anthon Genealogy*, 159.

5. Hall, *America's Successful Men of Affairs: An Encyclopedia of Contemporaneous Biography*.

6. Fish, *Anthon Genealogy*, 151.

7. "Columbia College," *New York Times*, June 29, 1871.

8. Fish, *Anthon Genealogy*.

9. "Railroads in the Late 19th Century," Library of Congress, https://www.loc.gov/classroom-materials/united-states-history-primary-source-timeline/rise-of-industrial-america-1876-1900/railroads-in-late-19th-century/.

10. *Atchison Daily Globe*, November 26, 1906.

11. "Stuyvesant Fish Is a Great Man," *Freeport Journal-Standard*, October 22, 1906.

12. *Osage County Chronicle*, January 14, 1876.

13. Fish, *Anthon Genealogy*, 179.

14. Fish, *Anthon Genealogy*, 179.

15. Fish, *Anthon Genealogy*, 180.

16. Fish, *Anthon Genealogy*, 187.

17. Fish, *Anthon Genealogy*, 158.

18. Fish, *Anthon Genealogy*, 185.

19. Drexel Lehr, *King Lehr and the Gilded Age*, 126.

20. Drexel Lehr, *King Lehr and the Gilded Age*, 126.

21. "Religion: Little Church" *Time*, October 19, 1931.

22. Fish, *Anthon Genealogy*, 117.

23. *Buffalo Commercial*, June 15, 1876.

24. *Buffalo Commercial*, June 15, 1876.

Chapter 4

1. Fish, *Anthon Genealogy*, 191.

2. *Rutland Daily Herald*, December 21, 1876.

3. Fish, *Anthon Genealogy*, 191.

4. Fish, *Anthon Genealogy*, 194.

5. Fish, *Anthon Genealogy*, 194.

6. Fish, *Anthon Genealogy*, 194.

7. Fish, *Anthon Genealogy*, 194.

8. Aaron O'Neill, "Child Mortality Rate (Under Five Years Old) in the United States, from 1800 to 2020," Statista, June 21, 2022, https://www.statista.com/statistics/1041693/united-states-all-time-child-mortality-rate/.

9. Stanford T. Shulman, "The History of Pediatric Infectious Diseases," *Pediatric Research* 55, no. 1 (January 2004): 163–176.

10. Fish, *Anthon Genealogy*, 196.

11. Fish, *Anthon Genealogy*, 213.

12. Fish, *Anthon Genealogy*, 213.

13. Fish, *Anthon Genealogy*, 195.

14. Fish, *Anthon Genealogy*, 198.

15. *Brooklyn Daily Eagle*, October 5, 1902.

16. "Then and Now," *Daily News*, July 11, 1943.

17. *Brooklyn Daily Eagle*, October 5, 1902.

18. Elizabeth, Lady Decies, *Turn of the World* (Applewood Books, 1937), 108.

19. Decies, *Turn of the World*, 41.

Chapter 5

1. "New York Urbanized Area: Population & Density from 1800," Demographia, http://demographia.com/db-nyuza1800.htm.

2. "A Street Cleaning Plan" *New York Times*, December 30, 1890.

3. "Hours of Pleasure," *Democrat and Chronicle*, June 21, 1889.

4. Metcalfe, "Metcalfe's Chat: A Run to Newport and What He Noted There," *Buffalo Sunday Morning News*, September 1, 1889.

5. Metcalfe, "Metcalfe's Chat."

6. Fish, *Anthon Genealogy*, 200.

7. Fish, *Anthon Genealogy*, 166.

8. Fish, *Anthon Genealogy*, 213.

9. "Jolly Times at Newport," *New York Times*, August 4, 1889.

10. *Boston Evening Transcript*, August 10, 1889.

11. "What Is Going on in Society," *The Sun*, August 10, 1890.

12. Fish, *Anthon Genealogy*, 221.

13. McAllister, *Society As I Have Found It*, 13.

14. McAllister, *Society As I Have Found It*, 31.

15. McAllister, *Society As I Have Found It*, 26.

16. McAllister, *Society As I Have Found It*, 113.

17. McAllister, *Society As I Have Found It*, 111.

18. McAllister, *Society As I Have Found It*, 114.

19. McAllister, *Society As I Have Found It*, 119.

20. McAllister, *Society As I Have Found It*, 119.

21. Virginia Cowles, *The Astors* (Alfred A. Knopf, 1979), 99.

22. Fish, *Anthon Genealogy*, 184.

Chapter 6

1. *Saint Paul Globe*, August 15, 1886.

2. Cowles, *The Astors*, 99.

3. *Saint Paul Globe*, August 15, 1886.

4. *Saint Paul Globe*, August 15, 1886.

5. Cowles, *The Astors*, 103.

6. Cowles, *The Astors*, 105.

7. Hal Boyle, "Two Famous Mansions Being Razed," *The Ithaca Journal*, November 17, 1947.

8. Vanderbilt, *Fortune's Children*, 129.

9. Stephen Turner, "Almack's and Society," *History Today* 26, no. 4 (April 1976).

10. McAllister, *Society As I Have Found It*, 212.

11. McAllister, *Society As I Have Found It*, 213.

12. McAllister, *Society As I Have Found It*, 217.

13. McAllister, *Society As I Have Found It*, 216.

14. Vanderbilt, *Fortune's Children*, 131.

15. Cowles, *The Astors*, 106.

16. "Mrs. Astor Is Dead, Society Loses Queen," *Daily Times*, October 31, 1908.

17. "Paradise in New York," *The Tennessean*, February 10, 1878.

18. Maury Paul, "Ward McAllister First to Use Term 'The 400,'" *Pittsburgh Sun-Telegraph*, March 16, 1941.

19. "Mrs. W. M. Astor Dead," *Evening Star*, October 31, 1908.

20. Drexel Lehr, *King Lehr and the Gilded Age*, 57.

21. Drexel Lehr, *King Lehr and the Gilded Age*, 58.

22. Drexel Lehr, *King Lehr and the Gilded Age*, 58.

23. "Paradise in New York," *The Tennessean*.

24. Drexel Lehr, *King Lehr and the Gilded Age*, 61.

25. Vanderbilt, *Fortune's Children*, 133.

26. Vanderbilt, *Fortune's Children*, 137.

Chapter 7

1. Cowles, *The Astors*, 101.

2. *The World*, June 11, 1893.

3. Bennett Cerf, "Try and Stop Me," *Herald-Sun*, July 30, 1948.

4. Cowles, *The Astors*, 102.

5. Cowles, *The Astors*, 98.

6. *Omaha World-Herald*, December 27, 1891.

7. McAllister, *Society As I Have Found It*, 313.

8. "One Man Who Rose Despite a Silver Spoon," *Rock Island Argus*, November 21, 1906.

9. "Mr. and Mrs. Stuyvesant Fish," *Rock Island Argus*, November 21, 1906.

10. *Muscatine News-Tribune*, November 25, 1906.

11. *Dixon Evening Telegraph*, November 22, 1906.

12. *Brooklyn Daily Eagle*, October 5, 1902.

13. "What Women Talk About," *Omaha World-Herald*, December 27, 1891.

14. "What Women Talk About," *Omaha World-Herald*.

Chapter 8

1. Vanderbilt, *Fortune's Children*, 116.

2. Consuelo Vanderbilt Balsan, *The Glitter and the Gold* (St. Martin's Press, 1953), 5.

3. Balsan, *The Glitter and the Gold*, 5.

4. Vanderbilt, *Fortune's Children*, 118.

5. Vanderbilt, *Fortune's Children*, 73.

6. Vanderbilt, *Fortune's Children*, 44.

7. Vanderbilt, *Fortune's Children*, 47.

8. Vanderbilt, *Fortune's Children*, 50.

9. Vanderbilt, *Fortune's Children*, 75.

10. "William K. Vanderbilt," *New York Times*, July 9, 1899.

11. "William K. Vanderbilt," *New York Times*.

12. Balsan, *The Glitter and the Gold*, 5.

13. *St. Louis Post-Dispatch*, April 2, 1883.

14. Paul, "Ward McAllister First to Use Term 'The 400.'"

15. "Gould and the Snorter," *Savannah Morning News*, December 24, 1883.

16. "Gould and the Snorter," *Savannah Morning News*.

17. Balsan, *The Glitter and the Gold*, 5.

18. "All of Society in Costume," *New York Times*, March 27, 1883.

19. "A Social Feud," *St. Louis Post-Dispatch*, April 2, 1883.

20. "A Social Feud," *St. Louis Post-Dispatch*.

21. "A Social Feud," *St. Louis Post-Dispatch*.

22. "A Social Feud," *St. Louis Post-Dispatch*.

23. "All of Society in Costume," *New York Times*.

24. "The Great Ball," *Buffalo Commercial*, March 28, 1883.

25. Frank Crowninshield, "The Vanderbilt Ball of 1883," *Vogue*, August 1, 1944.

26. "All of Society in Costume," *New York Times*.

27. "All of Society in Costume," *New York Times*.

28. "All of Society in Costume," *New York Times*.

29. "A Grand Social Event," *Fall River Daily Evening News*, March 28, 1883.

30. "All of Society in Costume," *New York Times*.

31. "All of Society in Costume," *New York Times*.

32. *Courier-Journal*, December 15, 1883.

33. "Gould and the Snorter," *Savannah Morning News*.

34. "The Great Social Event," *Brown County World*, April 12, 1883.

35. Rebecca Cope, "A Who's Who of the Gilded Age, Ahead of the Met Gala," *Tatler*, January 19, 2022.

Chapter 9

1. *Brooklyn Daily Eagle*, January 6, 1884.

2. *Buffalo Courier Express*, January 1, 1888.

3. *Buffalo Courier Express*.

4. "The World of Society," *New York Times*, February 15, 1885.

5. "The World of Society," *New York Times*.

6. "Society Topics of the Week," *New York Times*, December 26, 1886.

7. "The Big Parade," *Brooklyn Daily Eagle*, April 23, 1889.

8. "The Big Parade," *Brooklyn Daily Eagle*.

9. McAllister, *Society As I Have Found It*, 180.

10. Vanderbilt, *Fortune's Children*, 291.

11. Vanderbilt, *Fortune's Children*.

12. "Glory to Ward M'Allister," *The Sun*, January 3, 1890.

13. "May Dance, But Can't Drink," *Evening World*, January 1, 1890.

14. "May Dance, But Can't Drink," *Evening World*.

15. "May Dance, But Can't Drink," *Evening World*.

16. "Novelist Grows Vexed," *Philadelphia Times*, February 24, 1895.

17. "Novelist Grows Vexed," *Philadelphia Times*.

18. *Leicester Journal and Midland Counties General Advertiser*, October 31, 1890.

19. "Americanism in Politics," *Brooklyn Daily Eagle*, December 19, 1890.

20. McAllister, *Society As I Have Found It*, 190.

21. McAllister, *Society As I Have Found It*, 195.

22. "Gotham's Social Dictator," *Evening Star*, April 9, 1889.

23. McAllister, *Society As I Have Found It*, 51.

24. "The Only Four Hundred," *New York Times*, February 16, 1892.

25. "Today's Cafe Society Supplementing The 400 That Never Existed," *Charlotte Observer*, February 20, 1938.

26. "The Only Four Hundred," *New York Times*.

27. "The Only Four Hundred," *New York Times*.

28. "Men of the Day: Samuel Ward M'Allister," *New York Morning Journal*, February 14, 1892.

29. *Pittsburgh Post-Gazette*, May 20, 1893.

30. *Buffalo Enquirer*, April 20, 1893.

31. *Inter Ocean*, April 17, 1893.

32. Vanderbilt, *Fortune's Children*, 292.

33. "After His Critics," *Chicago Tribune*, April 16, 1893.

34. *Daily Democrat*, April 20, 1893.

35. *Minneapolis Daily Times*, May 6, 1893.

36. "Votes and Comments," *Brownsville Herald*, May 1, 1893.

37. "After His Critics," *Chicago Tribune*.

38. "After His Critics," *Chicago Tribune*.

39. "Talks from a Pulpit," *Chicago Tribune*, April 24, 1893.

40. *Chicago Tribune*, April 16, 1893.

41. "The World," *The Sun*, April 16, 1893.

42. "Floral Tributes to the Dead Leader," *Chicago Tribune*, April 16, 1893.

43. "Death of McAllister," *San Francisco Call*, February 1, 1895.

44. *Philadelphia Inquirer*, February 5, 1895.

45. *Delphos Daily Herald*, March 9, 1895.

Chapter 10

1. Drexel Lehr, *King Lehr and the Gilded Age*, 16.

2. Drexel Lehr, *King Lehr and the Gilded Age*, 22.

3. Drexel Lehr, *King Lehr and the Gilded Age*, 22.

4. Elizabeth Drexel Lehr, "King Lehr and the Gilded Age," *St. Louis Post-Dispatch*, May 17, 1936.

5. Drexel Lehr, "King Lehr and the Gilded Age," *St. Louis Post-Dispatch*.

6. Drexel Lehr, "King Lehr and the Gilded Age," *St. Louis Post-Dispatch*.

7. Drexel Lehr, "King Lehr and the Gilded Age," *St. Louis Post-Dispatch*.

8. Drexel Lehr, "King Lehr and the Gilded Age," *St. Louis Post-Dispatch*.

9. *Portsmouth Star*, December 29, 1897.

10. "How They Turned His Own Jokes on Once Funny Mr. Lehr," *Fort Worth Record-Telegram*, August 24, 1924.

11. "Squire of Dames," *Saint Paul Globe*, February 25, 1900.

12. Vanderbilt, *Fortune's Children*, 295.

13. Drexel Lehr, *King Lehr and the Gilded Age*, 56.

14. Drexel Lehr, *King Lehr and the Gilded Age*.

15. "Squire of Dames," *Saint Paul Globe*.

16. Drexel Lehr, *King Lehr and the Gilded Age*, 149.

17. "Revolution in Women's Dress Had Its Start at Sherry's," *Boston Globe*, February 22, 1936.

18. Drexel Lehr, *King Lehr and the Gilded Age*, 151.

19. Drexel Lehr, *King Lehr and the Gilded Age*, 48.

20. *Baltimore Sun*, August 31, 1924.

21. *News-Herald*, January 11, 1929.

22. Edith Wharton, *A Backward Glance* (D. Appleton Century, 1934), 175.

23. "Idiocy Gone to Seed," *Henderson Gold Leaf*, September 21, 1899.

24. Drexel Lehr, *King Lehr and the Gilded Age*, 130.

25. Drexel Lehr, *King Lehr and the Gilded Age*, 173.

26. Drexel Lehr, *King Lehr and the Gilded Age*, 173.

Chapter 11

1. Drexel Lehr, *King Lehr and the Gilded Age*, 23.

2. Drexel Lehr, *King Lehr and the Gilded Age*, 32.

3. Drexel Lehr, *King Lehr and the Gilded Age*, 23.

4. Drexel Lehr, *King Lehr and the Gilded Age*, 45.

5. Drexel Lehr, *King Lehr and the Gilded Age*.

6. Drexel Lehr, *King Lehr and the Gilded Age*, 28.

7. Drexel Lehr, *King Lehr and the Gilded Age*, 32.

8. "John Morris Sentenced: Pleaded Guilty to the Charge of Sodomy," *Star-Gazette*, September 9, 1899.

9. George Chauncey, *Gay New York: Gender, Urban Culture, and the Making of the Gay Male World, 1890–1940* (Basic Books, 1995), 36.

10. Chauncey, *Gay New York*, 36.

11. Chauncey, *Gay New York*, 37.

12. Drexel Lehr, *King Lehr and the Gilded Age*, 27.

13. Robert Armitage, *Edith Wharton, A Writing Life: Marriage* (New York Public Library, 2013).

14. Drexel Lehr, *King Lehr and the Gilded Age*, 16.

15. Mary Campbell, "Lust on Trial: Censorship and the Rise of American Obscenity in the Age of Anthony Comstock," *Panorama: Journal of the Association of Historians of American Art* (Fall 2018).

16. "Chose Death Rather Than Prison Cell," *Blue-Grass Blade*, November 2, 1902.

17. Drexel Lehr, *King Lehr and the Gilded Age*, 33.

18. *St. Louis Post-Dispatch*, May 17, 1936.

19. Drexel Lehr, *King Lehr and the Gilded Age*, 29.

20. Drexel Lehr, *King Lehr and the Gilded Age*, 52.

21. Drexel Lehr, *King Lehr and the Gilded Age*, 164.

22. Drexel Lehr, *King Lehr and the Gilded Age*, 40.

23. Drexel Lehr, *King Lehr and the Gilded Age*, 41.

24. Drexel Lehr, *King Lehr and the Gilded Age*, 42.

25. "Squire of Dames," *Saint Paul Globe*.

26. "Harry Lehr, Once Society's Playboy, Visits Hometown," *Kansas City Times*, February 23, 1927.

27. Vanderbilt, *Fortune's Children*, 308.

28. "Is American Society a Circus?," *Buffalo Sunday Morning News*, October 11, 1908.

29. Drexel Lehr, "King Lehr and the Gilded Age," *St. Louis Post-Dispatch*.

30. "Society Hostesses Prepare for Important Event," *Pittsburgh Press*, September 29, 1936.

31. Drexel Lehr, *King Lehr and the Gilded Age*, 91.

32. Drexel Lehr, *King Lehr and the Gilded Age*, 91.

33. Drexel Lehr, *King Lehr and the Gilded Age*, 91.

34. *Baltimore Sun*, August 31, 1924.

Chapter 12

1. Bob Kirchman, "Alva Vanderbilt's Marble House Became the Blueprint for Gilded Age Grandeur," *American Essence*, February 2023.

2. William H. Jordy et al., "Alva S. and William K. Vanderbilt House (Marble House)," SAH Archipedia, 2012.

3. "The Two Crossways," *Valley Spirit* (Weekly), August 3, 1898.

4. Cholly Knickerbocker, "Newport as a Summer Resort, Enjoys Enviable Position Among Foremost Spas," *San Francisco Examiner*, August 8, 1926.

5. "Society," *Brooklyn Life*, July 23, 1898.

6. Drexel Lehr, *King Lehr and the Gilded Age*, 106.

7. Drexel Lehr, *King Lehr and the Gilded Age*, 106.

8. "Mrs. Fish's Unruly Butler," *New York Times*, September 30, 1898.

9. Drexel Lehr, *King Lehr and the Gilded Age*, 106.

10. "The Two Crossways," *Valley Spirit* (Weekly).

11. *Standard Union*, August 20, 1898.

12. Caitlin Emery, "Caustic Wit and Lavish Parties: What You Should Know About Gilded Age Hostess Mamie Fish," *Newport Life*, August 19, 2021.

Chapter 13

1. *Star Tribune*, October 30, 1898.

2. *Star Tribune*, October 30, 1898.

3. "One of the Honored Dead," *Boston Globe*, June 26, 1898.

4. "The Two Crossways," *Valley Spirit* (Weekly).

5. *Star Tribune*, October 30, 1898.

6. *Brooklyn Daily Eagle*, October 5, 1902.

7. *Buffalo Sunday Morning News*, June 26, 1898.

8. *Brooklyn Life*, July 16, 1898.

9. *Brooklyn Daily Eagle*, October 5, 1902.

10. "The Two Crossways," *Valley Spirit* (Weekly).

11. *Brooklyn Daily Eagle*, October 5, 1902.

12. "The Two Crossways," *Valley Spirit* (Weekly).

13. "The Two Crossways," *Valley Spirit* (Weekly).

14. *New York Times*, September 17, 1902.

15. "Newport Social Doings," *The Sun*, August 9, 1898.

16. "Dinner Dance at Newport," *New York Times*, August 9, 1898.

17. "Newport Society Doings," *New York Times*, August 11, 1898.

18. "Dance in the Barn," *Fall River Daily Herald*, September 2, 1898.

19. "Mrs. Fish's Jolly Barn Dance," *Kansas City Star*, September 4, 1898.

20. Drexel Lehr, *King Lehr and the Gilded Age*, 46.

21. "Dance in the Barn," *Fall River Daily Herald*.

22. "Dance in the Barn," *Fall River Daily Herald*.

23. "Newport Society Events," *New York Times*, August 23, 1898.

Chapter 14

1. "Battle of the Gowns at Newport," *Kansas City Times*, May 28, 1899.

2. "Battle of the Gowns at Newport," *Kansas City Times*.

3. *Brooklyn Daily Eagle*, August 13, 1899.

4. *Northern Wisconsin Advertiser*, October 5, 1899.

5. "What Is Doing In Society," *New York Times*, August 5, 1899.

6. "What Is Doing In Society," *New York Times*, February 19, 1899.

7. "What Is Doing In Society," *New York Times*, February 15, 1899.

8. "St. Valentine's Day Fooleries," *Evening Sentinel*, February 16, 1899.

9. "What Is Doing In Society," *New York Times*, February 15, 1899.

10. "What Is Doing In Society," *New York Times*, February 15, 1899.

11. "Learning to Shoot," *Freeport Daily Bulletin*, December 26, 1899.

12. *San Francisco Examiner*, July 1, 1900.

13. *Topeka State Journal*, June 14, 1899.

14. *San Francisco Examiner*, July 1, 1900.

15. *Chicago Tribune*, June 4, 1899.

16. "Woman's World," *Savannah Morning News*, July 2, 1899.

17. *Wichita Eagle*, July 2, 1899.

18. "Struck a Stone Wall," *Boston Globe*, August 4, 1899.

19. "Struck a Stone Wall," *Boston Globe*.

20. "Struck a Stone Wall," *Boston Globe*.

21. Cleveland Amory, "Amory's People," *Marion Star*, March 2, 1978.

22. Amory, "Amory's People."

23. "Struck a Stone Wall," *Boston Globe*.

24. *Wichita Eagle*, July 2, 1899.

25. *Inter Ocean*, August 9, 1899.

26. *Boston Globe*, July 9, 1899.

27. "The Matrimonial Market Blooming," *Reading Times*, August 21, 1899.

28. "The Swell Set at Newport," *St. Louis Post-Dispatch*, August 20, 1899.

29. "Grandmothers Retain Youthful Appearance," *Salt Lake Herald*, August 27, 1899.

30. *Baltimore Sun*, August 29, 1899.

31. "Mrs. Fish's Novel Joke," *Atchison Daily Globe*, September 15, 1899.

32. "Mrs. Fish's Novel Joke," *Atchison Daily Globe*.

33. "Mrs. Fish's Novel Joke," *Minden Gazette*, September 7, 1899.

34. "Ellen Osborn's Fashion Letter," *The Journal*, August 2, 1899.

35. "Society," *Brooklyn Life*, September 3, 1898.

36. Richard Barry, "As to Bucking the Social Tiger," *New York Times*, June 30, 1912.

37. *Baltimore Sun*, August 29, 1899.

38. Frederick M. Winship, "A Mere Million Will Save New York's Historic Mansion," *Buffalo News*, January 7, 1979.

39. "Smart Set of the 100," *Baltimore Sun*, August 29, 1899.

40. "Smart Set of the 100," *Baltimore Sun*.

41. "Smart Set of the 100," *Baltimore Sun*.

Chapter 15

1. "Stuyvesant Fish Is a Great Man," *Freeport Journal-Standard*, October 22, 1906.

2. "Stuyvesant Fish Is a Great Man," *Freeport Journal-Standard*.

3. *San Francisco Examiner*, July 1, 1900.

4. *San Francisco Examiner*, July 1, 1900.

5. "Mrs. Fish's Vaudeville," *New-York Tribune*, January 21, 1900.

6. Renee Halm, "Hired Elephants as Waiters," *Reveille*, September 9, 1955.

7. *Evening World*, January 18, 1900.

8. "Mrs. Fish Gives a Vaudeville," *Philadelphia Inquirer*, January 21, 1900.

9. *New York Times*, July 29, 1900.

10. "Mrs. Fish's Day of Hard Labor," *Evening World*, January 18, 1900.

11. *New-York Tribune*, January 28, 1900.

12. *San Francisco Examiner*, July 1, 1900.

13. *Indianapolis Journal*, December 9, 1900.

14. "Harvest Home at Newport," *Davenport Weekly Republican*, August 29, 1900.

15. *Fall River Daily Herald*, August 23, 1900.

16. *Fall River Daily Herald*, August 23, 1900.

17. *Fall River Daily Evening News*, August 23, 1900.

18. "Society Has Fun," *Fall River Daily Herald*, August 23, 1900.

19. *Fall River Daily Evening News*, August 23, 1900.

20. *Fall River Daily Herald*, August 23, 1900.

Chapter 16

1. *Philadelphia Times*, August 5, 1900.

2. "Fine Theatrical Fete," *Lawrence Daily Journal*, January 3, 1900.

3. "Mrs. George Gould Wins," *Indianapolis Journal*, January 1, 1900.

4. "Mrs. George Gould in Society," *Boston Globe*, January 2, 1900.

5. "Mrs. George Gould Wins," *Indianapolis Journal*.

6. *Philadelphia Times*, August 5, 1900.

7. *Saint Paul Globe*, August 12, 1900.

8. *Saint Paul Globe*, August 12, 1900.

9. "Marie Dressler's Experiences in Fashionable Society," *Philadelphia Inquirer*, November 23, 1924.

10. "Marie Dressler's Experiences in Fashionable Society," *Philadelphia Inquirer*.

11. "Marie Dressler's Experiences in Fashionable Society," *Philadelphia Inquirer*.

12. *San Francisco Examiner*, March 10, 1901.

13. *San Francisco Examiner*.

14. "James Henry Smith Gives a Dinner Dance," *New York Times*, February 15, 1901.

15. "Smith Entertainment," *Transcript-Telegram*, February 15, 1901.

16. "Smith Entertainment," *Transcript-Telegram*.

17. *San Francisco Examiner*, March 10, 1901.

18. *San Francisco Examiner*.

19. *San Francisco Call and Post*, March 28, 1901.

20. "The Social Career of 'Silent James' Henry Smith," *Courier-Post*, September 27, 1906.

21. "The Social Career of 'Silent James' Henry Smith," *Courier-Post*.

22. "The Social Career of 'Silent James' Henry Smith," *Courier-Post*.

23. "The Social Career of 'Silent James' Henry Smith," *Courier-Post*.

24. "Count" Gregory, "Astonishing Confessions of a Bogus Nobleman," *Times Herald*, February 12, 1922.

25. Gregory, "Astonishing Confessions of a Bogus Nobleman."

26. Gregory, "Astonishing Confessions of a Bogus Nobleman."

27. Gregory, "Astonishing Confessions of a Bogus Nobleman."

28. Gregory, "Astonishing Confessions of a Bogus Nobleman."

29. Gregory, "Astonishing Confessions of a Bogus Nobleman."

30. Gregory, "Astonishing Confessions of a Bogus Nobleman."

31. "New York Urbanized Area Population and Density," Demographia, accessed April 25, 2024, http://demographia.com/db-nyuza1800.htm.

32. *Evening World*, January 18, 1900.

33. *Evening World*.

34. *Evening World*.

Chapter 17

1. Frederick Townsend Martin and Eveleigh Nash, *Things I Remember* (Kessinger, 1913), 169.

2. Martin and Nash, *Things I Remember*, 238.

3. Halm, "Hired Elephants as Waiters."

4. *Idaho Statesman*, July 8, 1900.

5. *San Francisco Examiner*, July 1, 1900.

6. *Idaho Statesman*, July 8, 1900.

7. *San Francisco Examiner*, July 1, 1900.

8. *New York Times*, May 27, 1900.

9. *Idaho Statesman*, July 8, 1900.

10. *San Francisco Examiner*, July 1, 1900.

11. "Mr. and Mrs. Stuyvesant Fish and Party in Chicago," *Chicago Tribune*, May 28, 1900.

12. *Philadelphia Times*, June 20, 1900.

Chapter 18

1. "Talk of a Dog Dinner," *Saint Paul Globe*, August 31, 1902.

2. "Talk of a Dog Dinner," *Saint Paul Globe*.

3. "How They Turned His Own Jokes on Once Funny Mr. Lehr," *Fort Worth Record-Telegram*, August 24, 1924.

4. Drexel Lehr, *King Lehr and the Gilded Age*, 168.

5. "Reader's Pulpit," *Austin Daily Herald*, January 18, 1902.

6. "Wholly Between Ourselves," *Standard Union*, September 14, 1902.

7. *Austin Daily Herald*, January 18, 1902.

8. *Brantford Daily Expositor*, October 12, 1901.

9. "Dogs or Babies," *American Eagle*, September 21, 1901.

10. Drexel Lehr, *King Lehr and the Gilded Age*, 168.

11. "Dennison Herald," *Purcell Register*, October 15, 1904.

12. Drexel Lehr, *King Lehr and the Gilded Age*, 168.

13. Mrs. Herbert B. Linscott, *Bright Ideas for Entertaining: Two Hundred Forms of Amusement or Entertaining for Social Gatherings of All Kinds* (Leopold Classic Library, 2016).

14. Drexel Lehr, *King Lehr and the Gilded Age*, 169.

15. Drexel Lehr, *King Lehr and the Gilded Age*, 169.

16. Drexel Lehr, *King Lehr and the Gilded Age*, 171.

17. "The Putrid 400," *Los Angeles Times*, October 12, 1902.

18. "The Putrid 400," *Los Angeles Times*.

Chapter 19

1. "Grand Duke Boris," *Hawaiian Star*, September 20, 1902.

2. *St. Louis Post-Dispatch*, August 23, 1902.

3. "Grand Duke Boris," *Hawaiian Star*.

4. "Grand Duke Boris," *Daily Telegraph*, September 9, 1902.

5. "Grand Duke Boris," *Inter Ocean*, September 10, 1902.

6. "Grand Duke Boris Reaches Newport and Is Rescued from Hotel by Mrs. Ogden Goelet," *Baltimore Sun*, September 1, 1902.

7. *Daily News*, March 3, 1929.

8. *San Francisco Examiner*, September 28, 1902.

9. *San Francisco Examiner*.

10. *San Francisco Chronicle*, August 9, 1902.

11. "Ye Olden Times," *Boston Globe*, August 23, 1902.

12. "Ye Olden Times," *Boston Globe*.

13. "Mrs. Stuyvesant Fish's Pleasantry That Started the Trouble," *San Francisco Examiner*, September 28, 1902.

14. "Mrs. Fish and Grand Duke Boris," *Baltimore Sun*, September 21, 1902.

15. "Some Aristocracy," *Oregon Daily Journal*, September 30, 1902.

16. "Some Aristocracy," *Oregon Daily Journal*.

17. "Mrs. Stuyvesant Fish's Pleasantry That Started the Trouble," *San Francisco Examiner.*

18. "Mrs. Stuyvesant Fish's Pleasantry That Started the Trouble," *San Francisco Examiner.*

19. "Stuyvesant Fish and His Family," *Buffalo Courier*, April 15, 1906.

20. Drexel Lehr, *King Lehr and the Gilded Age*, 96.

21. Frances E. Hadley and Paula A. Ironside, "Capers of Late Harry Lehr Proved Diverting to Newport," *Evening Courier*, December 1, 1934.

22. Hadley and Ironside, "Capers of Late Harry Lehr Proved Diverting to Newport."

23. Drexel Lehr, *King Lehr and the Gilded Age*, 98.

24. Drexel Lehr, *King Lehr and the Gilded Age*, 98.

25. "Mrs. Fish and Grand Duke Boris," *Baltimore Sun*, September 21, 1902.

26. *Baltimore Sun*, September 21, 1902.

27. *Baltimore Sun.*

28. Drexel Lehr, *King Lehr and the Gilded Age*, 98.

29. "$16,000 Sable Cloak," *Salt Lake Tribune*, November 9, 1902.

30. "Sneers at First Lady," *Detroit Free Press*, September 27, 1903.

31. *Evening Courier*, December 1, 1934.

Chapter 20

1. *New York Times*, September 17, 1902.

2. *Brooklyn Daily Eagle*, October 5, 1902.

3. *Kansas City Star*, October 10, 1902.

4. *Kansas City Star.*

5. *New York Times*, September 17, 1902.

6. *Boston Globe*, September 17, 1902.

7. *Boston Globe.*

8. *Richmond Dispatch*, September 17, 1902.

9. *Standard Union*, September 16, 1902.

10. "He Cleaned Out the Dive," *Kansas City Star*, October 10, 1902.

11. "Former Brooklyn Man Held for Banker's Murder," *Standard Union*, September 16, 1902.

12. *North Adams Transcript*, September 30, 1902.

13. *New York Times*, September 17, 1902.

14. *Brooklyn Daily Eagle*, October 5, 1902.

15. "The Putrid 400," *Los Angeles Times.*

16. *Brooklyn Daily Eagle*, October 5, 1902.

17. *Brooklyn Daily Eagle.*

18. *Vicksburg Herald*, September 21, 1902.

Chapter 21

1. "Glenclyffe, Garrison-on-Hudson, Putnam County, New York," American Aristocracy, https://househistree.com/houses/glenclyffe.

2. "Glenclyffe, Garrison-on-Hudson, Putnam County, New York," American Aristocracy.

3. Gary Stern, "Friars Land May Yield Housing," *Journal News*, November 12, 2000.

4. "Stuyvesant Fish," *Daily Nonpareil*, May 20, 1906.

5. "Glenclyffe, Garrison-on-Hudson, Putnam County, New York," American Aristocracy.

Chapter 22

1. Bennett Cerf, "Whatever Became of Old New York," *Richmond Times-Dispatch*, August 16, 1959.

2. "Stuyvesant Fish Roosevelt Critic," *Chicago Tribune*, March 22, 1907.

3. "The First Lady in the United States," *Star*, February 28, 1903.

4. Betty Boyd Caroli, "Edith Roosevelt," in *Encyclopedia Britannica*, September 26, 2023, accessed February 1, 2024, https://www.britannica.com/biography/Edith-Roosevelt.

5. Sophie Dweck, "The Evolution of First Lady Fashion, from Martha Washington to Jill Biden," *Town and Country*, April 17, 2022.

6. *Boston Evening Transcript*, October 16, 1903.

7. "Sneers at First Lady," *Detroit Free Press*, September 27, 1903.

8. *Boston Evening Transcript*, October 16, 1903.

9. *Transcript-Telegram*, September 28, 1903.

10. *Detroit Free Press*, September 27, 1903.

11. "The Extra Column," *Buffalo Times*, October 4, 1903.

12. "Fairly Rated," *Piqua Daily Call*, October 7, 1903.

13. "Would Be Aristocrats," *American Israelite*, November 26, 1903.

14. *Semi-Weekly Messenger*, October 6, 1903.

15. *Anaconda Standard*, October 4, 1903.

16. *Daily Review*, September 28, 1903.

17. *Buffalo Times*, October 4, 1903.

18. *Star*, February 28, 1903.

Chapter 23

1. "Harriman Attacks Fish," *Baltimore Sun*, February 27, 1907.

2. *The News*, February 27, 1907.

3. "National Affairs: Stuyvesant Fish," *Time*, April 21, 1923.

4. *San Francisco Examiner*, July 2, 1939.

5. "C. C. Rumsey Will Wed Miss Harriman," *Buffalo Commercial*, May 5, 1910.

6. "Love and the Money God Smash Dead Harriman's Empire," *Salt Lake Herald-Republican*, May 29, 1910.

7. "Cinderella Wins Her Prince," *Daily News*, October 28, 1934.

8. "Cinderella Wins Her Prince," *Daily News*.

9. "Cinderella Wins Her Prince," *Daily News*.

10. *Detroit Free Press*, September 27, 1903.

11. "Is Society a Circus?," *Buffalo Sunday Morning News*, October 11, 1908.

12. *Wall Street Journal*, April 28, 1910.

13. *Atchison Daily Globe*, November 26, 1906.

14. *Kansas City Star*, May 26, 1915.

15. "Ex Railroad President and Successor Whom He Struck with Fist," *Chicago Tribune*, August 29, 1907.

16. "Glen Gurnsey, Harriman-Fish Fight," *Billings Gazette*, December 15, 1907.

17. "Glen Gurnsey, Harriman-Fish Fight," *Billings Gazette*.

18. "Wall Street Version of the I.C. Rumpus," *Los Angeles Times*, August 30, 1907.

19. "Codirectors Chip in Advice," *Chicago Tribune*, August 29, 1907.

20. "Wall Street Version of the I.C. Rumpus," *Los Angeles Times*.

21. *Lexington Herald-Leader*, March 10, 1907.

22. "Railway War Has Reached Society," *The Province*, February 14, 1907.

23. *Topeka Daily Herald*, February 11, 1907.

24. "Trouble Between Fish and Harriman," *The Province*, April 11, 1907.

Chapter 24

1. "Mrs. Fish Snubs Mrs. Cornelius Vanderbilt," *Los Angeles Evening Post-Record*, August 13, 1907.

2. "Gay and Pretty Princess," *The News*, August 20, 1907.

3. Cholly Knickerbocker, *Buffalo Enquirer*, July 22, 1907.

4. "Sweden's Sailor Prince," *River Press*, September 11, 1907.

5. "The Heroic Penance of Gay Grand Duchess Marie of Russia," *The Tennessean*, January 17, 1915.

6. "Mrs. Fish Snubs Mrs. Cornelius Vanderbilt," *Los Angeles Evening Post-Record*.

7. "Mrs. Fish Wins Coup over Husband's Foes," *Los Angeles Herald*, August 15, 1907.

8. "Prince William of Sweden," *Boston Globe*, August 26, 1907.

9. *San Francisco Examiner*, August 23, 1907.

10. "Prince William of Sweden," *Boston Globe*.

11. *Chicago Tribune*, August 25, 1907.

12. "Society," *Washington Post*, August 25, 1907.

13. "Sweden's Sailor Prince," *River Press*, September 11, 1907.

14. "All Essential Tact," *The Journal*, October 20, 1908.

Chapter 25

1. *Buffalo Enquirer*, February 17, 1913.

2. "Mrs. Fish Makes Plea for Girls," *Oakland Tribune*, February 9, 1913.

3. *Labor World*, February 8, 1913.

4. Mary Boyle O'Reilly, "Mary Boyle O'Reilly on Picker Duty with Garment Workers," *Omaha Daily News*, January 27, 1913.

5. "Garment Striker's Bomb Wounds Two Guards," *Pittsburgh Post*, February 7, 1913.

6. O'Reilly, "Mary Boyle O'Reilly on Picker Duty with Garment Workers."

7. "Church Socialist Held in Garment Worker's Strike," *New-York Tribune*, February 7, 1913.

8. Jim Bishop, "When New Money Squeaked," *Morning News*, August 16, 1979.

9. "Mrs. Fish Talks to Girl Strikers," *The Sun*, February 8, 1913.

10. "Mrs. Fish Talks to Girl Strikers," *The Sun*.

11. "Mrs. Fish Talks to Girl Strikers," *The Sun*.

12. "Mrs. Fish Drops Out of Garment Strike," *New York Times*, February 9, 1913.

13. "Mrs. Fish Drops Out of Garment Strike," *New York Times*.

14. "Mrs. Fish Drops Out of Garment Strike," *New York Times*.

15. "Mrs. Fish Drops Out of Garment Strike," *New York Times*.

16. "Society Leaders in New York Assist in Garment Workers Strike," *Wagoner Weekly Sayings*, February 13, 1913.

17. "Noted Society Woman to Help Strikers," *Day Book*, February 8, 1913.

18. "Characteristic Pose of Mrs. Stuyvesant Fish at Whose Party $12,000,000 Worth of Gems Were Worn," *Grand Forks Herald*, August 5, 1913.

19. "Women of Smart Set Lend Aid," *Lima News*, February 9, 1913.

20. "Women of Smart Set Lend Aid," *Lima News*.

21. "Mrs. Fish Hurts Cause, Miss Barnum Fears," *New York Times*, February 10, 1913.

22. "Garment Workers Win the New York Strike," *Wichita American*, February 28, 1913.

23. "Mrs. O. H. P. Belmont, an Alabama Woman, One of the World's Foremost Suffrage Leaders," *Montgomery Advertiser*, May 25, 1913.

24. "Mrs. O. H. P. Belmont," *Montgomery Advertiser*.

25. *Charlotte News*, August 14, 1913.

26. *Evening Journal*, August 7, 1913.

27. Viola Rogers, "She Never Had a Higher Aim than to Be a Mother," *Kansas City Post*, August 2, 1913.

28. "Mother Goose Protest Against Suffragettes," *Oakland Tribune*, August 2, 1913.

29. Rose O'Neill, "Votes for Our Mothers," Breckinridge Family Papers, Manuscript Division, Library of Congress.

30. "Witch on Broomstick at Mrs. Fish's Mother Goose Ball Flies Amid Clouds," *Kansas City Post*, August 2, 1913.

31. "Witch on Broomstick," *Kansas City Post*.

32. *Norwich Bulletin*, March 7, 1913.

33. "Newport Affair Was to Remind Women of Their Old Ideals, Says Hostess," *St. Louis Post-Dispatch*, August 6, 1913.

34. "Mrs. Fish Fairy Queen," *Commercial Appeal*.

35. *Washington Post*, August 2, 1913.

36. *Kansas City Post*, August 2, 1913.

37. *Kansas City Post*, August 2, 1913.

38. "Mother Goose Ball Top Notcher," *Morning Journal*, August 2, 1913.

39. "Mother Goose Ball Top Notcher," *Morning Journal*.

40. *Kansas City Post*, August 2, 1913.

41. "Writing on the Wall," *Delta Independent*, September 5, 1913.

42. "Mother Goose Ball," *Knoxville Sentinel*, December 12, 1913.

Chapter 26

1. "Sneers at First Lady," *Detroit Free Press*, September 27, 1903.

2. Nina-Sophia Miralles, *Glossy: The Inside Story of Vogue* (Quercus Editions, 2021).

3. Edna Woolman Chase and Ilka Chase, *Always in Vogue* (Country Life Press, 1954), 115.

4. Woolman Chase and Chase, *Always in Vogue*, 115.

5. Woolman Chase and Chase, *Always in Vogue*, 115.

6. Woolman Chase and Chase, *Always in Vogue*, 120.

7. Woolman Chase and Chase, *Always in Vogue*, 121.

8. Woolman Chase and Chase, *Always in Vogue*, 122.

9. Woolman Chase and Chase, *Always in Vogue*, 122.

10. "The Poiret Collection of Gowns and Wraps," *The Record*, November 27, 1915.

11. "Fashion Fete Would Make the Queen of Sheba Gasp, King Solomon, He of Many Wives, Would Go Broke," *Lincoln Journal Star*.

12. "Fashion Fete Would Make the Queen of Sheba Gasp," *Lincoln Journal Star*.

13. Woolman Chase and Chase, *Always in Vogue*, 124.

14. "Paris Dressmakers to Give Fashion Fete in New York," *Detroit Free Press*, November 14, 1915.

15. "Paris Dressmakers to Give Fashion Fete in New York," *Detroit Free Press*.

16. Miralles, *Glossy*, 52.

17. "Fashion Fete Would Make the Queen of Sheba Gasp," *Lincoln Journal Star*.

18. "Fashion Fete Would Make the Queen of Sheba Gasp," *Lincoln Journal Star*.

19. "Fashion Fete Would Make the Queen of Sheba Gasp," *Lincoln Journal Star*.

20. *The Sun*, December 12, 1915.

21. Eleanor Hoyt Brainerd, "Debutantes Gowns Are France's Real Triumph," *The Sun*, December 12, 1915.

22. "Fashion Fete Would Make the Queen of Sheba Gasp," *Lincoln Journal Star*.

23. *Brooklyn Citizen*, November 14, 1915.

24. *Brooklyn Citizen*, November 14, 1915.

25. "Fashion Fete Millinery," *Pittsburgh Press*, November 26, 1915.

26. *Lincoln Journal Star*, December 3, 1915.

27. *The Sun*, December 12, 1915.

28. *Detroit Free Press*, December 19, 1915.

29. *Lincoln Journal Star*, December 3, 1915.

30. "Christmas Number Vogue," *Chicago Tribune*, December 21, 1915.

31. Adelaide Kennerly, "An Animated Poppy and Her Befrilled Harlequin at Burlesque Fashion Fete," *Mongomery Advertiser*, December 6, 1915.

32. "Fashion's Passing Show," *Brooklyn Citizen*, July 23, 1915.

Chapter 27

1. *Kansas City Star*, May 26, 1915.

2. "Mrs. Stuyvesant Fish Is Dead at Country Home," *The Sun*, May 27, 1915.

3. "Mrs. Stuyvesant Fish Is Dead at Country Home," *The Sun*.

4. *Boston Daily Globe*, May 26, 1915.

5. Fish, *Anthon Genealogy*, 215.

6. Fish, *Anthon Genealogy*, 215.

7. *Chattanooga Daily Times*, April 11, 1923.

8. *El Paso Times*, December 31, 1939.

9. "Stuyvesant Fish," *Great Falls Tribune*, May 1, 1923.

10. "Stuyvesant Fish," *Great Falls Tribune*.

11. "Turning the Tables on the 400's Joke King," *Fresno Bee*, September 14, 1924.

12. *Fort Worth Record-Telegram*, August 24, 1924.

13. Drexel Lehr, *King Lehr and the Gilded Age*, 208.

14. "Newport Looked Again at Crossways Doors," *Daily News*, June 2, 1924.

15. "Society Hostesses Prepare for Important Event," *Pittsburgh Press*, September 29, 1936.

16. F. A. M., "Mrs. Stuyvesant Fish Is in Reno Again," *San Francisco Examiner*, September 7, 1960.

17. Ama Barker, "The Passing of the Society Dictators," *Daily News*, March 3, 1929.

18. Barker, "The Passing of the Society Dictators."

19. *Daily News*, July 11, 1943.

20. Maury Paul, "Mrs. Fish and Oelrichs Unlike Originals," *Pittsburgh Sun-Telegraph*, March 19, 1942.

Epilogue

1. *San Francisco Examiner*, August 8, 1926.

INDEX